The Secret of Dreams

The Secret of Dreams

Pedro Meseguer, S.J.

Roman Catholic Books
Post Office Box 2286, Fort Collins, CO 80522
BooksforCatholics.com

Nihil Obstat:
Joannes M.T. Barton, S.T.D., L.S.S.,
Censor Deputatus

Imprimatur:
E. Morrogh Bernard,
Vicarius Generalis

Westmonasterii,
Die XI Januarii MCMLX

ISBN 1-929291-73-6

CONTENTS

v

III. DREAMS AND THE SCHOOLS OF DEPTH PSYCHOLOGY

IV. TELEPATHIC, PROPHETIC AND MYSTIC DREAMS

INTRODUCTION

1. *Is it worth it?*

This question of dreams is a particularly thorny one, wide open to discredit not only because the term *dream* is generally synonymous with *nonsense* or, at best, *unimportant curiosity*, *bagatelle* or *childishness*, but also because when one tries to take it seriously one is faced with memories of the abuses of occultists, magicians, diviners and astrologers, and no less, though in another direction, of Freudian psychoanalysts. These reasons lead many people to think that common sense must prompt them to ask: Are dreams worth bothering about?

Despite appearances, not all "serious people" are actually so lacking in desire to learn about man; and many are especially intrigued by this phenomenon of dreaming, as amazing as it is common, which is after all a part—and quite a large one—of our inner life. We spend a quarter of our lives dreaming—many as much as a third—and this without counting our day-dreams. So, does it seem logical that classifying insects and shellfish should be a worthy academic occupation, and that examining our own nature should not? If it were merely examination for its own sake, perhaps, but surely not if the knowledge gained can be useful to us?

There are glands in the human body whose function has only very recently been discovered, and there are a number of others whose functions are still unknown. But we do not doubt that everything in the body serves some purpose. Clearly the same is true of the psyche. So we can ask whether the function of dreams is quite clear, as well as whether their causes are known. Even more: just as knowledge of the glands has led to new preparations, natural or synthetic, known as

glandular or hormone, might not a systematic study of dreams lead to
the therapeutic or educational application of the knowledge gained?

As in other psychological matters, we all think we know too much
about the causes and the uses of dreams, and so we imagine that the
subject holds no further surprises for us: particularly because men
have from the earliest times devoted an enormous amount of attention
to dreams. Is there still anything to add? This world of fantasy,
arising from the shadows as soon as we cross the boundaries of our
waking lives, certainly justifies our curiosity and amazement. And if
amazement is the mother of science. . . . The body too, with its myriad
wonderful secrets, excited curiosity, for more urgent reasons, and yet,
till recently, it had not revealed many of those secrets. We shall see
how much progress has been made in our knowledge and management
of dreams.

I

DREAMS IN HISTORY

2. Dreams in early civilizations

It is a known fact that the most ancient civilizations were very pre-occupied with dreams. Those minds, still close to the primitive state, with a religious awe of natural phenomena, and accustomed to using and interpreting ideographs or written symbols, were more likely to see an ulterior, more consistent meaning in these seemingly illogical images and scenes than is modern man.

Many of the oracles worked through dreams. To consult them, one lay down to sleep in a sacred place, and the god gave his reply to the question in more or less explicit terms, which had to be eluci-dated by an expert (incubation dreams). In Assyria and Babylonia, dreams ranked high among the means of communication with the divinity. The cylinder of Gudea describes the consultations he had with the goddess Nina, who interpreted dreams, in order to find out the full meaning of one of his. Plutarch tells of a governor of Cilicia who sent a servant to the oracle of Mopsus, in Malta, with a question written on a folded sheet. In the temple the servant dreamed that a spirit appeared to him and pronounced the one word, "Black". When he returned with this reply, the courtiers all laughed, but the governor opened the sheet and showed them the question: Should he sacrifice a white bull or a black one? There were even cases when the person consulting the oracle could not produce an adequate dream, so the person in charge of the sanctuary dreamed for him. One can imagine what a fruitful source of deceit this practice could prove.

The Egyptians must have applied themselves assiduously to the interpretation of dreams, since they have left catalogues or dictionaries of oneiric symbols. The priests were the official practitioners of oneiromancy, as of other cultural activities. The reason for this does not appear to be only Comte's dictum (which must be taken with a pinch of salt), that sciences all pass through three stages: theological, metaphysical and experimental, but that dreams in those times always appeared to be divine, or sent by spirits separated from their bodies (sleep, the image of death). This sometimes led them to place "keys to dreams" next to a dead body, as though this might help the spirit of the dead man to understand the language of beyond the grave. Anything to do with death or the "great beyond" was the domain of religion and its ministers.

One can suppose that not only the priests interpreted dreams, just as now not only doctors try to heal the sick. The Old Testament gives clear evidence of this. When Joseph told his brothers his dream of the sheaves, they at once said without waiting for any wise man, "Shall we be subject to thy dominion?" And when he recounted his dream of the sun, the moon, and the eleven stars which worshipped him, his father immediately rebuked him, saying, "Shall I and thy mother, and thy brethren worship thee upon the earth?" (Gen. 37. 5 ff.) To jump from symbols to their meaning was a natural step for them to take.

As everyone knows, dreams appear frequently in Holy Scripture. They are usually considered as something sacred, a means of communicating with God. Yet normal human dreams are sometimes mentioned, either to be condemned as a source of vain disturbances or superstition (Ecclus. 34. 1-8), or regarded as instruments of God's ordinary providence. The first book of Samuel (28. 6) says that Saul "consulted the Lord, and he answered him not; neither by dreams, nor by priests, nor by prophets". Might this consultation of God, so that he may reply through dreams, refer to the use of dreams by incubation? Solomon's famous dream in Gabaon, after he has appeased God with a thousand victims for holocausts on the mountain, shows the ceremonial typical of dreams of incubation (I Kings 3). Many sacred dreams appear as clear, direct messages from the Godhead; others disguise their message in typical dream symbols and are interpreted in similar ways by prophets or others. The passage that deals most explicitly with dreams is Job 33. 14 ff, which will be more fully considered in Chapter V.

3. *The meaning of dreams*

The example of Joseph illustrates the prophetic meaning attached to dreams. The belief in prophetic dreams persists from the beginning of civilization to our own times—a mysterious business which, as usually happens, produces fanatical partisans, cynical unbelievers and the whole range of intermediate positions. In this connection it should be noticed that man's mind has a natural tendency to exteriorize, and the more primitive the mind the more it exteriorizes. Primitive peoples today attribute to the external world many things that civilized men consider subjective. Conversely, there exists a type of ultra-civilized man who subjectivizes more than is realistic. The exteriorizing tendency accounts for the existence of extremes of enthusiasm or cynicism. Those who hold that dreams represent objective realities must think of past (memories), present (telepathy or cryptaesthesia), or future events (prophecy, warning), and these events must hold some special significance for the individual or the community, since this is the mission of dreams, and, naturally, why they are considered important. Those who scorn them also have an exteriorizing mind: being unable to apply their objective criteria to dreams, which they regard as nonsense, they cannot see any other value in them. The more roughly the objective logic of the excessive intellectual is applied to their symbolic combinations of affective meaning the more nonsensical they seem. It cannot be easy for the human mind to strike a balance between objectivism and subjectivism: this is clear from the fact that so many centuries and vicissitudes have been needed for a few learned men—not the masses, who will never achieve such finesse—to find it.

Antiquity did, in fact, sometimes consider dreams to be the expression of a subjective state, either physical or mental. The Greek doctors, so Aristotle relates, observed dreams in order to diagnose the state of the humours or to nip certain morbid tendencies in the bud; Hippocrates and Galen deal with this specifically.[1] Conscious preoccupations and feelings are also considered as dream-conditioning factors. But the aspect of "mere expression of the psyche" was not considered important, except that it occasioned recommendations to go to sleep with a good disposition, since one's disposition could affect the good or bad auguries of one's dreams. It is extraordinary to watch century after century go by and men living with this idea—that dreams indicate psychic states—without knowing what to do about it. Not until the coming of psychotherapy, little more than half a century ago, was the idea emphasized, elaborated, and applied. This is really understandable, since only a psychotherapy based largely on theories of a dynamic unconscious could value dreams as being the surest way to approach the depths of the unconscious, with its affective complexes, ramifications and influences. Many minerals have been in the same case: known of old, they are only exploited when some industry has need of them.

4. The Greeks—Artemidorus Daldianus

In Homer, dreams are usually sent by the gods and the dead, but also by the absent living (telepathy), as can be seen from at least one passage, Penelope's dream of the eagle and the geese in the *Odyssey*, in which the eagle, speaking in the first person, explains the meaning, saying, "I am your husband".[2] The later Greeks generally followed this approach: dreams are a gift of the gods, their oracle, and a communication from the dead. As such they belong to religion, and the temple was the best place to have them interpreted. I have already suggested that this led to the specialization and even mechanization of oneiromancy, which has survived to this day.

The best-known surviving manual of this special skill is by Arte-

1. Hippocrates, 1 *Epid.* and 3, test. 1 com 2, *de humoribus.* Galen has a little book called *De praesagio ex insomniis.*
2. *Odyssey.* XIX, ll. 531 and ff.

midorus Daldianus, and it has been edited countless times in many
languages, certainly being corrupted in the process. Although it
belongs to the second century A.D., I am going to say something about
it before dealing with Cicero and Aristotle, since it expresses a more
primitive outlook than theirs.[3]

He begins with a general interpretation, and defines dreams like this:
"A dream is a movement or conformation of the spirit which, under
the most diverse appearances, announces future goods or ills." This
immediately gives us the chief preoccupation of occultist oneiromancy.
But at the end of the first chapter he says: "It is the custom to call all
dreams divine unless they are natural or ordinary." This shows us
something which was and always has been generally held—that not all
dreams are significant (mainly from the prophetic standpoint), and
that there are ordinary, natural dreams. Modern psychotherapy, on the
other hand, holds that all dreams mean something, that all are a version
or copy of something within us, something that we do not always
possess the necessary data to identify.

Artemidorus gives the following criteria for the interpretation of
dreams:

1. To judge a dream and determine its consequences, it should be
    considered from beginning to end; in certain cases, however, one
    should begin at the end and go back to the beginning, since the
    end explains the beginning and makes the whole dream clear.

    To judge a barren dream, which seems to offer no point where
    it can be grasped, so to speak, certain suppositions are necessary,
    to supply a missing link or to find the meaning.

2. The interpreter must, above all, be a wise man, and have
    learned from long experience to apply his methods with prudence.

    Firstly, he must not make any initial error, since this will sub-
    sequently be increased and eventually falsify the whole meaning
    of the visions in the dream.

    Secondly, he should not interpret a dream unless he knows its

---

3. Artemidorus Daldianus, *Oneirocritica*. (There is an English translation, by Wood,
1644 and later editions.)

circumstances thoroughly. These must all be studied, one by one, if he is to give an accurate judgement. He must not pronounce on what he cannot understand, nor give a spontaneous verdict, but a well-meditated one, thereby avoiding controversies. If he has told the dreamer that he will be unfortunate and he turns out to be fortunate, or if a dream of happy augury produces only a minor happiness, the harm done will not have been very great; the interpreter should in all cases know the dreamer's state of mind.

3.   To judge dreams that do not correspond to any known cause, the interpreter must know whether they occurred by day or by night, since their effects will vary according to whether they came in the hours of light or those of darkness, at dawn or at dark. He must also know what kind and quantity of food the dreamer had taken before going to bed, since an abundant, heavy diet disturbs and distorts the visions that occur in dreams, even though they may not come till dawn.

The main body of the work is a catalogue of dream subjects, with an indication of what each one prefigures, not arranged alphabetically, as in other books, but classified by subject matter. The author occasionally interposes short notes. He insists several times on the ambiguity of some dreams and the difficulty of tying up all their loose ends. He ends by saying that for a dream to presage something important, it must have made a deep impression on the sleeper. This remark, and others (such as those transcribed above), though intended as oniromancy, can validly be transposed to psychoanalytic interpretation, since they are general principles. For instance, to say that the same dream dreamed by two different people, or by the same person at different times, can have very different meanings is universally valid. And experience confirms that a dream that makes a profound impression on the dreamer deserves particular attention; that the end sometimes clarifies the beginning; that the circumstances in which the dreamer finds himself at the time of the dream must all be taken into account; that certain external stimuli, such as light, can introduce accidental variations which should be considered as such if the essential theme is to remain undisturbed; that only a prudent man, free (as the Greek *sophos* demanded) from passions that might cloud his judgement and experienced in interpreting dreams, can hope to do so with any degree of certitude: these and others are still perfectly valid norms even for modern dream study. Apart from these considerations, the book is the product of the most ingenuous observation; its author believes that all facts and events and their ideas and representations are bound together, and to the mind, by mutual bonds, and that if predictions fail, their failure is generally due to defective consideration of all the elements that should be taken into account. His concept of the universe found a large following in the Ancient World.

5. *Aristotle and his treatises: "On Dreams" and "On Prophecy in Sleep"*

As the founder of scientific psychology, Aristotle deserves a place of honour. The section of his works called *Parva Naturalia* contains three most interesting chapters: *On Sleep and Waking*, *On Dreams*, and *On Prophecy in Sleep*.[4] Leaving the first aside, I shall summarize the principles contained in the last two.

His main question is to which faculty dreaming belongs. After some deliberation, he decides, "It is clear that dreaming belongs to the sensitive faculty and is related to it in the same way as imagination". But this does not prevent the understanding, though weakened to a greater or lesser extent, from playing some part in dreams, nor from realizing that dreams are unreal: "Moreover, in a dream we have some other concept, just as if we perceive something while awake; for we often have some thoughts about what we perceive. And so in sleep we sometimes have other thoughts beyond the mental pictures. This will become obvious to anyone if he reflects on it, and tries to remember his dream when he has awakened." From this he deduces that not everything that appears in dreams is illusion.

4. Aristotle, *Parva Naturalia* (London, 1935), pp. 310-83.

B

To explain the mechanism of dreams, he establishes that sensory stimuli do not only affect the senses at the moment they are received, but continue to do so for some time after. He gives various examples, such as the persistence of one colour in sight, the dazzle that results from looking at the sun, a strong smell remaining in the nostrils, the deafening effect of a loud noise, and others not so clear. His explanation of this retarded influence is unacceptable today; but if his arguments are sifted, the following conclusion emerges, that sensations leave a more or less lasting impression. But how, he asks, can imagination draw such clear pictures from such slight impressions? To this he replies that it is like a person in the grip of a strong feeling, whether of fear or love, who is reminded of his enemy or loved one by the slightest resemblance, the more so the stronger his feeling. This is the cause of both the error and the clarity of the image, despite its slight basis. When awake, the intervention of other senses, and judgement, allows us to correct the error, but not in dreams; there we are at the mercy of feelings and appearances. The reason why such slight stimuli are sufficient to produce such a strong illusion is that in dreams they are not swamped in a mass of concomitant sensations and preoccupations, as they are in waking: still water will reflect the tiniest details. This stillness allows images and likenesses that have lain dormant in its depths to come to the surface. Aristotle compares this process, charmingly, with a children's toy of his time: a frog made of cork, covered with a layer of salt thick enough to make it sink in water; when the salt dissolved, the frog rose to the surface.

This simile of a liquid surface also leads him to an acute observation. When the water is inordinately disturbed, it will not reflect any image at all; this happens with the ordinary preoccupations and sensations of our waking lives, and in sleep with digestive or other disturbances. If the surface is disturbed at only one point, however, regular concentric waves are caused, which distort the image somewhat, but in a systematic manner, leaving it still recognizable. If two or three disturbances are made, more waves are produced, larger or smaller, and then, though this is a more complicated task, the different distortions in the image

can be corrected, restoring it to its original shape. Now these focal
points of waves represent bodily affects or *movements*. In dreams,
reality (whether external or internal) is reflected, but subjected to
as many distortions as the dreamer is subject to affects or humours.
This is a most acute observation, applied literally today in the theory
that complexes can be unconscious to a greater or a lesser extent:
just as the conformation of the waves indicates the centre from which
they radiate, so the nature of the distortions imposed on reality can
indicate the complexes, often deeply hidden, at their source. So the
interpreter's whole art, says Aristotle, consists in visualizing the original
reality through the distortions. Today the aim is to discover, not the
original reality, but the sources of the disturbing elements.

From these considerations he later concludes that one should go to
bed having eaten moderately, and undisturbed in one's mind. Concerning the modifications undergone by oneiric images, he says that all
changes wrought in them suggest new likenesses and evocations,
which establish the "somnial flux" spoken of by St Albert the Great,
in which certain species change gradually into others. Aristotle compares this flux of phantasmagoria to the changing shapes of clouds.

He does not appear to deduce the magnifying of small stimuli—
those left by previous sensations or new ones reaching the sleeping
senses—only from the effect of contrast produced by the silencing of
conomitant sensations, but also from the concentration of vital heat
that takes place during the dream, and from the effect of these modified
impressions or sensations on the inner consciousness. So the slightest
noise can become a thunderstorm, and a little extra heat in one limb
can become a fire. Meunier and Masselon say the same: that dream
images are a veritable microscope of sensibility.[5] Precisely because of
this, Aristotle encourages doctors to observe dreams, since "as the
beginnings of all things are small, it is true that the beginnings of illnesses
and other affects will be slight; but for the aforementioned reasons,
they will appear more intensely in dreams than during consciousness...."

5. Meunier and Masselon, *Les rêves et leur interprétation* (Paris, 1910).

He also says that dreams can include other sensory impressions actually received, such as the cock crowing, the light of a lantern, etc., almost without distortion. Hence it is sometimes possible to converse with a person dreaming, following the thread of his remarks so as not to wake him. He also describes, for comparison, the different classes of vision and hallucination that can come to people when awake. His final definition of a dream is this: *A mental image, originating in the move-ment* (actuation) *of the senses* (stimuli), *which comes to animals during the repose of sleep.*

He also asks whether everyone dreams, and whether during his whole sleep, or only a small part of it. While recognizing that it is unusual, he admits that some people never dream, while others dream throughout the whole of their lives; others do not in their youth, but do so when they grow older. This he explains by connecting it with his remarks on digestive disturbances preventing dreams; he appears to consider youth too troubled by excessive vegetative commotion. Remember: the disturbed surface does not reflect an image.

A few words about the chapter on prophecy. He asks whether one should believe in its existence; so many people say one should, that some must have experienced it. He carefully states that he will not venture an outright "Yes" or "No", and so he goes on to study various cases. He at once rejects the view that dreams are sent by the gods, on the grounds that they can be sent to all, which is unworthy of the gods, who would surely send them only to the best and wisest. And if the gods do not intervene, he continues, there is no apparent reason for thinking that dreams represent fortuitous happenings, or events far away in time and space. It is quite another matter when the dream tells of what is going to happen to the dreamer himself, either physically or morally: physically, by virtue of his remarks on the beginnings of affections; morally, because just as conscious actions predispose one to dream the same things, dreams predispose one to put their material into action. He dismisses the claims made for coincidental dreams, such as of a naval battle dreamt a long way away which is later learnt to have taken place, by saying that since dreams are legion, it is natural for them to hit the mark once in a while, quite by chance, just as sometimes happens when one mentions someone, and he appears—"Talk of the devil".

There is, however, one class of telepathy that he accepts, explaining it by a theory of his own about transmission of movement and other influences through the ether. He claims that actions and even objects (sensible stimuli) leave certain vibrations in the air, which last for some time and eventually die out. The effects of these movements of the ether are best felt in dreams, and by uncultured, simple people whose empty minds are free from distractions, and so obey the influences that act upon them, with the docility of a weathercock. This, according to Aristotle, explains why even the stupidest people sometimes have knowledge or foreknowledge of distant events in their dreams.

He lists two other categories in the same class: close relatives, whose mutual love enables them to recognize each other from afar with a minimum of perception, which will be paralleled in dreams by the vibrations produced by new arrivals; and "melancholics" (psychopaths) and lunatics, who vehemently follow any of these movements, their minds unaffected and unclouded by subsequent different impressions. He ends with this little paragraph, which is weightier than it might appear to those unacquainted with modern psychotherapeutic interpretation of dreams: "But the most skilful judge of dreams is the man who possesses the ability to detect likenesses, which are often scattered and distorted in dreams, disturbed by different movements".

Such, very briefly, are Aristotle's views on dreams. Here, as in all his work, we find his wonderful combination of experimental orientation and reasoning. Neither his predecessors, nor, until very recently, his successors, showed these qualities in such degree, free from the errors to be expected from the state of knowledge at the time he wrote. When he talks of the meaning of dreams, it is notable how briefly he deals with those produced by a subjective mental state. The time for that had not yet come.

6. *Greek treatment of other problems relating to dreams*

Greek writers raised other problems about dreams, but in view of the
impossibility of tracking down all the isolated references in their
numerous works, I shall only mention two. Such was the scope of their
intellectual activity, that they scarcely left a human or scientific
problem untouched in some form, though we must always make
allowances for the knowledge at their disposal.[6]

Heraclitus of Ephesus (fifth century B.C.) asks: Why is one's dream
world a personal world, and one's waking world a common one?
Certain theorists, sunk in the morbid depths of modern gnostic
speculation, have raised a storm of words around this question. At the
risk of appearing to simplify unduly, I shall answer Heraclitus by saying
that even the waking world is, for many reasons, a "personal" one for
each individual, constructed from a personal point of view, just as a
coloured glass colours everything seen through it; the dream world is
far more personal, owing to the invasion of tendencies and subjective
affects which can mould the pliable matter of the subconscious at will
without the constant corrective provided in waking hours by the
evidence of the senses and the comparative critique of reason. The
waking world, which is to a certain extent "common", is a world lit
and coloured by abstractions, a world of ideas and words, based on
reality, and offering sufficient ground for agreement for men to understand one another. This is the view of critical or moderate realism.

The second question, raised by Plato in the ninth book of the
Republic, is more interesting. He says: "There dwells in all of us a
vehement concupiscence, wild and lawless, even though some of us
seem so moderate; this can clearly be seen in dreams". Here is the
dramatic problem of the dualism which affects man's moral life: one
part of us acts deterministically and anarchically as mere brute force,
but very early on in life it is limited by another part, more lucid,
hierarchical, free, loving law and order. From these two opposing
principles stems an instability that can be resolved in one of two funda-

6. Dr Ludwig Binswanger: *Wandlung in der Auffassung und Deutung des Traumes von
den Griechen bis zur Gegenwart* (Berlin, 1928), pp. 7 and ff.

mental ways: in the wise man, by virtue; in the fool, by vice (for vice, it must be remembered, is essentially the ultimate stupidity). Even in these extreme cases, and far more in the indeterminate ones which are the most frequent, dreams provide a stage on which the "other self" can emerge from the shadows, released by the relaxation of conscious control, and finally restrained only by automatisms, which go deep as a result of long practice, or by the occasional flicker of reason which penetrates into dreams. Contrary to Jung's oft-repeated dictum, the more the "old Adam" is mortified in situations where equilibrium has been achieved, the less is his influence in dreams. Virtue can become "second nature" to an extent where dreams no longer clash with conscious thought. The plasticity of human nature makes this possible. But before reaching this degree of conformity and firmness, the "other self" makes its escape in dreams; the less stable the balance between the two extremes, the more frequent and prominent these escapes will be. I shall come back to this in Chapter V.

The contrary is equally true, that the "good self" frees itself in dreams from the yoke of the "bad self" when the latter is dominant in conscious conduct. This should not be forgotten, since noble and ethical aspirations are also part of human nature; they are natural, and so imbued with force; it is this force that urges them on to the dream stage. It is certain that this natural force is moulded by cultural environment into different forms, right or wrong. So, for example, a Buddhist and a Christian may disagree; but however the concepts of "good self" and "bad self" may be understood, both are contained within all of us, and Plato means that when one dominates conscious conduct, *the other*—he only mentioned the bad—gets the upper hand in dreams.

If we want to know ourselves, this is worth remembering. But I am not saying this in the way that some modern psychoanalysts do: they crudely judge a person's morality by his dreams, for which he is not responsible, and not by his conscious acts, which are the product of his free will, calling the latter hypocrisy and the former sincerity. Aristotle, in his *Nichomachean Ethics* (Ch. XIII), long ago denounced this error.

When certain authors, Epictetus among them, say, "Do you wish to know yourself? Consult your dreams", this means that dreams can give us invaluable information, but it must be interpreted with great care.

7.   Cicero's "De Divinatione"—Other authors

Although belief in prophetic dreams was certainly very widespread, it also had its opponents. Cicero says that these were innumerable among the people, but among philosophers he mentions only Xenophanes, Carneades, and Epicurus. Aristotle admits a special presentiment in dreams in certain cases, based on natural causes. Cicero deals systematically with the opposition between belief and disbelief in prophetic dreams, in the two books of *De Divinatione*, more than two centuries before Artemidorus.

The books are in the form of an imaginary dialogue between his brother Quintus and himself. In a short introduction he states the universality and antiquity of belief in some foretelling of the future, particularly through oracles "possessed" by gods, sacred "furentes", such as the famous pythonesses of Delphos, and still more through dreams. The whole of the first book is a defence of this belief by Quintus, quoting many authorities, Socrates and Plato in particular, and producing an abundance of curious examples and arguments, always with particular reference to dreams and always repeating that, even if the cause or explanation of such phenomena cannot be discovered, the fact of their existence must be recognized. The theory he takes from Socrates, Posidonius, etc., is expressed in these lines:

> When the soul has been called away by sleep from its intimate association and contact with the body, then it recalls the past, clearly discerns the present, foresees the future. For, though the body lie as if life were extinct, yet the soul lives in full vigour—yea, and how much more truly shall it live and flourish when death frees it completely from the flesh! That is why its prophetic powers increase as the last hour of mortal life approaches. Thus, they who are in the grip of grave and fatal illness know that death is at hand; and so, the

images of those who have passed on flit before their mental vision, and it is at that moment that they most passionately long for fame. But for men who have not lived as they should have lived, the end brings only the bitterest sorrow for their sins.

I may add that the ability of the dying to foretell the future is established by Posidonius' famous tale of a certain Rhodian who with his last gasp called the names of six persons of about the same age and then announced which one of them would die first, which second, and so on through the list (which afterwards happened).[7]

Complementary to this theory, still trying to explain how prophecy is possible, especially in dreams, is the other that Quintus puts forward later, by which everything is subject to destiny—*fatum*—understood as a certain determinism flowing from cause to effect and linking them together from all eternity, so that causes already contain the future in some measure. In order to foretell the future, therefore, it should be enough to devote oneself to a thorough study of causes. This, he adds, is a difficult study, and so predictions are not always accurate. God alone knows all causes, and so he alone can never be mistaken. Men can only collect indications and venture a prophecy.[8]

The whole of this doctrine, which Cicero puts in the mouth of his brother Quintus, making him the mouthpiece of Stoicism and of a very ancient and widespread tradition, is a theory of *natural knowledge of the future*, which existed alongside the more primitive belief in divine inspiration or supernatural knowledge of the future, which Quintus would presumably also allow. To finish, he launches an imprecation against the whole tribe of plebeian soothsayers, fortune-tellers, quacks and magicians whose tricks and usury discredited "true and reasonable divination".

In the second book, Cicero himself speaks and, one by one, refutes all the arguments advanced by his brother and his masters; always supposing, however, that the question is one of foretelling the future.

7. Cicero, *De Divinatione*, I, Ch. XXX. Trans. H. M. Poteat (Chicago, 1950), pp. 366-7.
8. Cicero, *De Divinatione*, I, Chs LV-LVI.

He denies that dreams are given by the gods. He denies any connection between oneiric visions and the natural course of events, and any possibility of foretelling the future arising from such a connection. Finally he denies that the interpretation of prophetic dreams can be based on experience, on a long study of the correspondence between dreams and happenings. He concludes:

> Therefore, let divination by dreams be jeered off the stage, along with the other tricks of the soothsayers. . . .
>
> Now sleep is esteemed a refuge from the anxieties and burdens of life, but actually very many apprehensions and fears are born of it. Dreams, indeed, of themselves, would carry less weight and would be more lightly regarded were it not for the fact that they have been taken under the wing of philosophy, and not by incompetent bunglers, but by men of the highest degree of intellectual power— men who are able to distinguish between consistency and inconsistency and who are looked upon as models of all the philosophical virtues.[9]

This paragraph shows how strong and deep-rooted was the belief in prophetic dreams, and how strongly men's minds were bound to the exteriorizing tendency already mentioned. Only when speaking of doctors does Cicero admit that dreams may predict the course of an illness, or its nature, since here he sees that there may be some relation between dreams and physical condition. Other aspects of dreams he passes over, pausing only to quote Aristotle as saying that they are remains of waking experiences and memories which combine with each other, stirred up by the natural movement of the mind, which never ceases, since, as nature abhors a vacuum, so life abhors inertia, which would be death.

Of the poets, Lucretius deserves prior mention. He devotes some seventy hexameters to dreams in Book IV of *De Natura*. He considers them to be reminiscences of the past, either satisfaction of desires or results of the humours. Horace, Ovid and Virgil make only brief

9. Cicero, *De Div.*, II, Ch. LXXII, pp. 460-1.

allusions. Macrobius, commenting on the *Dream of Scipio*, distinguishes five classes of dreams. Petronius has these verses:

> *Somnia quae mentes ludunt volitantibus umbris*
> *Non delubra deum, nec ab aethere numina mittunt,*
> *Sed sibi quisque facit. . . .*

The dreams that haunt our minds as the shadows flicker do not come from the temples of the gods, nor are they sent by fate from heaven; everyone fashions his own. . . .

In Plotinus, with his all-embracing "soul of the world" and mystical neo-platonism, we need notice only the theory that during sleep the human soul is closer to the divinity. The idea is an old one, like the assertion that madmen, epileptics, etc., are equally privileged. These manifestations of irrational energies seemed to the ancient world to have a sacred quality, just as some meteors did. Tertullian, St Gregory of Nyssa and others have their comments to make on dreams, but the next important treatment of the subject comes from the most acute psychologist among the Fathers, the great St Augustine.

8. *The oneiric psychology of St Augustine*

St Augustine was tremendously preoccupied with the problem of phantasy in all its manifestations, waking as well as dreaming, visions, hallucinations, ecstasies, etc., with or without divine or diabolic intervention. He makes most acute observations and analyses, quotes a great many examples, puts forward different hypotheses, and several times confesses that these phenomena have always filled him with amazement. Naturally, I shall not give an account of every passage in which he mentions this subject, but only of some of the most significant.

His friend Nebridius, also intrigued by these problems, wrote and asked him how superior powers, good or evil, could make us dream something at their command. "This", replied St Augustine, "is a very large question, which would have to be answered in a personal conversation or in some treatise rather than in the space of a letter", and, coming to grips with the subject, he says:

I am of the opinion that every act of our mind produces some effect in the body, and that, however heavy and slow our senses may be, they feel this effect, in proportion to the intensity of the mental act, as when we are angry or sad or joyful. From this it may be concluded that, when we think of something which has no apparent effect on the body, it can nevertheless be apparent to the supernatural and heavenly spirits, whose perception is so very keen that ours does not deserve the name of perception in comparison with it. *Therefore, those traces of activity which the mind imprints, so to speak, on the body can both remain and take on a certain appearance; and when they are subconsciously aroused and activated, they easily produce in us thoughts and dreams, according to the intention of the arouser and activator.* For, if our earth-bound and utterly unresponsive bodies can be so unbeliev-ably affected by the playing of organ music, or by rope-dancers and numberless other such spectacles, as it is clear that they can, then it is certainly not unreasonable to suppose that spiritual and heavenly beings, acting with faculties that have a penetrating natural effect, possess a far greater ability to arouse in us whatever they wish, without our being aware of it even while we are the subjects of it. We are likewise unaware of how the overflow of bile drives us to frequent anger—yet it does so drive us—while, as I have said before, this very overflow is caused by our being angry.[10]

There is much to consider here, but I want to draw attention only to the lines in italics. These form the most complete and exact definition that could be desired of what is today called the "dynamic uncon-scious", which is still attacked by many authors—including important ones such as Bumke[11]—suffering from an inexplicable blindness in this

10. *Letters* 1-82. Trans. Sister Wilfrid Parsons, s.n.d. (New York, 1951), Letter 9, pp. 21-2.

11. Oswald Bumke, *Psychoanalysis and its Satellites* (Barcelona, 1944), pp. 35 ff. "In other words: nobody denies that a latent consciousness exists. But Freud aims at proving some-thing quite different: that these memories which are not for the moment in the conscious mind can produce our reasonings, meditations and thoughts; that we act in accordance with them, and that our consciousness is deceived as to the effects of this psychic process. It has not been definitely proved. . . ."

Christian ascetic works and books of Spiritual direction are full of warnings against the deceits of nature and the subtleties and tricks of pride.

respect. St Augustine says here that not only does a repository of memories exist, but that it is "aroused and activated" by the hidden (unconscious) design of heavenly beings or of the will, that is by individual and affective tendencies, since in ancient and current modern usage the concept of *voluntas* has this meaning as well as that of "rational will". There is a further reason for understanding the passage in this way: the word *latenter* means "secretly": this fits those tendencies that are more or less unconscious—at least at the moment referred to—but not the rational will, which, understood in the fullest sense as free and deliberate, is by definition something conscious and so quite unsuited to the adverb *latenter*. Finally, all these subconscious processes force their almost finished products on the conscious mind (*cogitationes*), and on dreams. In the latter particularly, the dreamer is the first person to be surprised by the unsuspected combinations produced, some of them astonishingly original and apposite, and this surprise is a clear sign that he has not consciously assisted in their elaboration. That they do fit some design, some ordering process which selects particular elements from the vast storehouse of possible memories, is patently obvious. Also, the different ways, now scientifically catalogued (displacement, condensation, etc.), in which dreams order their material, show an extent of ingenuity that we lack in waking life. The particular clarity of vision we enjoy in dreams does not show us scenes being produced and arranged, but ready-made. Finally, the study of thousands and thousands of dreams indicates that what is first and foremost manifested in them is affectivity, taken to include, naturally, the tendencies indissolubly linked to it, which the ancients considered to have their seat, by and large, in the *voluntas*.

Modern writers say precisely this about the dynamic unconscious. All this talk about design, etc., cannot be held to apply only to heavenly beings, since it is obvious that *cogitationes* and dreams are a continuous human process, and neither St Augustine nor anybody else maintains that they always come from outside sources. What is of interest here is the psychic process itself. Also, he quite naturally mentions something subjective, the predominant humour, in this case bile, which can transpose itself on to the psychic level with spontaneous pretexts and manifestations which also clearly show an unconscious design. Finally, Nebridius in his letter, to which St Augustine is replying, speaks of the wonderful way the language of fantasy reproduces the affective—instinctive—physiological human condition.

St Augustine holds that all images come from the senses, contrary to the opinion put forward by Nebridius that there are innate images existing in the soul before its union with the body. Otherwise, asks Nebridius, how does the mind produce the strange figures of dreams, never seen by human eyes? To which St Augustine replies: "How else do you think, but by a power innate in the mind, of increasing and diminishing?"[12] "It is possible for the imagination to alter the data brought in by the senses, and by subtraction, as we said, or by addition, to produce things which in their totality have been experienced by none of the senses, although parts of them have been experienced in one or another instance." "Thus it happens", he says in the preceding sentence, "that, when people are accustomed to deal in such fictions, images of this sort break in on their thoughts almost spontaneously." Note the details of these sentences, and of those I shall quote later, for they round off the explanation I gave of the lines in italics in the previous passage.

Book XII of the treatise *De Genesi ad Litteram* is largely devoted to a study of the nature and origins of visions, particularly those he calls "spiritual" visions, opposed to corporeal visions on the one hand and intellectual on the other—in other words, imaginative visions. The following paragraphs explain his theory of the production of dreams:

But in those cases in which the body is the cause of such visions being seen, we do not wish to say that the body shows them, for it has no power to form anything spiritual. What happens is that volition being drugged or disturbed, or excluded by the brain, which directs the movement of feeling, the mind itself, which on account of its own movement cannot cease this operation, since the body will not allow it fully to feel physical things or direct the force of its

12. *Letters* 1-82 (N.Y., 1951), Letter 7, p. 18.

intention to them, goes its own way: that is to say, it either makes images of physical things, or contemplates those offered to it. Now if it is the mind itself which makes them, they are pure phantasy; but if they are offered to the mind, then they are visions or apparitions. Finally, when one's eyes hurt or go blind, since the cause is not in the seat of the brain, which diverts the very intention of feeling, visions of this kind are not produced, although this obstacle may be placed by the body in the way of seeing physical objects. The blind see things more easily when they are asleep than when they are awake. For when they are asleep, the way of feeling which takes the intention (or point of application of the mind) to the eyes, is drugged in their brains, and so the intention, switching to another object, sees the dream visions as though the objects seen were actually present, so that the sleeper believes himself to be awake and seeing, not semblances and shadows of objects, but the objects themselves. But when blind men are awake, the intention of seeing is diverted through those channels to the eyes, and on reaching them and being unable to go any farther (since the eyes are blind), remains there and gives the sensation of being awake, of being awake in darkness, even in day-time, and not asleep.

Many of those who are not blind are asleep even when their eyes are open, and can see nothing with them (somnambulism), but this does not mean that they see nothing at all because with the spirit (imagination) they see the visions of dreams. On the other hand, if they are awake and close their eyes, then they see neither visible objects nor dream visions. It is of great importance that the way of feeling should be able to go from the brain to the eyes, without the obstacle of lethargy, disturbance or exclusion, so that the strength of the intention can reach the same parts of the body (senses), even though they may be closed, so that when physical images are seen, one will in no way think that these are the same objects as perceived by the senses.[13]

Notice the resemblance established between dreams and delirium, in accordance with the theory put forward in the previous passage, a point that is now again under discussion (Jackson's Law).

13. Migne, *Patrologia Latina*, Vol. 34, col. 70.

As to the meaning of dreams, St Augustine follows the idea that some dreams are meaningful and others not; this was generally accepted, though some of the Greeks held that all dreams had a meaning, whether human beings could see it or not. By claiming that dreams could be versions of either a physical state or a mental situation, St Augustine is naturally admitting the psychic meaning of dreams discussed by psychoanalysts. This meaning—today the most interesting —had not concerned the ancients in the least.

When he refers to the "meaning" of dreams, St Augustine, like most of the ancients, is referring to their prophetic, telepathic or premonitory meaning, or sometimes to their educative value. Sometimes significant dreams are clear and expressed directly in terms of their meaning, as when one dreams that a person is drowning as a direct premonition of the event. Most often, however, the meaning is hidden behind allegories and symbols. The ancient belief in the divine origin of dreams, attacked by Aristotle and Cicero, was fully reinstated with the coming of Christianity, under the influence of both the Old and the New Testaments, with their frequent use of dreams as a means of communication between God and man. No one doubted or could doubt the possibility of such God-given dreams, with or without an intermediary. St Augustine goes further and considers that visions in ecstasy are psychologically dreams, with the difference that the senses are suspended by supernatural means instead of the natural means of sleep. He allows these "significant" dreams to come from a preternatural source (God, angels, demons), not from some natural *vis divinatoria* natural to the human soul as "some writers claim"—such as St Gregory of Nyssa and even, to a certain extent, Aristotle. As for the apparition of dead people in dreams, he inclines to the opinion that their souls are not normally responsible for this, but that, as in the case of seeing living people in dreams, those concerned are not aware that they are being seen and do not feel any sort of virtue or influence emanating from themselves. He relates that a disciple of his in Carthage saw him in a dream and that in the dream he solved a difficulty in a passage of Cicero for him, while in fact he was in Milan at the time with his thoughts far from

Cicero. Naturally, he does not reject the possibility that God may command souls to appear in dreams, just as he commands angels to do so. He supports all these points with curious examples concerning well-known people of his time.

In the context of these ideas it is worth noting that a person can have a significant dream without understanding it. As he says:

> How is it that we sometimes see significant images in our spirit without realizing that they are significant? Or that we feel that what we see has some significance without knowing what it is? And how is it, finally, that thanks to a fuller demonstration we not only see the image with the imagination but understand with the mind what it signifies? These matters are very difficult to know, and once known, even more difficult to express and explain.[14]

To finish with St Augustine, I am going to quote one more passage, taken from a later chapter in the same book:

> But there are other normal human visions (or dreams) which either originate in diverse ways in our spirit (imagination), or are suggested to it in some way by the body, according to our physical or mental state. For men not only turn over their preoccupations in their thoughts while they are awake, personifying them in physical likeness, but, even when they are asleep, dream what they need; if they are mercenary, they dream that they are doing business, and if they happen to go to bed hungry or thirsty, they dream of huge meals and drinks.[15]

It may seem that I have devoted too much time to St Augustine (as indeed Aristotle and Cicero), but in fact these ideas on dreams form the basis of a common heritage that was transmitted through subsequent ages with scarcely any major addition, and we can pass very quickly from them almost down to our own times.

9. *Arabic and Jewish oneiromancy*

Leaving aside China, India and other distant civilizations, we can

14. Migne, *P.L.*, Vol. 34, col. 473.   15. Migne, *P.L.*, Vol. 34, col. 479.

c

consider the Arabs, who took great account of dreams. The Koran, partly the result of a dream revelation, says that dreams reveal the secrets of Allah. Muslim potentates always kept interpreters of dreams at their Courts. Many treatises on oneiromancy were produced, the most famous of which seems to have been Ibn Shahin's *Kitab-al-Tabir*, a collection of thirty-one earlier works. Arabic authors also wrote commentaries on Aristotle, Hippocrates and Galen. They brought back ideas on dreams from their contact with Persia, Chaldea, Hindustan and even China. Yet their works do not show any particular novelty in the most important aspects of the subject.

Dreams play an important part in the Talmudic[16] tradition. The documents collected by Kristianpoller[17] show a fairly well-developed system of jurisprudence concerning the natural or supernatural origin of dreams, different classes of dream—prophetic, oracular, therapeutic, spontaneous, provoked, etc. They also show that interpretations frequently developed into complicated, cabalistic arbitrary decisions.

The Jews on the whole held much the same principles of oneiromancy as the Greeks and the other nations with whom they came in contact. Sceptics on the subject were the exception.

They insist that a dream cannot be effective unless it is interpreted and, further, that an unfavourable dream can be corrected and neutralized by a favourable interpretation. They even took money and other gifts to the interpreter to induce him to favour a benevolent interpretation. This is not far removed from modern psychology, which generally claims that within certain limits, dreams admit of varying interpretations, and that psychic energy can be directed in one way or another according to the explanation given. Jung attacks this idea that a dream can be forced to reveal an unintended meaning, since he regards dreams as immutable manifestations of psychic spontaneity. He condemns any interpretation that voluntarily or involuntarily departs from the dream's intended meaning, as therapeutically useless;

---

16. See A. Stocker, *Les rêves et les songes* (St Maurice, 1945), pp. 101 ff.

17. Kristianpoller, "Traum und Traumdeutung", *Monumenta Hebraica*, Vol. IV. (Berlin, 1923). See also *The Jewish Encyclopaedia*, "Dream".

the dreamer may momentarily accept such an interpretation as valid, but only on a superficial level; a permanent cure must be based on acceptance at a deep level. I do not deny that Jung may be right in certain cases, but it also seems contrary to experience to deny that dreams—in common with so many other human matters—may have a variety of meanings. The fact that a patient has dreamt one thing is an excellent opportunity to introduce helpful suggestions into his inner consciousness, through the interpretation of the dream. Also the psyche, being a complex entity, expresses itself in complex dreams.

10.   *Scholastics and other Western writers up to the nineteenth century*

St Gregory the Great, St Isidore, the author of the treatise *De Spiritu et anima*, and most of the Christian writers of the High Middle Ages, pay scant attention to dreams. They are generally content to repeat the well-known essentials, adding at most some personal comment of no great importance, some new classification, or some new example from their own experience.   St Albert the Great (1193-1280) paraphrases and, with some digressions, comments on Aristotle's treatises, but without adding any new data or psychologically interesting viewpoints, although his text is considerably longer than the original. He is particularly interested in prophetic and telepathic dreams, as indeed were most of the ancients and to a lesser extent most writers down to modern times. He admits some degree of natural prophecy, and relates that he himself once dreamt of a child falling into the water near a mill and being killed by the mill-wheel. Soon after waking, he heard a woman bewailing her son who had just been killed in this way. But he expressly says that he is giving the views of the peripatetics, rather than his own personal opinions. Dealing with the interpretation of metaphorical dreams he gives the usual advice, and remarks that poets have the greatest facility since they are most used to handling symbols.

St Thomas Aquinas deals only very briefly with dreams, in their relation to prophecy and superstition. He recognizes that natural prophecy is no more than a certain fallible prognostication based on knowledge of the causes of future events. This knowledge may come from the stars and is more or less blurred and tenuous. Apart from this, he gives the generally accepted views.

The well-known doctor, philosopher and visionary Arnauld de Villeneuve deals with dreams in his writings, as was to be expected, but with him the mixture of physiology, astrology, metaphysics and theology, so common in the Middle Ages and often well into the Renaissance, is more prominent than in the other writers.

The good scholastics—Suárez can be taken as typical—reached a moderate position on natural and supernatural causes, classification of dreams, lack of moral responsibility, etc., which did not change much over the centuries. As always, ordinary, normal dreams are discounted because of their irregularity, uncertainty and disorder, and doctors are said to be able to profit from observing them only in the case of illness, in order to determine the dominant humour (as the ancients taught). Dreams as a psychotherapeutic or psychopedagogic instrument are unknown. Most attention is paid to their kinship with magic, superstition and theology. Among those who devoted most space to dreams is the Portuguese doctor Gaspar de los Reyes, who practised in Spain.[18] A Spanish doctor and philosopher, "the divine" Vallés, deals with dreams in several works, and wrote the following sentences, which are the most accurate description we have yet seen of what Jung was to call the "prospective function of dreams":

> In dreams we are often advised of our future actions, since our first thoughts about what we are going to do are often continued in dreams, where most commodious means are found for attaining our desired aim; these means please us when we awake, and we put them into effect, attributing this to a divine revelation of what was to be done, whereas the cause is in fact natural.[19]

Doctor Huarte de San Juan would have had something interesting to say on the subject, but it falls outside his scope and he barely men-

18. *Elysius jucundarum quaestionum campus, omnium litteratorum amoenissima varietate refertus*, etc. (Brussels, 1661).

19. Francisco Vallés, *De his quae scripta sunt Physice in libris sacris, sive de sacra Philosophia, liber singularis* (Turin, 1587), Ch. 30, p. 249. This passage is worthy of note in connection with the quotation from Bumke, see note 11, p. 28.

tions it. Luis Vives, in his treatise *De Anima*, has a short chapter which is as sensible as all his writings, but adds nothing new.

For Campanella, the neo-platonist, the *anima mundi* is the basis of all instincts, intuitions, dreams and prophecies, which the *anima hominis* understands through a special mysterious sensitivity. This theory could be considered as a sort of exaggerated version of the facts that Jung was to explain with his doctrine of the "collective unconscious".

Descartes initiated a more dangerous attack on the integrity of the human being in his psychological explanation, which is too rationalist on one hand and too mechanical on the other and so leads to a dualism that renders the relation between the soul and the body an insoluble problem. The wake he left shows how wrong his principles were: sensationalism, idealism, positivism and mathematicism—a bad time for psychology which had to take refuge among the moralists. The *Discours de la Méthode* brought the problem of criticism into the limelight. Knowledge and its attendant problems gradually became the most absorbing question. After centuries and centuries of belief and confidence in itself, the human mind suddenly seemed to be seized with an insatiable thirst for verification. Descartes was responsible for this. After him, the Enlightenment, drunk with intellectual and scientific optimism, moved farther and farther away from the volitional and affective life.

11. *Romanticism and positivism*

It was precisely this tendency that gradually led to a reaction that was to reach its peak in Romanticism. Some minds grew tired of the burning torch of knowledge, of all this logic, mechanics and dissection, and turned, with varying degrees of success, to a study of the complex experiences underlying human behaviour. They examined the extraordinary originality of life, the hidden faculties, telepathy, dreams—everything instinctive and emotional. Dionysius rebelled against Apollo, the life force against pure intellect, the unconscious against the conscious. This took place above all in Germany, where, perhaps due to racial characteristics, this pressure of primitive, even orgiastic, forces has always been felt very strongly by the classically disciplined mind, and even more strongly by the ascetic. These states of equilibrium seem very difficult to attain there, since they do not appear to correspond (in the writers at least) to that balance between the two extremes which alone can guarantee stability. No other European literature is so full of excessively rationalist criticism on one hand and truly volcanic eruptions of irrationalism on the other. The latter take the form either of an exaltation of vitality or of a terrified delight in transcendental myths and forms of nature mysticism.

Certain circles at the beginning of the nineteenth century were beginning to create an atmosphere favourable to mystery, emotion and phantasy; a good preparation for the understanding of dreams. It is significant that Maine de Biran should have written a treatise on dreams. The names of those who prepared the climate in Germany are legion: Goethe, Hamann (called "the wizard of the North"), Herder, Novalis, Schlegel, Tieck, Schelling, Schleiermacher. By the middle of the century, while empirical positivism continued on its way, there was a strong introspective current that produced many works on dreams. By the last quarter of the century, these works had become very numerous indeed. Every aspect of dreams was studied: psychophysiological, artistic, pathological, occultist or, if one prefers, metaphysical, therapeutic, etc., both in theory and in practical application. Finally, Freud opened up a new epoch, the age of psychoanalysis, with his publication of *Traumdeutung* in 1900.

II

DREAMS IN SCIENCE

12. The coming of the "scientific era"

As the natural sciences, particularly in the nineteenth century, gradually separated themselves from natural philosophy, of which they had formed part for centuries, and as their triumphs became clearer and their promises grew to Utopian dimensions, so men's minds became more and more impressed with everything verifiable by experiment, everything visible and tangible, solid and positive: understanding was firmly wedded to the material world. The old "speculations" of classical psychology paled at the first approach of the new "scientific" psychology, nurtured on physics and physiology. The names "psycho-physics" and "psychophysiology" belong to this time—the middle of the last century (which is not to say that such sciences do not have their proper place, but they must be confined within their limits and not considered simply synonymous with psychology). At that time a psychological explanation had to lead, apparently naturally, to some biological and, if possible, physical substratum if it was to be believed. The wind of experimental science swept through all domains of knowledge, blowing hardest in every dark corner where some remnant of mystery might be hiding.

Dreams, so prone to obscurantism, also had their "hour of truth". In 1848 Maury began his first study. According to Vaschide, Maury was the first to study dreams in a purely scientific spirit, though even he could not entirely forsake the philosophical method.[1] More and more

1. See A. Stocker, Les rêves et les songes, p. 212.

39

students followed his lead. Unfortunately, as has happened so often in psychology, the different writers did not all link their work to previous studies but generally began independently. They not only had different viewpoints and used different terminology, which can always be brought into line eventually, but reached diametrically opposed conclusions, owing to an excess of confidence in their own limited experiments and a tendency to generalize from insufficient evidence, on points already complex and largely dependent on personal characteristics. However, a fairly respectable body of sufficiently sound knowledge can be sorted out from among their works and I shall attempt to sum up their most important conclusions.

13. *Sleep a condition for dreaming*

Our progress through life is geared to the two rhythms of sleeping and waking. Both are part of our double psychophysiological life, but on a different level. Awake, we stand on the firm ground of reality; asleep, we move into the fantastic world of dreams. Awake, our nervous energies are directed towards action, immediate contact with the world, and the solution of its problems; in sleep, we plunge into solitude and immobility, we curl up into ourselves, saying "Enough!" to our daily preoccupations. This rejection of daily reality and this indifference are the keys to the world of sleep; they are given to us when we come into the world. In fact we go to sleep lulled by the persuasive all-embracing desire to forget our worries. We can of course combat and put off this desire, but if our will does this too much, nature will intervene and impose its own rule. Thus, willy-nilly, we begin to lose contact with reality and to descend into the soft, dark world of sleep. As Bergson says, "Sleep is loss of interest";[2] this phrase came into psychological terminology with Claparède: "Considered globally—from the biological angle—the sleeping state consists of a rejection of interest in the present situation; it is a state of negation".[3]

2. E. Bergson, *L'énergie spirituelle* (Paris, 1944), p. 103.

3. Claparède, "Le sommeil et la veille", in *Nouveau Traité de Psychologie*, Vol. IV, p. 472.

Though sleep is not the central object of this study, it must be considered as the physiological framework and the negative condition for dreaming. The door from waking to sleeping is as it were bewitched: no one can go through it with his eyes open. We know that at a given moment we are awake; we can even feel ourselves approaching the door, and then we realize later that we have been asleep, but we are never conscious of the actual process. Those who have the impudence to attempt to find out are punished with insomnia. Only those who simply let themselves slide through gently are rewarded with sleep. The process is one of the simplest and most natural when one allows oneself to go along with it, but one of the hardest and most deceptive when one tries to understand it.

Our normal physical and mental preparation for sleep is the same as that of the animals: we look for a quiet corner away from disturbances such as light, noise, heat and cold; we adopt a comfortable position which will allow us to relax our muscles without moving or falling; we close our eyes; we renounce control over our train of thought; we say farewell to cares and worries; we let our will fall into a bottomless pit of passivity and nihilism. . . . Then there begin to appear those first messages of a new world—hypnagogic phenomena (with which I shall deal later). Generally in a few seconds, perhaps instantaneously, we disappear into a sort of universal blankness and for some time—which varies with different people—we swim about in the dark waters of total unconsciousness. This is the first onset of sleep.

Apparently the restoration of physical energies, which mysterious vegetative forces bring about after the day's expenditure, demands a break from the bonds and functions that condition waking life: a ship must be put into dry dock before a hole in the hull can be welded. But it must not be thought that sleep is simply a consequence of expenditure of energy or fatigue. One can be exhausted and not sleep, and vice versa. The brain has a mechanism that acts as a switch between waking and sleep. Usually, when our physical forces are in need of restoration, we feel sleepy, and if we have no reason to want to stay awake, but decide to give in to the desire for sleep, this mechanism begins to function and we fall asleep. But if these processes are upset, we can suffer from insomnia even with a great need and longing for sleep. The need for sleep is clearly greatest during the first hours—the length of time will vary with the degree of fatigue. All who have made a study of sleep have discovered that its depth curve descends rapidly to a maximum at the end of about the first hour; in the second hour it rises again fairly sharply to a middle position, and from the third to the seventh it comes gradually up towards the surface, till we automatically wake up. These different levels of sleep have been studied by a variety of ingenious methods, chiefly by the different intensity of stimuli, generally noise or light, necessary to wake the sleeper. Lately, electro-encephalograms have been used.

So it appears—as in fact we all know—that sleep is not uniform, but follows an uneven course. And different people have different maximum and minimum points on the depth curve. To deal with normal differences between individuals, and the borderline between normal and pathological, with the hairsbreadth transitional stages, would be a long task. In general, one can say that for an hour or an hour and a half we are in a very deep sleep, which gradually becomes shallower until we wake up. The relation between this and dreams is the important factor here.

First, during the brief period of actually falling asleep, there come about what are called "hypnagogic images". Next, during the deep sleep, it would appear, though some disagree, that there are no dreams. In the intermediate sleep there are indefinite dreams which leave a vague impression that something was happening in the imagination, but no memory. In the light sleep dreams become clearer and more vivid, particularly in the last and lightest phase, when situations and stories appear in which the faculties of waking consciousness become more and more apparent. This leads one to think that mental activity increases in proportion to the restoration of physical energy. Some authors insist that mental life is a continuous process, with no sharp break between sleep and waking, but reality suggests that there is in fact an essential break between waking consciousness and oneiric consciousness.

14. *Hypnagogic images and other phenomena of the drowsy state*

The intermediate phases of consciousness—falling asleep and waking up—have their own particular characteristics, very different from those of sleep proper. There is naturally little to say about these fringes of sleep in the case of people who are asleep before they are in bed, or wake up, or are woken up, with a jerk, but when this state between sleeping and waking is prolonged for any reason, particularly when one wakes up slowly, there is a strange oscillation between lucidity, semi-lucidity and dreaming, with shadowy images, illusions, hallucinations, cataplexies (paralysis), nightmares, shocks and flashes of dream. However inattentive we may be to our own mental processes, we must surely have noticed this at some time, and it leaves a particular impression. It happens in those lazy awakenings when, tired of sleep, we feel a desire to get up, and yet, reluctant to leave the warm bed, we allow ourselves a little more creature comfort. It happens if we go to sleep on a summer afternoon, particularly if we lie down (heating of the cerebellum?), perhaps with digestive troubles. . . . It happens also before we fall asleep at night. Sometimes certain features predominate, sometimes others.

These "shadowy images" are largely what are known as "phosphenes", or appear to originate from them: flickering points which hover undecided, jump, meet and separate, luminous filaments, tangles of shaded light, whirls of orange or greenish light, little sparks of clarity, perhaps a sketch of a ghostly face, fragments of figures. . . . All these pass in a confused blur, or perpetually changing against a dim opaque background occasionally relieved with flashes of brightness, depending on the light.

In this state snatches of thoughts and preoccupations also generally appear, and originate an essential part of dreams, their symbolism, except that in this state we are not completely unconscious and can surprise the symbolism in its early stages.[4] The strangest of all these

4. A. Caruso, "Uber den Symbolismus der hypnagogischen Vorstellungen", in *Revue Suisse de Psychologie*, Vol. VII (1948), pp. 87 ff.

hypnagogic images are undoubtedly those which are so close to waking sensations that (even with the remnants of our critical faculty) it is hard to distinguish between the two. In 1830, Johannes Müller called them "pseudo-hallucinations", and many people nowadays just call them hallucinations. I cannot see that they have the strength and scope of typical hallucinations, and I shall call them "semi-hallucinations". They seem to be a complete copy of reality, one is conscious of them, and they can be delayed for a few moments for observation, like Jaensch's eidetic images. They are isolated images and distinct from thoughts. These characteristics all distinguish them from oneiric images. Leonhard states that acoustic and tactile sensations predominate in them, but Ey, on the other hand, considers these the least frequent. One can only conclude that this varies with the individual.

These half-waking states are not common. There is something compulsive about them. They are sometimes accompanied by cataplexy, a paralysis full of a sense of oppression, from which one forces oneself to escape, but which seems to drag one further and further down. The will to get up produces not movement but some hallucinatory deception which really makes one believe one has got up, but this is followed by the realization that one is still in the grip of the cataplexy. A desperate effort must be made in order to escape. But one does not completely lose control of the situation; the critical faculty intervenes and can modify the course of events. It is a truly nightmarish state. Sartre, who with all his faults is a master of introspection and of description of fleeting, indefinable experiences, has some penetrating pages on these phenomena in *L'Imaginaire*.

15. *General characteristics of dreaming*

Some authors consider hypnagogic images the first links in the chain of images of which dreams are composed. These first dreams, however, if they do occur before and during the deepest sleep, are, for practical purposes, impossible to record. It seems that these images may appear in the intervals of light sleep which may for some reason or other occur during the first two hours; it seems doubtful that they appear in the normal deep sleep. This leads us straight to normal dreams.

One cannot hope to give a complete definition of dreaming, since calling it "the imaginative representation of events or things during sleep" merely refers in general terms to a basic individual experience, leaving the amazing peculiarity of the dream world practically untouched. The best way is to compare it to other states, and, firstly, to waking.

Dreams and waking.—There have been philosophers, oriental ones in particular, who have tried to minimize the difference between dreams and waking. "Tchuang-tse dreamed one day that he was a butterfly, and now does not know whether he was then a man who dreamed he was a butterfly or a butterfly who dreamed he was a man."[5] "The ever-dreaming Orient", one might say. Hervey de Saint-Denis, in his famous book on dreams,[6] also tried to minimize the difference, but it can be objected that he was a specialist in Chinese, who might easily have assimilated the oriental tendency to subjectivity, in which psychic realities count far more than in the more objective and positivist West. But examples abound, and amongst others a certain Delboeuf in France has claimed that dreams make use of all the mental activities of waking. Furthermore, Descartes himself, the foremost exponent of western rationalism, showed considerable hesitation in separating dreams from reality, and made this the starting point of his philosophical discussion. Calderón makes his characters wonder whether dreaming is life or life is a dream. It is true that there is such a thing as a "daydream", a transitory state for some people, a moderate habit with others, a vice in others, and yet in others a near approach to delirium, until for many lunatics it becomes the essence of their mental life.[7] The scale goes from one extreme to the other. But here I am

5. F. Oliver-Brachfeld. *Como interpretar los sueños* (Barcelona, 1949), p. 5. See *Quelques aspects de la Philosophie Védântique*, by the Swami Siddheswarananda (Paris, 1954), pp. 197-220.

6. H. de Saint-Denis, *Les rêves et les moyens de les diriger* (Paris, 1867).

7. On "daydreamers", see the fine work by A. Borel and G. Robin, *Les rêveurs éveillés* (Paris, 1925).

dealing only with normal people, and neither I nor anyone else who has written on the subject seriously doubts for a moment that despite the numerous similarities which are bound to exist between the two states, there is in fact a fundamental difference between dreaming and our waking perception of reality.

One cannot discuss how and why to distinguish dreams from reality without alternate reference to waking and dreaming. Remembering a dream when awake, we can distinguish easily enough by applying the usual criteria of our knowledge of reality, such as the principle of contradiction, comparison with definite memories, observation of physical laws of time and space, etc. But when we dream we feel dream sensations as though they were produced directly by real stimuli; we believe ourselves in direct contact with reality, exactly as in cases of hallucination. Even when our sleep is lighter and critical intervention filters through into the dreams, enabling us, paradoxically, to realize that we are dreaming while we actually are, the hallucination still remains, because these critical interventions are only momentary. In fact, when we are dreaming, we are a defenceless prey to hallucination. We cannot resist the internal stimuli, because our critical apparatus is inactive.

Dreams the product of a central origin.—Actual sensory impressions only penetrate occasionally into dreams, unlike when we are awake, and even then they pass through some sort of mysterious filter which transfigures them completely before they reach the dreaming consciousness: so an insect bite can become a thrust in a duel; thunder can become the roar of a mob. Dream images come from a central, not a peripheral, origin, although their elements may indicate some relation to the outside world. When we embark on a dream we carry with us, like Noah's ark, sufficient provision to establish a personal world which can survive without any external contact.

Dissolution of the space-time framework.—In waking consciousness, everything is ordered by fixed co-ordinates in time and space. In dreams this framework either disappears or becomes pliable and extendable, so that the most impossible situations become perfectly natural. One can be everywhere, inside and outside at once, if needs be.

Objects can change shape without causing any surprise. In one dream a man was hitting another with a ruler—an instrument he often used —when the man he was hitting turned into a giant colander, which did not deter his attacker from thinking him dead and hiding the body carefully. In another dream a man was swimming in a hotel corridor, without it occurring to him that the water might run out. In a dream of mine I once saw a friend of mine with the head and beak of a stork, and still recognized him easily enough. Distances, of course, are elastic: however much we walk we can never reach something close at hand, and the next instant we can be miles away without having flown. The scene of one action becomes another far away without any attempt at continuity, and then the two become hopelessly confused. One can die and return to life, be old and grow young, glide gloriously through space. In short, time and space no longer exist as limits to actions. Any impressions of time and situation that remain are purely subjective reminiscences, liable to any change. Furthermore, on a different plane, there are telepathic dreams in which separation in space does not hinder perception, and prophetic dreams (their existence or non-existence will be discussed in due course) in which time counts for nothing.

Collapse or alteration of the intelligence.—Intelligence may become infantile or be undermined in many ways, but it is not annulled. It still retains some remnants of its normal resources, but these are confused to a greater or lesser extent. Its essential power of reasoning is disturbed and robbed of the basic principles by which it interprets reality and constructs the appropriate syntheses. The images themselves seem to bring a certain faculty for fitting objects together, sometimes well, sometimes very badly from an objective point of view, although the combination may form a marvellous psychic language. We watch and agree to all this with amazement and unlimited credulity.

Criticism is lacking, because there is no comparison. There is none, for one reason, because of the extreme narrowness of dream consciousness; at any given moment, it grasps only the present, which is so fragile and fleeting that we hardly realize when it is past. Take the metamorphoses we accept so readily, for example: if a book became a cat, then a tub, then the entrance to a cinema, without preventing us from thinking that it is still "something" we want for some reason or other, the process should be understood like this: there is a thread running through the series—the idea of that "something"; but in dreams the idea is compatible with a thousand forms, one for every given moment; since there is no connection between one moment and the next, the oneiric consciousness, which cannot grasp series (before and after), perceives no metamorphoses; the waking consciousness does, since it can remember and see the series. This is why there can be no criticism. The explanation is Leonhard's, and, in many cases at least, seems a good one.[8]

Sometimes, however, dreams produce higher syntheses which elude us when we are awake. Many inventions have been made in this way. Poincaré found solutions to difficult mathematical problems in dreams. Zorrilla, according to his memoirs, added a stanza to a poem in a dream when he had not been able to work it out before going to sleep. The following morning he was astonished to find it written in his own handwriting, in its proper place.

Language disturbances.—The absence of intelligence is also reflected in language disturbances, which have been extensively studied by Kraepelin and Bleuler. How fine certain phrases and lines seem to us in our dreams! Why do we never make a note of these masterpieces, we wonder. Han Ryner once dreamt that he was a barrister defending Chateaubriand, who had been accused of some crime. The judge was Napoleon, and so eloquent was the plea for the defence that the Emperor was moved to tears. Ryner had trained himself to wake up immediately and note his dreams, so he at once wrote out the final sentence. It was, "You see before you Chateaubriand accused accusingly of carrying unjust accusations under his arm and of carrying a former secretary under his arm." He could have wept with disappointment.[9] Sometimes the words have no meaning at all but are simply a jumble of sounds in an unknown language—yet pearls are hidden in all this

8. K. Leonhard, *Die Gesetze des normalen Träumens* (Leipzig, 1936), pp. 66 and ff.
9. Han Ryner, "Simple note sur le songe", *Action et Pensée* (Sept., 1949), p. 67.

nonsense—not literary pearls, but ones of great value in understanding the psychology of the dreamer; but this is a matter for psychoanalysis, which I am not considering at the moment.

Procedure through images.—The most striking feature of dreams is that they proceed almost entirely by way of images. It is amazing how easily abstract ideas, critical judgements, allusions or relationships, affective currents, indeed the whole of psychic life, take shape in symbols, recognizable shapes drawn from the storehouse of personal experience. This makes them largely incommunicable. When common symbols appear, as they do in many typical dreams, it is due to the existence of a common culture and language with a common stock of stereotyped symbols. In the case of more basic images, it is due to the fact that we all share the same human nature, which acts in the same way in the face of the same objective reality. This produces paradoxical, oddly assorted conglomerations of images, which "scientific" psychology refuses to investigate, saying that this incoherence and strangeness are typical of dreams, without bothering its head any further, and perhaps being "scientifically" scandalized by the tentative interpretations of psychoanalysis. In any case, even those who admit that dreams have a meaning (where it is sufficiently clear) would not deny that sometimes the significant thing about a dream is that it has none. Children's games are also significant; so is the way a horse rolls and kicks in a field. Why should imagination not be allowed to play in the same way? These natural relaxations cannot take place in a vacuum, so must take some form or other, hence the problem: which is more important, the specific form each one takes, or their general overall characteristics?

Summary of some of the general characteristics of dreaming.—Removal of the senses from the objective world; relaxation and capriciousness of the time-space framework; infantilism or senile decay of the intelligence; impossibility of adequate criticism; extreme credulity; modification of many objective relationships; narrowness of consciousness; procedure almost entirely through images; autonomy of the course of images; incoherence and strangeness of combinations of images; dis-

D

turbance of affects, so that horrors can be viewed with indifference and harmless objects arouse undue alarm and despondency. Other distinguishing features will emerge during further discussion of dreams.

16.   *The self in dreams*

Imagine an artist like Walt Disney assembling abstract thoughts to form the basis of a work, dramatizing them around a central figure, visualizing them in form and colour in a film and then, as though by magic, putting himself into the film, becoming the central figure and living the action as though it were a part of his own life: this is roughly what each one of us does when he dreams. Awake, we think ideas; asleep, we live them. Our waking ideas take shape in words and phrases; in dreams they become persons and situations. Psychoanalysis, which in this respect has made many converts from among the "scientific" psychologists, claims that these ideas, particularly at times of crisis, are often an exposition and appreciation of our psychic state and of measures to remedy it, which our waking consciousness sometimes rejects or resolutely ignores. In dreams, these latent ideas, freed from the compulsion imposed upon them by our waking selves, unfold to form an exact allegorical transposition, as if on a cinema screen. Here consciousness can watch a version of itself that is sometimes clear and convincing, but more usually cryptic, enigmatic, and in need of interpretation.

The position of one's actual self in dreams presents a curious problem. It is said that no one ever sees himself as he actually is, at least alive. I once saw myself dead, like the German writer and teacher Jean Paul Richter (1763-1825) who "saw himself dead" on 15th October 1790.[10] One sometimes sees oneself projected in another shape or figure, which may be singular or plural. We see dreams as we see the world, as we experience life. Sartre, who has observed these phenomena so acutely, says in *L'Imaginaire*:

10. See Charles Baudouin, *Découverte de la personne*, p. 94.

How are we to take this apparition of the sleeper himself in this imaginary world? Must we suppose that it is really *he*, in person, as a real consciousness, who steps into the world of oneiric imagery? This hypothesis strikes me as senseless. Because for the sleeper to introduce himself, as a real consciousness, into the drama of his dreams, he would have to be conscious of himself as a real being, existing in a real world, at a real time marked with real memories. But these conditions are precisely those that define the waking state.[11]

I am not satisfied with this way of posing and formulating the problem. The dreamer feels himself a part of oneiric phantasmagoria with direct and immediate, not reflected, consciousness of himself; in some dreams he may see himself with reflected oneiric consciousness and at moments even with awakened or almost awakened consciousness. This should not be surprising, since we spend a large part of our waking lives looking outward, without turning our thoughts inward on ourselves and our experiences. The dreamer lives his dream with his own subjective existence active in the background, independent of real time and space or, rather, of a certain way of consciously co-ordinating himself with real time and space. Personal subjectivity gives sufficient light to illuminate this process. The dreamer actually lives the events of his dream, with full faith in them, but is incapable of placing himself in a critical observation post from where he can see every side of the actual situation. Because of this, we say he is dreaming. Most men spend their waking lives in this same simple state without in fact using the critical observation post. But they have the power to use it, and it is the possession of this power that distinguishes waking from sleep.

When we go to sleep we abandon one world and one way of being, and cross over to another. The problem is whether we cross over to different inner experience. We seem to continue living as ourselves, with our memories somewhat mutilated and disordered, but still substantially ourselves. Used to seeing ourselves in our waking lives as the centre of our experiences, we feel that this vital spark is not extin-

11. Jean Paul Sartre, *L'Imaginaire* (Paris, 1940), pp. 218-19.

guished in dreams but continues, in a particular way and after an
interlude of darkness, to be the same centre of reference and experience,
held together by an implicit sense of continuity; whatever our surroundings, we remain conscious of ourselves. We may be sad or
happy for illusory reasons, but the person who is sad or happy is as real
in dreams as he is awake.

17. *The elements of dreams*

Writers who deal with dreams sometimes contradict each other. One
may say that dreams reflect the preceding day's preoccupations, while
another thanks Providence that dreams take us away from everyday
life into a completely different world, which seems a more restful
opinion. Each is partly true: the error lies in generalizing.

Scientific study of a phenomenon means definition of its nature and
discovery of the laws that govern it. But dreams exist on different
levels, which behave in different ways, so one has to be very cautious
in stating general laws to apply to all dreams, because the number of
exceptions will be vast. The dream world is too often considered a
simple whole. In fact it is precariously made up of elements that do
not all obey the same laws. For example, the regularity of the *central
image* does not apply to *peripheral images*; the laws of *visual images* are
not quite those of *tactile images*, and visual images in themselves have
one set of rules for form and another for colour.

So the various elements must be distinguished and studied separately
before undertaking an overall study of the dream world.

First, the *central image* must be distinguished from *peripheral images*.
Consciousness, both waking and in dreams, is like the field of sight: it
has a point of maximum focus and minimum extension, and the
remainder is in a sort of marginal haze.

Another distinction is between what may be termed the *dream theme*
and the various forms in which it expresses itself. The succeeding
images are grouped round a central idea (which may be a business
worry or an affective complex), which determines the general course

of the dream. Various dreams can be dramatically different entities, but have a common link, the same dream theme.

Other elements which can be distinguished are: authentic *memories, pseudo-recollections*, legitimate *discursive actions, paralogisms* or *fallacies, beliefs, desires* and *affects*. The various elements must now be considered in turn.

18. *Oneiric images*

These are more distinct than the images of waking consciousness, but less so than semi-hallucinatory hypnagogic images (already discussed) and still less than true hallucinations. The will to govern one's train of thought, characteristic of the undistracted waking consciousness, is inhibited during sleep. Then the images seething in the imagination, freed from control and corrective criticism, are masters of the field, as fascinating as if they were real, and free to follow their own course. Yet though dreams dazzle and enslave the mind to such an extent, they still retain a "dream atmosphere", an artificial light, a dim colouring, an after-taste of incompleteness which—according to some observers—make them immediately recognizable as dreams, even when we are in the grip of their magic persuasion. But it is, I repeat, dangerous to generalize. In many dreams, quite probably most, the hallucinatory effect is complete and we see them in true perspective only when we awake.

There are undoubtedly others in which the feeling, "it's only a dream", is more or less prominent, particularly when the intelligence appears on the scene almost fully awake but without destroying the magic of the illusion. It divides the psychic flow into two levels, the "critical self" and the "dreaming self", which somehow do not destroy each other but remain in a paradoxical compromise. Though this position is highly unstable, fleeting and intermittent, Hervey de Saint-Denis, in his famous book on how to direct one's own dreams, managed, by extreme virtuosity, to stabilize and control it, thus making two mortal enemies—understanding and the active will on one hand and dream phantasmagoria on the other—live together in peace.

19.   *Optic images—Separation of form and colour*

Optic images, which form the vast majority, can be divided into form, colour and luminosity. Of these three aspects, by far the most prominent is form. Dreams are usually visions of forms which cannot be called either light or dark. Colours are generally very faded and hard to define when one tries to remember them alone. In certain cases, how- ever, colour may play an important and even central part—a blood- stain, for example. Sometimes, also, luminosity is specially important. But form is the commonest indication of persons and things, and since the attention is generally concentrated on a sequence of events, the other aspects are generally faint, unless some special reason brings colour or light to the fore. People who do not examine their dreams carefully may be surprised to hear this and may not believe it; some people do in fact tend to dream more in colour than is usual, but more frequently they try to reconstruct their dream when they wake up and add the colours that naturally fit the objects.

This separation of form and colour has another very curious aspect: there is a different incubation period, so to speak, between a sense perception of a form or colour and its apparition as a central image in dreams. Colours may appear the following night, whereas forms usually take several days. This means that a colour which belongs, in fact, to a certain object can appear in dreams attached to another object. Leon- hard observed this minutely, and was led to the conclusion that forms which appear in dreams simply because they were a recent experience, and not for any other reason, took a minimum time of ten days, and usually took twenty. Whether the time taken was nearer ten or twenty days depended on various factors: the intensity or duration of the perception, how often it had been recalled in the meantime, its affective content, the opportunity of associating general evocative force with mere repetition of recent experience, etc. He considered that these time limits should not be thought merely casual, but related to some physiological process which controls the repetition of sensations. I should object to this theory on the grounds that forms and colours can hardly be separated in this way when perception of form ultimately depends on reception of colour through the retina. The distinction between light-dark and chromatic scales would have to be more complete than is generally thought and they would each have to follow separate laws, which seems to be indicated by some of Professor Michotte's experiments on perception. Goldstein observed one case which tends to confirm this, a soldier, Schneider, who was wounded in the head and at first saw forms without their colours.[12] This is a psychophysiological problem posed by dreams. It seems beyond question after all Leonhard's observations that colours do reappear as central dream images (*central* is important) far more rapidly than forms.

Another peculiarity is that forms that were the central object of waking attention can appear, not as central images, but as peripheral ones, that same night. And vice versa, forms that were peripheral and unnoticed can appear as central images that night. All this applies to sensations.

As regards the reappearance of fantasies, that is of things not seen or heard the preceding day, but only imagined, much the same can be said, but the differences are less pronounced. If we think intensely about some person or thing, this seems to prevent its emergence as a central dream image; on the other hand, a fleeting or peripheral idea often becomes the focal point of a dream.

20. *Law of tangency*

It must not be thought, however, that the person or thing seen or imagined the previous day does not appear in that night's dream. What happens is that he or it appears in analogous or related forms. This is a very general and very important law of all dreams, and one

12. See P. Laín Entralgo, *La Historia Clínica* (Madrid, 1950), p. 549.

that has many implications. Leonhard calls it the "law of *Beitraumen*";
we can call it the law of tangency or, if one prefers the Greek, of
paranoiria. It means the tendency to look at things obliquely, to allude
to, indicate or hover round an object, run parallel, or find a substitute
for it; dreams can apparently never reproduce an object in its exact
and proper form, but always produce a copy, imitation or
parody.

For example: a man is worried about a bill, and dreams of a bill,
but not the same one; he has been explaining the exact details of something he wants made: he dreams of a similar thing, but not the one he
wanted; he has been with a friend, and dreams of the friend's brother;
he has been invited to a dinner, and dreams of a different dinner which
resembles it in some way; he has been involved in some financial
transaction, and dreams of another. The object never appears in its
correct shape; anyone can prove this for himself. Leonhard relates that he
was explaining this law to a friend, who replied that he did not agree,
because the day before his car had broken down and he had dreamt
that he was repairing the engine. "The same car?" asked Leonhard.
"Well, no, as a matter of fact it was a lorry." In fact, careful observation
will show that the object never appears in its proper shape.

There is an exception: certain very intense, usually *unpleasant*,
experiences do reappear in dreams from time to time, apparently
exactly as they happened. The process is rather like an echo, and grows
fainter each time until it finally fades away. The moment of being
wounded, or an operation without anaesthetic, for example, may be
repeated exactly; as such they form a category that obeys its own
laws.

Why not relate the law of tangency to the law of different incubation periods for form and colour? If the delay in the reappearance of
forms were in fact the result of a process of maturation, or of a physiological mechanism, as Leonhard holds, this would be a tempting
explanation of the law of tangency. Why do objects not appear in their
proper shapes? Simply because forms arrive later than the *idea* of an
object, and the urgent need to dream of the object clothes it in different

forms, which, for their part, reveal the concern of the dream with that particular object.

This law robs the Freudian "censorship" of a large part of its force and prestige. It has always been known that the changes attributed by Freud to the action of a "censor" take place not only when the dream material is censurable, but even when it is completely harmless. (And, incidentally, "X-certificate" subjects often ignore the supposed censor.) I do not think this means that the idea of a censorship mechanism must be completely abandoned; dreams as well as real life do show cases in which the operation of such a mechanism seems a plausible explanation. Once again, it is dangerous to generalize.

21. *Acoustic images*

Acoustic images, though less common than optical, are also very frequent. Speech, one's own and that of other people, deserves special mention among the different sounds heard in dreams. We are aware of our own speech from inside, distinguishing words, as when awake. One's own is very often the least acoustic of all, not only because the echo of the voice in one's head prevents one from hearing it correctly, but because human thought, especially on abstract topics, can hardly be conceived without an inner language. Hence it is very difficult to decide whether in our dreams we speak phonetically or think verbally. The same sometimes applies to the speech of other people in dreams; we can understand them in some strange way, without hearing any sound; on other occasions we may hear sounds with perfect clarity. Also very frequent, usually when we are particularly interested in what is being said, is an indistinct noise of words which leaves us anxious and unsatisfied. This is particularly noticeable if we expect to be told something we do not know; this is not surprising, since we can hardly expect someone else to tell us, in our dreams, something we do not know ourselves. Remember that in our dreams we are author, producer, actors, theatre and public all combined. If we say something in a foreign language we notice the oral articulation more clearly, since the idiomatic material, being less familiar, is a spur to the attention. When we hear, in a foreign tongue, a reply we cannot understand to a question we managed to ask—just as often happens in waking life—the deception is usually even more marked. We hear sounds of talking, but no words are formed; this is very typical of dreams. Finally, there is no incubation period for sounds; they can reappear the night after being heard, particularly if heard intensely for a long time. I shall say more later about sounds actually heard at the time and their incorporation into dreams.

22. *Other images*

Tactile sensations also occur, but far less often than the others. Leonhard and Hoche both say that they have found no evidence of taste and smell in dreams. This does not mean that dreams of eating and drinking are rare, but they must be produced by hunger and thirst. I myself have never noticed taste in my dreams about food, but I do remember once being offered some biscuits in a dream, and, still in the dream, no doubt prompted by the subconscious desire to observe taste, thinking, "And people say there is no taste in dreams!" Since memories of taste and smell exist in waking life, it should in theory be possible to experience them in dreams, but of course they are particularly evanescent. One has a certain ingrained intuition about the feel and taste of food.

Coenaesthetic and also proprioceptive, or intracorporeal, sensations, as pure images, and not illusions built up from an actual sensation, are very rare. This may be because the muscles are relaxed and their movement cannot be felt: in dreams we glide or fly instead of walking, or appear in different places without knowing how we got there. In some nightmares, too, when a wild beast or a man with a knife is about to attack us and we feel an immediate need to use our legs, we find ourselves tragically glued to the ground, so tragically that the terror of it wakes us up. On the other hand, one does dream of walking and climbing stairs, with the fatigue they bring.

To sum up and compare what has been said about different images:

forms reappear as the central image after an interval of between ten and twenty days, unless they were a marginal perception, in which case they may appear as the central image the same night. Colours, fully observed, appear that night, as do sounds if heard long and clearly enough. Tactile sensations also reappear immediately.

Another question is the persistence or tenacity with which images can reoccur in dreams after their perception. Visual images seem able to last a long time; the others fade away very rapidly, perhaps lasting only from a day to that same night.

It must be remembered that the force that causes an image to reappear in dreams can come from two different sources: one is the freshness of a recent impression; the other is the law of association taken in its widest sense, to include likeness, contrast, contiguity, affective homotonality, in fact any relationship or resemblance, however accidental or absurd. However weak and tenuous these connecting threads may be, they can at any given moment bring the most forgotten image in its entirety out of its obscurity into the light for an instant—and let it fall back, perhaps never to be disturbed again. These two sources of apparition of images can of course work together in certain cases.

23. *Actual sensations incorporated into dreams*

Actual sense-impressions have, since earliest times, been known to penetrate into the sleeping consciousness and be incorporated, more or less altered, into the fabric of dreams. Aristotle gives a series of examples. Later authors do the same, the most famous of them being the one recounted by Maury: lying face downwards, he dreamt that he was being tried during the French Revolution; he was condemned, taken to the scaffold, and felt the guillotine fall on his neck. Waking up in terror, he found that in fact a piece of wood from the canopy of the bed had fallen on his neck.

The problem posed by this and similar cases is the incredible speed with which a story can be built up round an actual sensation, in such a way that the climax coincides with the sensation itself; which would mean that, contrary to the laws of time, the dream must begin before the sensation that provokes it. Various solutions have been proposed.

Some authors say that this dream was unconsciously arranged by Maury when he was awake and told the story—an easy thing to do, particularly after a lapse of time.

Others say that dreams follow their natural course, and if one of the many sense-impressions being received by the sleeper is an apt one, it will be included however much skill is required; if none is suitable, none will be included and the sleeper will remain unconscious of the sensation. Of the millions of dreams that people have, they recount only those that offer a good combination of sensations and dream-theme, and ignore the rest.

A third explanation is that at least some dreams do not work with successive images, but simultaneous ones, that they give a panoramic view of every page of the story at once, in much the same way as the whole Passion is represented in some medieval altarpieces. When we awake we naturally arrange the scenes into their correct chronological order, because our reason works that way. Other cases of this panoramic vision are related: a man who has an accident, or is drowning, is said to see his whole life, or a large part of it, in a sudden flash of clarity, which would seem to indicate that he sees it all simultaneously. If this is so, it does not seem unreasonable to suppose that some sensations provoke, at the moment when they are felt, an historical setting which gives them meaning. There are other examples.

A friend of mine, who was very worried about his heart condition, dreamt that he was suffocating, went to the window to breathe, leant out and saw to his horror that his breast was opened and that he could see his "poor little heart" in every detail, contracting and expanding in time to . . . He woke up and found that it was beating exactly in time to the ticking of his alarm clock. This is an acoustic sensation becoming optical in the dream through the common factor of timing. Such transformations are very common.

Another example: when I was a child, one of my brothers once amused himself by tickling my face with a handful of pine-needles. I can still remember the horror of a swarm of mosquitoes biting my face in the dream at that moment. A fairly common nightmare is caused by too many bedclothes: one may dream of a huge black cat asleep on top of one, or an enemy trying to strangle one. The crowing of a cock might become a brass band in a procession, and an alarm can become a peal of bells, the actual sensation in each case being neatly fitted into an appropriate story.

These sensations and the startling results which follow naturally arise most often in those senses, such as hearing and touch, which cannot be shut off as eyelids can shut off sight. Internal sensations, pleasant or unpleasant, are in the same case. A man dreamt he was climbing a long staircase and that at each step his knee hurt; he woke up and discovered that in fact his knee was hurting. These sensations are sometimes keener in dreams than when we are awake; this is the basis of the time-honoured practice of observing dreams in order to diagnose an incipient illness. Arnauld de Villeneuve tells of a patient of his who dreamt twice successively that he was being hit on the ear with a stone; a short while later he developed inflammation of the ear. Perhaps dreams of water mean an excess of lymph, and perhaps dreams of fire have some special physiological significance. Hunger, thirst and other natural necessities produce dreams about the corresponding satisfaction.

This correspondence between actual sensations and dreams readily lends itself to the more orthodox type of scientific experiment. Practically every possible stimulus has certainly been tried: bringing a red-hot poker near the face, firmly tying one arm, putting on lights, setting one limb or the whole body in a certain position, different sounds and smells. The subject is then woken up and asked to relate his dream. A copious amount has been written about these experiments, which have not in fact revealed anything of any great moment.[13] In normal

13. M. Vold, *Uber den Traum*, 2 vols., 1910-12.

life, actual sensations—except perhaps internal ones, and some reputable authors have their doubts about them too—play a very small part in dreams. What is important is the conclusion that the dreamer is not completely cut off from contact with the outside world, and that the mental powers are not completely asleep. This leads to the next subject, partial sleep.

24. *Partial sleep*

The psyche does not give itself over to sleep without making provision for remaining sensitive to some stimulus or other during its inertia. It has a sort of selective filter, through which some impressions can pass and others not. A miller will sleep through the grinding of his mill, but if it stops he will wake up. The classic example is a mother with a young child, who will sleep through a thunderstorm and wake up at the infant's slightest wail. There is precision as well as beauty in the phrase from the Song of Songs: "I lie asleep, but oh! my heart is wakeful". Hearing one's name will wake one up more easily than any other sound. If you are anxious to catch a train in the morning, you can hear the preceding hours strike with indifference, but the right one will wake you up even though you are used to sleeping longer. Some people do not even need this but seem to wake up in time with the light from the window, even though their eyes are shut. Others seem to be able to wake themselves at the right time by merely telling themselves to do so before they go to sleep—but they often wake up too early.

This discriminating permeability of the subconscious during sleep can be useful. For example, a child was in the habit of illtreating his little sister, and could not be corrected. His mother consulted a doctor, and the advice was to whisper persuasively into his ear while he was sleeping lightly, "I love my little sister very much and treat her kindly", or some such formula. Little by little the child's attitude towards his sister changed for the better. Curiously enough, positive formulae only are effective; it is no use saying, "I will not hit my sister": this produces the same effect as, "I will hit my sister"—a useful law to remember in fighting against temptations.

This reminds me of an even more curious example. At the Paris Fair in May 1934, I was visiting the famous section of the Concours Lépine for amateur inventors, and I saw a man with a white beard by an ordinary looking gramophone with some attachment by which the needle could be moved from any point of the record back to any previously selected point, so that the same passage could be repeated over and over again. I was intrigued by such a strange invention and still more so by the look of its venerable inventor. I asked him what it was for and he replied:

"You know, in this life we fight conscientiously against our failings with great expenditure of energy and very little result. And we leave out of account certain natural forces that could give us the victory with far less trouble. One of these is suggestion. Suggestion acts through the unconscious; it slips into us by a sort of unguarded back door. As is well known, the two states in which we are most open to suggestion are natural sleep and the hypnotic trance. Well now, the latter is not always easy or convenient to come by, or even possible, whereas natural sleep is always at hand."

"All right", I interrupted, "but where does your invention come into all this?"

"I am just coming to that", he replied. "If you have some failing, phobia, bad habit, anxiety, or obsession, it can be cured like this. Draw up some suitably suggestive corrective sayings for whichever of these you may suffer from. They can then all be put (one after the other) on to a record, which will murmur insinuatingly into your ear. The record might be called a box of psychic pills. You take them like this: choose the defect you want to overcome and find the part of the record that has the appropriate saying. Put the gramophone on your bedside table with my apparatus set so as to repeat only that saying. Fit an alarm system to the starting mechanism of the gramophone to switch it on at a suitable time—say, three or four in the morning. You just go to bed and don't worry about it any more. When you wake up you will not remember anything, but while you were asleep you were for a time listening to a friendly, persuasive voice giving you a special message. This message will have a subconscious effect and will do its duty, never fear. It will be even more effective if someone else has prepared it for you and you do not even know you have been subjected to its influence."

This strange toy of course contained more philosophy than the happy-go-lucky visitors were bargaining for.

To return to partial sleep, electro-encephalograms[14] have confirmed what other psychological data had suggested, and what has been more definitely asserted since Herbart, that the whole organism does not sleep at the same time; without going to the excesses of phrenology, it is known that, within certain limits, different parts of the brain perform different functions. So in dreams the motor area can be asleep while the imagination shows a thousand movements: they are put into pictures, but not into action. In somnambulism, the opposite happens: the movements are made, but not imagined, so the sleep-walker remembers nothing when he wakes up: the motor area was awake while the imagination slept. In the obsessive drowsy state discussed in Section 14, there is an even greater contrast between motor and imagination, since there is hallucination—maximum image—on the one hand, and cataplexy—minimum movement—on the other.

Ewald says that acoustic dreaming occurs only in the lightest sleep, whereas optical dreaming can occur in both light and deep sleep: this would suggest that in deep sleep the centres of acoustic dreaming are asleep, while those of optical dreaming are awake. Logical reasoning, the critical faculty and the will, are all more active (or closer to their waking selves) in light sleep than in deep. All of which leads one to the conclusion that an understanding of these different levels of sleep in the various parts of the psyche is indispensable to an understanding of sleep and, above all, of dreams.

The obvious reason why some parts sleep more than others is that

14. Henry Roger, *Elementos de Psicofisiología* (Buenos Aires, 1948), Vol. II, p. 249. See also Jean Delay, *Les ondes cérébrales et la Psychologie* (Paris, 1942).

they need more sleep, they need to recuperate more because they have been more tired. An immediate corollary is that when all the faculties have been equally tired, sleep will be more even, all parts sleeping simultaneously. But since life, particularly modern life, involves one-sided or at least uneven activity, this uniform tiredness and total sleep are not normal. Furthermore, it cannot be decided *a priori* that this would be most beneficial, though at first sight it would appear to be. Some authorities say that the sphere of volition, being the most synthetic, needs most sleep. Be that as it may, it would accord well with the theory that inhibition of the will is the necessary condition for imaginary pictures to become oneiric images, with their greater sharpness and feeling of reality. From this it follows that, as oneiric images are the basic characteristic of dreaming, so inhibition of the will (as I said when discussing sleep) is the fundamental characteristic of sleep. This is worth remembering in connection with responsibility in dreams.

25. *Memory in dreams*

Some authors say that there is an intensification of memory in dreams —hypermnesia. If memory here means the mere emergence of subconsciously perceived or completely forgotten elements, one must agree. In both cases, these elements are not *recognized as having been seen* (normal memory) but perceived as though they were new. Macario relates the following case:

A man had inherited a piece of land and remembered hearing his father say that it had been bought and paid for, but he could not show any legal documents because he had forgotten where they were kept. This had rendered him liable to lose the lawsuit in which his right to the land was being contested. On the eve of the hearing, he dreamt that his father had told him that the documents were with a certain retired notary. When he woke up he went to see if this was true and in fact found them there and so won his case.[15]

15. Jean Lhermitte, *Les rêves*. Coll. Que sais-je? (Paris). For a similar example see Section 51 of the present work.

E

Some people will doubtless take this as a preternatural intervention by the father rather than a case of memory. I shall not venture to decide either way. What is certain, though, is that there is no need to have recourse to the preternatural for an explanation, since the heir might well have heard his father mention the documents and say where they were kept, without paying much attention, and the faint trace left in the memory, while insufficient for conscious recollection, would be enough to bring it to light in a dream under the stress of worry about the lawsuit.

There are many other cases like this. The biographer of Amor Ruibal tells that his prodigious memory could find anything in his apparently disordered library without an index. Once, however, when he was looking for a rare pamphlet on the Codex of Hammurabi, the system failed and he spent hours looking for it. He summoned his assistants, who hunted book by book and dossier by dossier, but also failed to find it. He went to bed that night annoyed and worried, and dreamt clearly where the text was. He got up early, went to see, and it really was there.[16]

Sometimes languages that one heard spoken, or perhaps spoke, in infancy, apparently completely forgotten since then, are heard in dreams. Often in these cases they appear, not as something once known, but as quite new, reminiscences rather than actual memories.

In other cases, although the memory of time, space and other circumstances of the previous knowledge may be lacking, there is a vague impression that this is not the first time. Maury tells of a dream in which he went back to his early childhood in the little town of Trilport, where he saw a man in uniform; he asked him his name, and was told it. He was not sure whether this was just imagination, or memory. He happened to see his old nurse, and told her the dream. She told him that when he was a child, his father had built a bridge in Trilport and that there had been a watchman of that name.[17] This told

16. A. Gómez Ledo, *Amor Ruibal o la sabiduría con sencillez* (Madrid, 1949), p. 40.

17. A. Maury, *Le sommeil et les rêves* (Paris, 1878), p. 92. Quoted by Freud, *The Interpretation of Dreams*, and by Lhermitte, *Les rêves*, p. 66.

him that it was a definite memory. But for the nurse, he would have retained a vague impression of having seen it before, which all the authorities say is often misleading. But cases like this lead one to think that this "seen before" impression is often considered fallacious through mere lack of verification. On the other hand, it has been proved beyond a shadow of doubt that dreams do very often produce false memories.

Leonhard, unlike other writers on the subject, devotes a great deal of attention to this phenomenon; he says it is a much used device for clarifying an obscure situation in dreams. False memories are usually accompanied by a firm feeling of certainty. If we have not in fact known the person, thing or event in question, it is possible that we may have dreamt of them before; in which case this would be memory from dream to dream. Leonhard says, however, that a careful study has led him to the conclusion that this does not happen. But with all due respect, I think there are cases in which these "false memories" can be explained as memories from dream to dream. Dreams, after all, can be carried on after a waking interval, which seems impossible without some sort of dream-to-dream memory; they can also be repeated, not only in normal sleep but, more usually, in oneiric delirium.[18] Leonhard, on the other hand, considers this so-called repetition a typical example of false memory. Whatever explanation is given, there is no doubt that the phenomenon is a very frequent one. Leonhard holds that almost every dream has false memories. The mere fact of seeing a thing in dreams gives us a certain amount of information about it. Completely strange and fanciful people and things appear quite normal ("seen before"). In dreams a bachelor can feel himself married and even a husband of long standing, with no sense of strangeness. One dreams of a garden and then "remembers" that it is one's own, when it is nothing of the sort. In all these cases, the certainty felt is not a product of reasoning, not even of the false reasoning of dreams, but a direct

18. Lhermitte, p. 66. See also G. Siegmund, *Der Traum*, pp. 51-2, where he tells of his own experiences when suffering from typhus, when his dreams carried on the same stories for days and days, repeating some scenes.

and primitive phenomenon. In dreams, one can "explain everything", or rather everything must be explained somehow or other . . . the explanations, of course, are taken to be excellent. False memories are one of the easiest and commonest of them. The differences between them and true memories are seen when one wakes up and is robbed of what a moment before had seemed a permanent possession.

Another question is: which are more prominent in dreams, old or recent memories? It is common knowledge that childhood scenes and friends occur frequently, mixed in with a thousand other details of later years—rather as in old age one is supposed to keep distant memories fresher than recent ones. This may be due to their having been revised and organized more often, or to the fact that they were received at a time when retention was easier. This suggests a parallel: that the collapse and dissolution of the intelligence and the biological factors governing it, in sleep, are strongly reminiscent of the collapse that takes place in madness and senility. The fact that memories of infancy seem to occupy a privileged place in dreams may be clearer from this parallel.

While this may be true, there is another law based on other principles which must also be recognized: within certain fairly strict limits, recent memories are more distinct than earlier ones. This has constantly been observed but other factors can modify it, since some older memories obviously remain clear if they have a great affective content, if they have left a deep impression, if they have often been revived in the meantime, or for a variety of other reasons.

26. *The memory of dreams*

This is another question which arises when discussing memory. The first point to note is that under normal circumstances memory of dreams is extremely fragile. Most people can hardly remember their dreams at all, and quite a large number are completely unable to remember them and so say they never dream. Others have a vague impression of having dreamt, but retain no definite impression.

Dreams are extremely elusive, so they lend themselves readily to later interpolations. Unless special measures are taken they are irrevocably lost. Sometimes, though, at some stage during the day, a chance association will suddenly bring last night's dream to mind, when one thought it completely forgotten.

Hervey de Saint-Denis particularly states that in order to remember dreams, one needs special interest and long practice, as one does to see in the dark. One of the best ways, he suggests, is to keep a diary of dreams. On waking, with the dream still fresh in your mind, carefully make an intense revision of it, as though it were a speech you were learning by heart. These precautions are usually necessary because as soon as you open your eyes and set about the new day's business, nocturnal fancies fade beyond recall. Therefore you must write it down as soon as possible so as to forestall the arrangements, links and additions that the mind's ordering instinct will normally tend to make. When you make a special effort to remember dreams, by this and other means, it gradually becomes easier and you find that you have several each night. You even think you are dreaming more than before, but it would appear that this is not the case: in fact you are simply remembering more.

These procedures are considered necessary to remember ordinary dreams, but there are also extraordinary ones, which affect one profoundly, engrave themselves on the mind with a wealth of detail and remain there for years without any effort to remember them. These dreams are letting us know by these means that they are important. Psychoanalysis tells us that they would surely tell us something interesting if we could understand them. Nature has good cause to select a few privileged dreams to place in front of our eyes, from the vast number that we dream, and forget, every day.

We do not, by all accounts, remember all the dreams we have—in fact only a very small proportion. One could discourse at this point on the modesty and humility of this amazing process which creates so many marvels with so little care that we should ever see them in the light of day. They come from the unconscious, flit through its domain

for a few moments, and, generally without emerging from the unconscious, are then plunged back into perpetual oblivion. The process is
like a sort of psychic gland: its secretions flow into its own channel,
for its own use: everything remains in the dreams themselves, or rather
ni the unconscious.

We ourselves, in all probability, do not know what effect it produces.
Who knows whether a dream—of which memory retains no trace—
may have been the necessary, or at least contributory, condition for a
psychic or even a physiological process, whether it has excited different
moods or produced changes no less real and efficacious for being
infinitesimally small? Exactly the opposite might be held to be the
case: that a dream is nothing but a psychic epiphenomenon, a faint
glimmer or purely expressive mirage produced by the physiological
process in action. But it is surely possible that both cases can be true.
A dream might receive its first impulse from an affect, produced in its
turn by a humour; once it has been set in action in a purely expressive
capacity, it continues on its own—for reasons I shall go into later when
dealing with the course of sleep; through an inherent finalism it then
promotes, elaborates, distributes, directs or dissolves the original affects
so that it can bequeath a vitally useful state of mind to the conscious,
which remains quite unaware of this operation. We do not know
exactly how much we owe to dreams. I shall continue these considerations later.

27. *Volition in dreams*

I have already discussed understanding in dreams while setting out the
general characteristics of oneiric consciousness (Section 15). As for the
will, I have said that inhibition of conscious direction of psychic events
is one of the basic conditions of sleep and dreams. However, we do
sometimes dream that we want something. Hervey de Saint-Denis
flatly assigns a preponderant role to the will. He exaggerates. In deep
sleep automatism is more active; in lighter sleep understanding and
will function more, but even then not the full will, but a series of

impulses resembling will.[19] And dreams seem to take a malicious pleasure in thwarting what little will is left. You want to run away from a danger and cannot. You want to shout for help and no sound comes. You can run or shout well enough at times, but only when you have no particular desire to. You are in a train going through landscape well known to you; you say, "Now such-and-such a landmark is coming", and a different one appears. You are shooting rabbits and a man appears in the sights. You look for a canoe on a lake to go boating and find a cart (which of course you get into thinking somehow that it is a boat). These are all actual examples. In some in-between states, such as the half-awake state following a brusque awakening, the will appears able to dictate certain actions with almost hallucinatory rapidity, but these states have their own characteristics even though they seem like dreams.

The central image in a dream always acts of its own free will. This is why dreams are so full of surprises and why it is impossible to do what you want in them: you are tied to what they want to make you see. Often, however, though a dream may not give you what you want, it will give you something similar or related. You might see a bather dive under water; you can sit and wait for him to come up, and when he does, he appears under a tree. The exception to this rule seems to be the expectation of something unpleasant. I once dreamt I saw a waiter at the top of some stairs, carrying a tray laden with bottles and looking behind him. I thought, "He's going to drop them", and he did, with a crash, down the stairs. Fortunately, dreams have their own ideas, and though the contents were spilt, the bottles did not break. In nightmares, which are no more than intensifications of some worry through anxiety, the terrible expectation is always fulfilled: the bull catches you, the knife reaches you, the axe whistles about your ears—but at this point, when you have given yourself up for dead, you wake up. (Though I once actually felt the cold steel of a sword thrust into me.) Nightmares usually destroy themselves by leading one into too intolerable a situation.

19. Lhermitte, *Les rêves*, p. 96.

28. *Affectivity*

Some writers have solemnly affirmed that dreams are devoid of emotion, except when they depend on a mainly physical disposition.[20] This is an unjustified generalization of the fact that in dreams we can sometimes watch blood-curdling situations with complete equanimity. In the intellectual sphere, we can watch complete absurdities without surprise. But dreams are closest to affective life, since they express the most primitive layers of the psyche, in which images and affects predominate. Charles Baudouin says that "dreams, and imagination in general, are symbolic of the affective life, and of the subconscious affectivity in particular".[21] With all due respect, I consider this assertion—though far nearer the mark than the other—still an exaggeration. Since man himself is more than his feelings, his dreams and his imagination will also consist of more. They include thirst for knowledge, delight in form, and quasi-mechanical repetition (as when we give our imagination free rein without any particular direction of feeling); they attempt to find solutions, and produce symbols of purely notional concepts, or of intentions and plans more or less devoid of affectivity, such as business routines and duties. All these also belong to the human condition. I do not intend to quibble as to whether the instinctive inclinations and various affects which originate with them, are, directly or indirectly, the motor of all mental life. If one insists on seeing at least some affectivity in every single psychic phenomenon, the discussion can become very awkward, and I am not prepared to enter it on this level.

It is really a question of vocabulary: whether normal usage can refer to certain purely instrumental and automatic psychic mechanisms as "affective", or whether perception in its various aspects can manifest itself in dreams and the imagination, when the cognitive faculty operates freely, alone, on neutral material, moved by ends that are either not at all, or only remotely, tinged with affect. In many cases

---

20. *Affekte doch sonst dem Träumen fremd sind*, K. Leonhard, *Die Gesetze des normalen Traumen* (Leipzig, 1939), p. 55.
21. *Introduction à l'analyse des rêves* (Geneva, 1945), p. 36,

nobody, I think, would speak of affectivity. I do not think that even those who believe—as I do—that the affective life is essentially and functionally linked to the instincts by virtue of their nature, and to them alone, would claim that every instinctive movement must necessarily carry an affective resonance. The word affectivity does seem to demand a certain degree of intensity. For the theory to be universally applicable, one would have to postulate a sort of subliminal affectivity, like rays that do not quite make light. The initial movement, imperceptible, but related to what, when increased and perceptible, will be called an affect, is not yet properly speaking a psychological affect, but at most a physiological one. But I do not want to labour the point.

Baudouin has devoted a fine book to a demonstration of the role of affectivity in dreams and in association of ideas generally.[22] Psychoanalytical schools of course lay great emphasis on this point, and Schmid goes so far as to say that dreams are a product of the "emotional memory".[23] They are undoubtedly largely right. Yet, without further proof, I cannot admit such a generalization of the theory to the exclusion of every other possibility.

Some writers have also stated that ethical feelings do not feature in dreams. This is true of some dreams, in which man appears as a purely natural force following his imperturbable course. But it is very often not true, and is another dangerous generalization.

In dreams we can feel hesitation, worry, sadness, compassion, humility, pride, shame, joy, haste, irritation, love, appetite, fear, panic, anxiety—in fact the whole range of affects and emotions. They generally insinuate themselves into the oneiric consciousness gradually, not suddenly or forcefully. It is certainly a curious fact that objects often appear without their corresponding affect; the contrary is not so common, since affects usually produce their appropriate images. From which it appears that an image cannot arouse the corresponding

22. *Introduction à l'analyse des rêves.*
23. G. Schmid, *Die seelische Innenwelt im Spiegel des Traumlebens.* Quoted by Siegmund, *Der Traum*, p. 56.

affect, at least in any significant degree, as easily as the affect can produce the image. In waking life, where the imagination is controlled by the critical intelligence, one can feel an affect, such as rage, without remembering why, or inventing a reason. I remember a friend shaking his fist and saying, "I don't know whom or why, but I pity him!", as though a discharge of purely physical feeling, not due to psychic causes, had produced the impression of being possessed by an affect without content or material objective. Melancholia and euphoria or enthusiasm are often like this: Tolstoy wrote of himself, " 'I love, I love so whole-heartedly . . . Oh, their courage, the brave men!' he repeated, and burst into tears. Why? Who was brave? Whom did he love? He could not say for certain."[24] Such a state of mind, which can exist with no apparent cause in waking life, cannot be satisfied with a vacuum in dreams (or in illnesses involving loss of control) but must create an adequate situation and react according to the sedative or cathartic effect involved. Incidentally, there are good reasons to suppose this to be one of the principal objects of both dreams and day-dreams.

Another question, already touched upon, is whether dreams create a state of mind, or at least either intensify tenuous ones or eliminate them through the appropriate reaction. It seems that they do. I shall certainly never forget some dreams that have brought me deep and lasting consolation, and other people have told me of the same experience. False generalizations have also been made about this.[25] It is enough to reaffirm what has been held from the time of the Greeks onwards: that dreams can in fact produce states of mind that are propitious or unpropitious for certain actions, even though the dream itself may be forgotten. For example: Tissie one day met a person with whom he had quarrelled, but without knowing why, greeted him amiably. Surprised at himself, he hunted for an explanation, and remembered dreaming the night before that they were friends.

24. Quoted by Charlotte Bühler in *The Course of Human Life as a Psychological Problem,* p. 89.
25. Leonhard, *Die Gesetze des normalen Traumen.*

Classical authors saw in this predisposition towards certain actions an explanation of prophetic dreams, since the dream prepared the way for a future action.

29. *The dream theme*

Having seen the different elements that make up a dream, it is time to discuss their synthesis: theme, situations, and course. The central idea of the whole dream is called the *dream theme*. At least in part, it naturally has its origin in waking life. An anxiety, for instance, is like a sore place or affected organ on which thoughts converge, to perform their primary task of finding solutions to vital problems. The same is true of joys and desires. This may lead one to think that every waking mood will be reflected in dreams, but this is fortunately not the case. Some are and others are not, following the caprice of an unconscious selector, often puerile and sometimes very wise. This function is particularly obscure, and clearly stamped as irrational.

The waking preoccupation, or current problem, say an affective complex with its various roots, connections, perspectives, desires and unexpressed fears, forms the basis and deep meaning of the dream, but it is not the dream theme. This is the trajectory of expression traced and directed by the psyche across the field of affectivity. Hence one of its primary characteristics: it persists right through the dream. This is understandable, because it is nurtured in a permanent state of mind. Its persistence is the more remarkable in contrast to the extreme fragility and constant changes of the images, which cling like ivy to the supporting trunk: the faintest breeze will shake the leaves, but the trunk will stand firm.

30. *The dream situation*

The dream theme produces the *dream situation* (or situations), which is the next step forward in the scenic realization of the theme. It is conditioned partly by the theme and partly by the images available at the time, their availability being governed by the laws of reappearance,

persistence and association. Sometimes the available images are sufficient
to enable the action to proceed without a hitch, but they sometimes
lead to a dead end from which an escape is only possible by jumping to
another series of images—another dream situation—or, if the obstacle
is too disturbing to the affectivity, one simply wakes up, as in nightmares.

The dream theme can also change, since dreams may be generated
not only by one complex, but by several. Laws of association can use
one incident in the dream situation to touch off another complex and
so produce a new theme. Or else two themes may combine and continue bound up in each other, producing doubly significant situations:
this would be an example of the *condensation* of which Freud speaks,
and allows for a wide variety of solutions. Secondary themes, like
eddies or short-circuits, also appear in the course of a dream, usually
produced by the dream situation, but are soon exhausted and have no
effect on the main current.

Dr Leonhard gives the following example:

My attention was called one day by my department in the hospital
to a problematic case of cretinism, and I was thinking of my diagnosis. That night I dreamt of an anthropoid creature with a wrinkled
face (nothing like the slightly cretinous face of the young woman),
lying in a bed. A man was examining it, and other figures, presumably students, were grouped round the bed. I saw the strange creature
again, and it turned out to be a very special sort of animal with two
wings like sea-shells growing out of its back. One of the students
handled it rather roughly, and it said "Ouch!" in a human voice.
I examined it to see if it was hurt, and noticed that it had grown
more wings. Then I watched it with the students until it emerged
from under the bedclothes, whereupon it looked like a lobster.
Meanwhile, only one student was left, a girl, and she slowly pushed
her foot towards the animal. I told her to be careful not to tread on it,
and then it began to run, passing over her foot, but by now it had
stopped looking like a lobster and was round like a hedgehog, but
without prickles. Other students reappeared and I heard a voice.
I went to hear what was being said and one student said that in his

opinion it was a case of schizophrenia, not cretinism. This opinion displeased me considerably. The animal by now had a pig's body but legs like a basset hound's. I said, "Anyway, it's more like a pig", wanting to relate it with cretinism, since cretins often have a facial expression rather like a pig's.[26] Then I woke up, remembered the dream clearly and fixed it firmly in my mind.[27]

The dream theme here arises from the preoccupation with the diagnosis of the day before and consists in a visualization of different opinions on the disease, in the form of metamorphoses of the creature in an atmosphere of discussion and clinical examination. Despite the prolonged process of metamorphosis and the incidents it occasions, note how the idea that "it" must be identified runs right through all the changes. A meticulous interpreter might attempt, perhaps rightly, to find some parallel between the different zoological states of the creature and the different forms of mental illness under consideration, but the general line of possibilities and opinions is sufficient. In the end, the doctor's view won the day. The dream situation was always coincident with the dream theme. There were no secondary themes added to the main theme, though one nearly started when the student pushed her foot forward. The central image—the patient—changed continually, while the peripheral images—the vague students who are seen there or somehow just known to be there—remained unchanged. And the central image was altered according to the law of tangency, while the peripheral images stayed closer to reality.

31. *The dream course*

The question of the dream theme is closely linked to that of the *dream course*. How is it that dreams do not consist of a series of static, disconnected images, but have some organized movement and for a time go through some action or fragment of action with many of the attributes of real life? An adequate reply demands the same sort of

26. One might add: Because *Schwein* (pig) recalls *Schwachsinn* (cretinism). Leonhard's extreme hostility to Freud prevents him from recognizing this type of association, which Freud considers so important. But this strikes me as a clear case of it.

27. *Die Gesetze des normalen Träumen*, pp. 58–9.

insight into the esssence of the process of dreaming as does another different question: why, when we shut our eyes, can we see the shapes and colours of objects we have seen? Dreams, like imagination, thought and feeling, are basic facts which have to be recognized and taken as a starting point; if any explanation of their distinguishing characteristics is going to be made, it must be with due reservation.

So, in this case, one can say: the sensitive memory, which plays such a large part in dreams, by its nature bears a close resemblance to the sensations which furnish it with its material. Now these sensations perceive not only static objects, but living pictures in which the various impressions—of shape, colour, movement, sound, etc.—combine to form a whole. Accordingly, the impressions left on the memory go in series, one giving rise to the next by association, in much the same way as the reflex actions of walking stimulate one another, so as to provide a continuous movement. This is one side of the question.

The other is that dreams must contain a greater or lesser degree of underlying action on the part of the intelligence, the degree depending, most probably, on the level of sleep in the centres most closely responsible for the exercise of that function. When one pictures imaginary scenes to oneself while awake, the intelligence supervises and intervenes to prevent absurdities. Diminished by sleep, the intelligence tolerates a greater or lesser degree of incongruity, according to the depth of sleep. In both sleep and waking, the automatic play of associations tends to produce images and more images, with reference to nothing except the chain of association; these images are either connected to the preceding ones or remain unadopted. Here one may suppose processes of *selection* —choosing between the images offered, *adaptation*—fitting some elements to others, and *completion*—evoking the images required to fill the gaps which occur in dream situations. It is this intellectual need to form a comprehensible whole, more or less degraded, that Bergson considers to be the mechanism for prolonging dreams.[28]

Images, he says, are presented in a formless way. To impart some meaning to this senseless jumble, explanatory reasons are sought;

28. E. Bergson, *L'énergie spirituelle*, 1932 edn, p. 94.

they may be very extraordinary, but are accepted as quite satisfactory in dreams, and give rise to new images. Images arise to fill the gap, more or less, but other inopportune ones appear with them, or are dragged in by them, and they create new gaps and fresh nonsense. More images are called in to remedy this, and so the process continues.

This explanation is acceptable once its scope is reduced somewhat. In any case it should be taken in conjunction with what has been said about the dream theme, which is a sort of canalization, determined in extent by the psychic complexes in action, and by the materials related to them, which the intellect has elaborated from current problems.

The images are not completely incoherent. They already form groups, cursory schemes and tendencies; then they as it were warn the memory to prepare the elements that interest the consciousness at the moment, awake or asleep. Every sensitivity of the consciousness with regard to a particular theme (an anxiety, a desire, a fear, an intention) at once produces a sympathetic disposition of all available images bearing on the case, of whatever kind they may be. Memories that have slept for years suddenly seem affected by some movement order which emanates automatically from the psychic situation, by the mere fact of consonance. So when the right movement arrives, they emerge freely and help the consciousness to a more congruous resolution of the problem in hand.

This is the case with simple perception. The bare data furnished by sensory stimuli are prepared, filled out and illuminated by memories to produce what is known as "apperception"; which is what reaches the lucid consciousness with some degree—even a considerable degree—of complexity; as when certain subjective desires intervene. Hence one can say of someone, "He sees things as he wants them"; this is unconscious desire, which is responsible for much that is afterwards supposed to come from elsewhere, from objective reality in this case.

An orator in full spate will often produce ideas and expressions that in cold blood would surprise him as much as anyone else; many other situations also produce such moments of maximum achievement. They would seem to postulate this previous polarization or magnetization of the resources of memory, as well as a sharpening of intuition and other faculties. In dreams, too, the psyche retains this method of functioning. In this too, despite the imperfections and lacunae proper to sleep, dreams sometimes show a hyperaesthesia, a synthetic power, and an originality that the waking consciousness lacks. Cases of dreams providing solutions to problems which have otherwise proved insoluble are numerous enough to place this phenomenon of interior mobilization in dreams beyond doubt. The direction of reason and the nostalgia for great things sometimes produce dreams astonishing in their nobility and wise handling of a human problem. But this is inexplicable unless one supposes dreams to be directed by previous conditions analogous, as we have seen, to those that facilitate the course of waking thought.

Here we must also recall the speculations about ideomotor impulses inherent in ideas and images, called the *idée force*. Nor must one forget, in particular, that images in movement, such as those of living pictures, are images of actions, which, by their nature, require continuity. In fact, the magic of associative evocations consists merely in putting the image of an action on the stage and leaving it to reach its fulfilment alone by spontaneous impulse. The *ideomotor* concept, so popular with some writers, seems to be merely another way of expressing this. The term has only the advantage of emphasizing one aspect: the unity of the different phases of an action, and, consequently, the associative force linking the various parts together.

It is now less difficult to understand why dreams follow a course and find more or less successful ways out of their various situations. If something goes wrong and the emotions are disturbed, the dreamer is freed from the trap by waking up. But normally one particular vein is exhausted and the dream comes to an end, giving place to another.

32. *Principal general laws of dreams*

By way of summing-up, some general laws governing dreams can now be formulated. There may be exceptions to some; there certainly are to others. This shows that one cannot at the same time survey every level at which the regular features which we are trying to catalogue take place; the general rule may be subject to a certain set of conditions, while the exception may be subject to a higher or lower set, and so appear an exception. These laws, then, are approximations which it would need a more systematic and exhaustive study to bring closer to reality. As they stand, they do, I think, at least give some idea of these phenomena. I have included one or two ideas that for some reason or other were not touched upon in the exposition.

1. In dreams, images predominate—mainly visual and acoustic, not inert, but living, imitating life. In lesser proportion, all the other psychic activities intervene, their degree of intervention depending on the depth of sleep.

2. Oneiric elements behave with a certain amount of autonomy in their appearance and development, and are also subordinated or co-ordinated to a certain extent under the influence of the dream theme and intellectual, affective and imaginative habits. Hence many sensible pictures and also many absurdities.

3. *Forms* seen do not usually appear as the central image till between ten and twenty days later, unless they are either unpleasant or peripheral. *Colours* and *sounds* usually appear in the same night's dreams (Leonhard).

4. Dreams usually comment on, repeat or elaborate thoughts of the preceding day or a few days before, not in identical form but in a similar or related form. The scheme is the same, or similar, but expressed in a different way. However, one point in a problem may persist, as in inventive dreams.

5. Generally, unless another law interferes, the preceding day's peripheral and rejected sensations will appear as the central dream image before its more important and meditated ones; emotive sensations before affectively neutral ones; recent ones before old. Images of infancy are privileged, and often provide elements or scenarios.

F

6. External and proprioceptive sensations often provoke dreams in which they appear distorted or fitted into a dramatic context.

7. The preceding day's desires and fears, particularly unconscious, tend to become dreams, but not all and not always, since other laws of selection also apply. The most active function seems to be auto-suggestion through affective fixation of the idea. The law of compensation can be reduced to this, since lack of satisfaction produces auto-suggestion.

8. In dreams, ideas and feeling take on sensible forms more or less correctly called "symbols", generally in dramatic form, through a selection based on analogy or on relationships established by the dreamer's subjective experience.

9. The law of association, understood in its widest sense, is the most prominent in the selection of dream images.

10. Though oneiric images generally imitate reality, they are often, for symbolical purposes, syncretic images with several meanings, with contributions from several different sources.

11. The dream theme and a group of peripheral images persist to a certain extent throughout the dream. Central images change continuously, usually contradicting or at least surprising the dreamer's expectations.

12. Depending on the level of sleep, some order is sought in dreams, and some attempt is even made to avoid absurdities. This means that ideas and images are aroused which, through the law of association and under the influence of the dream theme, produce a sequence of scenes, or a dream course.

13. Memory in dreams often seems different from waking memory; it reproduces seen objects as "never seen" and vice versa. False memories are very common. Memory can also stretch from one dream to another.

14. Generally speaking, affects are only moderately excited. If they become intense they usually wake the dreamer.

15. We remember only a small part of our dreams; hence one cannot give a total judgement on the presumed adjustment between oneiric expression and mental state.

16. Some dreams contain hardly anything besides playful flickers of the imagination; others repeat past experiences, especially unpleasant ones; others try to find solutions for the future; others produce unexpressed opinions, repressed desires or hidden aspirations; others echo a physical state or a nascent affect; others clearly seem to contain telepathic influence, and so on.

17. Throughout his dreams and according to circumstances, the dreamer reveals the whole of himself, either as an actor or as a spectator (in which case he often attributes his own characteristics to others). Innate and acquired habits, social influences and personal achievements, ethics, religion, culture, animal instincts, amorality, and natural self all feature. If personal discipline has led to mature balance, this will appear. In fact, the whole of human nature is there.

18. Significant dreams are most usually provoked by personal crises.

19. Devoting attention to dreams seems to increase the function.

20. Some dreams leave a lasting impression, but most are very easily forgotten.

There are many other laws that could be formulated, particularly if the different schools of psychoanalysis are taken into consideration, but they can be left till later, so as not to mix "scientists" and psychoanalysts on paper when in life they hold themselves so jealously apart. If some psychoanalytical theories appear among these laws, they are those that the scientists find most acceptable.

33. *The "scientific" analysis of dreams*

"Once the laws governing the origin and formation of dreams are known, there is not much room for interpretations that try to give significance to what apparently has none." Thus Leonhard at the end of his book.[29] He alludes of course to Freud and the others with their esoteric discussions of latent meaning. This he considers unworthy of science, a sort of intrigue in which all sorts of uncontrolled fantasies are involved. Any attempt to seek an ulterior meaning in dreams is, for Hoche, a "mystical and dangerous game". Leonhard holds that the truly scientific analysis of a dream is that which accounts for its elements and its course by comparing them with waking memories and by applying laws of dreams to them; in other words, the purely formal genetics and mechanics of dreaming.

For him, one of the main laws is that of tangency, by which, we have seen, one never dreams of objects in the same form in which they were seen, but of substitutes and related objects. This he considers possibly due to the purely psychophysiological fact that sense-impressions need to mature for a certain length of time before they become dreamable. Another well-established law is that waking thoughts determine dreams, so the dream is forced to reconstruct the situation; this it has to do not with the elements of the situation proper—these are still immature—but with others at the disposition of the psyche, summoned by association (likeness, contiguity, contrast . . .). This being so, the scientists ask, why bother, like Freud, to search for dramatic explanations involving theories of the super-ego, censorship, camouflage through hypocrisy or modesty, when there is a simple and adequate explanation at hand? Why should stupid and timorous scruples affect people in dreams, when awake they have no hesitation in thinking and doing exactly as they please? The true reason, says Leonhard, is tangency, which operates indifferently in the sexual and non-sexual fields, and sometimes, if it suits its purpose, even gives a sexual colouring to perfectly innocent matters. Adler is continually insisting on this point, claiming that many sexual dreams originate not in sexuality but in the "will to power".

Leaving concrete cases aside and recognizing the law of tangency, I do not believe that it and other "scientific" laws can fully explain a dream; but I shall discuss this later.

29. Leonhard, p. 122.

A few examples will show what scientific analysis consists of:

Dream 1: "I have to go to a class given by one of my tutors. I am standing alone in front of a closed shop. I begin to listen to the class which has begun. I wake up and realize that the voice I heard was not the tutor's as I thought, but a newspaper vendor's in the street." (M. Foucault, *La rêve*, p. 257.)

Here the explanation is clear. A thought from the preceding day: go to class, listen to my tutor. Substitution for the class, a closed shop. An actual sensation transformed into the tutor's voice: hearing the newspaper vendor. That is all, according to "science".

Dream 2: "I am visiting a Limoges porcelain factory with my mother and Mrs X. But the vases are being made by girls sewing them. The plates are also sewn at the edges." (Foucault, p. 240.)

Some months before, the dreamer had visited a porcelain works in Limoges. Mrs X., who was with his mother, had a dressmaking shop in the town. The dreamer himself explained that he had recognized a seamstress from her shop among the girls in the porcelain works. The two works are confused.

Dream 3: "I go into a room and begin to open doors and windows on to a garden, to air the room, since I had seen a brazier with glowing coals in the room. 'Very dangerous'—I thought in the dream—'because of the poisonous fumes it gives off.' "

When he went to bed he was worried because he had not aired the room.

Dream 4: "I am carrying pieces of something in my pocket. I put my hand in and very distinctly feel splinters of glass sticking into me." (Leonhard, p. 53.)

When he went to bed he had put the clock on top of his spectacles on the bedside table, and was worried in case the lenses were damaged.

Dream 5: A doctor dreamt that he was going up a tower with a friend. The friend showed symptoms of fatigue, anxiety and dyspnoea. The doctor diagnosed *angina pectoris*. (Lhermitte, *Les rêves*, p. 35.)

When he woke up he realized that he himself was suffering the
very symptoms that he had projected on to his friends.

And so on. We have already seen other examples in the preceding
chapters. Leonhard says that he does not see what more is necessary.
He finds a great attraction in relating dream elements to waking
memories and in verifying how the various laws are fulfilled. But this
sort of analysis appears pretty short sighted to the psychoanalysts.
True, the dreams quoted here seem fairly harmless. Those that occur
in a nervous crisis are generally far more involved. One could certainly,
without departing from "scientific" principles, find a basis for a far
deeper analysis—in the principles of oneirology. Since the dream
theme comes from the day before, all depends on how the day's problem is interpreted. The difference between one type of analysis and
another is not so much in oneiric psychology as in waking psychology,
or human personality. A rich and comprehensive personality will find
many things in dreams. A poor and abstract character will make a poor
analysis. The least satisfying aspect of Freudian interpretation is its
human psychology, its underlying view of man. Adding to this the
fact that it often pushes its juggling and subtleties to an absurd extreme,
one can understand why it has encountered so much serious opposition.
But one is bound to recognize the many benefits of psychoanalysis and
its brilliant intuition into the idiosyncrasies of the dream world.

With a balanced and complete personal make-up and a sensible use
of the laws of dreams, it is possible to find deeper and richer meanings
in dreams than those produced by academic "scientific" analysis.
The devotees of the latter, it must be said, are now fewer and less
opposed to the findings of psychoanalysis, understood not as orthodox
Freudianism, but as all the psychological movements provoked,
stimulated or encouraged by him in one way or another.

34. *Psychophysiological theories of dreams*

If one good overall theory of dreams were possible today, it would have
to be partly psychophysiological and partly psychological. It would
have to explain the different forms, degrees and elements of dreaming:

day-dreams, hypnagogic images, hallucinatory images of compulsive drowsiness, central and peripheral oneiric images, somnambulism, imaginative symbolism, different behaviour of the various elements, transformation and amplification of actual sensations, the dramatic course of the dream, etc. And this includes dreams only, since I am not concerned now with a theory of sleep, though this would doubtless be related to the various aspects of dreaming.

The nearest approach to a theory of dreams on the psychophysiological side is one of progressive and uneven dissolution of the consciousness and its various functions, in relation to the electro-chemico-biological state of the various anatomical centres which control those functions; this state is closely linked to the workings of metabolism. The experiments and observations carried out by Marinesco, Kreindler, Saguer, Von Economo, Demôle, Sture, Berggren, Môberg, Martel, Vincent and others show that the centre that regulates sleep is in the diencephalon, from which the inhibiting influence of dormitive action spreads unevenly, by modifying the neuronic chronaxies, to the various cortical regions.[30] It would be superfluous here to give details of these mechanisms. The expression "dormitive action" was used deliberately, since it is recognized today that sleep is an active intervention on the part of the controlling centres, which in turn are connected to other regulating centres, to inductory and subsidiary psychic factors, and to physico-chemico-biological organic conditions. This is the difference between sleep and the mere blocking that takes place in full narcosis (lethargy produced by certain drugs). This theory has outdated many others, which it would be lengthy and useless to enumerate.

To return to dreams: the cortical regions are those that condition the most differentiated psychic functions. Electro-encephalograms and experiments with various narcotics, which attack different centres, have shown, together with the accounts of people who underwent these experiments, that dreaming ceases when the whole cortex is asleep, and is very active when it is awake, even though the other parts

30. See López-Ibor, *Angustia vital*, p. 390, Note 11. Also Robert Bossard, *Psychologie du rêve* (Paris, 1953), pp. 11-54.

of the brain—and so the person—are asleep. Between these two extremes, intermediary levels of sleep in these parts, or different levels in different parts, have been produced, and their repercussions on dreaming noted. That is to say that while some centres are asleep, others are awake; some dream and others do not, or some dream more than others. Bearing in mind the psychological aspects of partial sleep, it will be seen that the two series of experiments, physiological and psychological, parallel and confirm each other. Thus Roger gives the following definition of dreaming, based on recent studies. "The contemplation, by a partially sleeping consciousness, of images arising in the parts of the brain that are still awake."[31]

Another very promising approach to the problem of finding an overall theory of dreams is the study of various psychopathological states, which are nearly always closely linked to dream manifestations. From the time of the Greeks onwards the close relationship between madness and dreams has been emphasized. This problem, often tackled, has been of passionate interest to psychiatrists for rather more than a century. Henry Ey has recently produced a new approach to the problem with a wealth of observation and reasoning.[32] These investigations, like those of dementia and any dissolution of the psychophysical entity in general, can help in the study of the phenomenon of sleep, understood as a process of dissolution, though normal and reversible. It will be seen that all these organo-dynamic theories spring from Jackson's Law, which is that when mental functions are disturbed or annulled by illness, the first to be affected are those that appeared last: that is to say that the order of degeneration is the reverse of the order of development.

A piece of common knowledge can show how well-founded is this theory. This is the ancient observation that the maximum degrees of waking are those of greatest concentration and synthesis, while any weakening of this state, such as distraction, easily produces day-

31. Henry Roger, *Elementos de Psicofisiología*, Vol. II, p. 250.
32. Henry Ey, "Le rêve, 'fait primordial' de la Psychopathologie", in *Etudes Psychiatriques* (Paris, 1948), pp. 164-261.

dreams; the maximum relaxation and passivity, reached in sleep, produce dreams.

In speaking of man, however, it is wise to be on guard against theories that tend to excessive division. It should not be forgotten that when the human entity is broken up, and some of its parts or functions suspended or merely weakened, the resultant state is not simply the difference between the whole and what has been taken away, as in straightforward subtraction; the whole proceeds to re-group itself entirely and adapt itself, more or less organically, to the new situation, thereby acquiring fresh overall characteristics: X asleep or X dreaming. This is one of the basic definitions of the living being.

Garma's theory of the reason for oneiric hallucinations can be taken as the borderline between psychophysiological and psychological theories. An impression of reality is produced, he says, when the energy of the stimulus is greater than the resistance that the ego is capable of setting up. This normally happens with real stimuli, so their impression is completely vivid. However, when the reaction—or resistances—of the ego are greater than the force of the physical stimuli, objective vision fails—negative hallucination. And when internally originated images have such energy content that they overcome the ego's resistance, then they appear as visions of objective reality—positive hallucination. There are three possibilities in dreaming. Either images are heavily charged, or resistance is diminished, or both at once. Garma says that "the totality—basis of the dream—formed by remnants of the day's experience and latent repressed desires, cannot normally be elaborated by the ego" in the waking state; this creates a miniature traumatic situation. Now traumatic situations, being very acute, tend to produce hallucinations, except when the ego's resistance is greater. In dreams the difference in potential between the charge of the stimulus and the resistance of the ego will be much the same, owing to the diminished resistance produced by sleep. Hence, though the miniature traumatic situation may not have a great charge of energy, it has sufficient to produce hallucinations in dreams.[33]

33. Angel Garma, *Psicoanálisis de los sueños*, 3rd edn (Buenos Aires, 1956), Chs IX and X.

This theory is either a truism or an excessive simplification of the conditions which produce hallucinations, both inside and outside dreams.

35. *Psychological theories of dreams*

A general idea of dreams cannot be considered complete without considering their purely psychological aspects, and even psychophilosophical and psychotheological ones. For example, what purpose do dreams serve in the totality of human life? Why is all consciousness, including oneiric consciousness, not suspended completely in sleep? Since some toxic drugs and certain illnesses produce an intensification of dreaming, is it not a deficiency, a damage to nature caused by intoxication through work? Or might it be a primitive function with a positive end, to integrate human nature at its most uncontaminated level?

One way or another, evidence could be produced; for my own part, I hasten to add that I consider dreaming a normal process with a positive purpose. Sleep must not be considered a weakness because it is a result of fatigue, though it can be considered an imperfection. This should not alarm anyone, since man occupies a definite place in the scale of creation, ordained by the Creator, and this place has its merits and its limitations. Man has a spirit, but he is also subject to a thousand disadvantages proper to material life. All animals get tired and go to sleep. Even Adam alone in Paradise, according to Genesis, slept, though theology must decide on the nature of that sleep, which had such profound consequences.

So what end, or rather what ends, can be assigned to dreams? I have already touched on some of them. I shall now mention them again, together with others that I have not yet discussed, and even anticipate some that belong more to psychoanalysis or depth psychology than to "scientific" psychology. This will give a wider view of the matter.

First, the end of make-believe or "play" which has long been considered to be similar to dreams. Here one must ask what purpose is served by dream make-believe. As an outlet for energy? Since these outlets need no organization, many supporters of mechanical association, who see nothing but chaos in dreams, will be content with this explanation. But dreams themselves show that they are not always chaotic. Perhaps make-believe serves to exercise various functions so that they will be skilled and ready when they are needed for serious work. Or again perhaps it is a consolation—certainly a necessary one—which provides illusory enchantment at least, when life refuses real satisfaction. Make-believe involves all these. It could also be a completion of interrupted processes, very beneficial in centralizing the tensions or disturbances usually provoked when a course of energy is broken off in full spate.

All these purposes are possible, at least at different times. All, and others which will be mentioned, can without undue forcing be included in Freud's dictum that every dream is a wish-fulfilment. By substituting "tendency" in its widest sense for "wish", this theory may become universally valid. As "wish" is generally understood, Freud himself had to recognize that his theory could not be applied to every dream, though he insisted that wish-fulfilment was the most important, even primordial, function of dreams. Innumerable pages have been written both for and against this expression of wishes in dreams.

Freud also makes dreams the guardians of sleep; the enchantment produced by their visions and by the fulfilment of one's wishes prevents one from waking up too easily, just when the bonds of sleep have been stretched thin. To them could also be assigned the mission of waking us when something threatens our well-being, which nightmares do perfectly when, for example, we are in an uncomfortable position.

Dreams can also be considered to try out solutions to current problems or to plumb the future as seen through our fears, presentiments, knowledge and desires: that is, they have a prospective function.

They can also ponder something that waking consciousness has ignored or passed over lightly, by showing it in an exaggerated form or in its final consequences, in order to warn us. Or the opposite, what

Jung calls their "reductive function", when our appreciation of some-thing, including ourselves, is excessive; dreams put everything, including the dreamer, in its proper place without hesitation—the wonderful "neutrality" of dreams, as some writers call it.

The abreactive—or cathartic—function consists in offering occasions, as only dreams can, for discharging unfettered affects and emotions which have been repressed—of disgust, fury or desire perhaps; by this means the psyche is purged (which is much the same as the completion of interrupted processes already mentioned).

Sometimes dreams seem to have an informative function, telling us not only about our own mental states and inner problems, but also about our own or other people's state of affairs, according to their bearing on our personal situation, making them a basis for personal elaboration. In doing this they show a power of synthesis of essentials which we often lack when awake, if we are distracted by a host of accidentals, or for other reasons. This is how dreams make discoveries and find solutions which have kept us puzzled all day: many cases of this have been reported.

With certain repetitive dreams—particularly about unpleasant shocks—the fact that we continue to dream the same thing even when our feelings on the subject are exhausted seems to be a means of assuring us that we are safe from the unpleasantness; of dissipating its power, easing the shock that had affected us, gradually erasing its impression.

At critical moments in our lives dreams may perhaps be—for many people certainly have been—a providential guide. Certain intuitions fundamental to the human capacity for sensible judgement take on a very definite and instructive shape. So do certain elevated desires which may have been trodden underfoot in waking life. This is particularly true of well-educated or idealistic people who through erroneous ways and through becoming involved in tricky situations have finally lost their bearings and found themselves on the rocks of a painful crisis. St Jerome's famous dream in which he was whipped by angels for reading Cicero was one of these crucial dreams. There are many examples.

Dreams can also be supersensitive states in which we receive telepathic accounts—there can no longer be any doubt of this—of distant happenings, according to laws of selection that are still only dimly understood.

Finally, innumerable trustworthy cases show that God has used dreams as an open door with which to communicate with men in one way or another. There are many cases of God granting great favours through dreams.[34]

It will be seen that dreams are not lacking in uses: one could certainly think of more. Now an attempt must be made to find a definition that will accord well with them all and explain the salient features of dreaming as a psychological function. Until something better is found, I suggest the following:

The oneiric function, through the inhibition and uneven weakening of psychic resources in sleep, offers conscious and unconscious life an imaginative screen on which to express themselves, and a testing ground for their reactions, which are mainly affective, and characterized chiefly by hallucination, symbolism, subjectivism, and sincerity.

This, I think, expresses what belongs strictly speaking to dreams and to no other function. Everything else that emerged from our consideration of the various finalities of dreams consists of diverse instincts and virtualities, manifested in dreams, but with an independent existence of their own and also manifested in a thousand ways in waking. These are functions of the human psyche, with its two closely linked spheres, spiritual and material. The particular contribution of dreams can be defined in psychological terms much as I have done. They open wide the gates of sincerity, to facilitate the play of psychic energies through their expression and their reactions.

34. See Alois Wiesinger, *Okkulte Phänomene im Lichte der Theologie* (Graz, 1948; 2nd edn, 1953. English trans, *Occult Phenomena in the Light of Theology*, London, 1957).

III

DREAMS AND THE SCHOOLS
OF DEPTH PSYCHOLOGY

36. *Essential contributions*

Depth psychology is concerned with unconscious motives of conduct: those motives that are hidden in the depth of the psyche—hence its name. It originated in modern times with Sigmund Freud and psychoanalysis. Several dissenters broke away from his school to found their own, the most famous being those of Alfred Adler and Carl Gustav Jung. In the field of dreams, Adler's contribution is not important, since he followed Freud's method, merely substituting the will to power, or instinct of domination, of transcendence, for the sexual libido. Jung on the other hand has made a particularly extensive and original study of many aspects of dreams.

There are numerous other eclectic writers, who have not made a sufficiently original contribution to the theory of dreams and their interpretation to merit separate mention. The disciples of existential analysis, despite their critical vigour, can be counted among these. The only one who deserves fuller treatment is Schulz-Hencke, who has interesting things to say in his book, though he is fundamentally a Freudian-eclectic, but this would involve too lengthy a discussion. I believe the essential contributions of depth psychology to be those of Freud and Jung, and it is with these two that I wish to deal in this chapter.

I. FREUD AND THE INTERPRETATION OF DREAMS

37. *How and why Freud was interested in dreams*

Freud's place in the study of dreams is so central that two perspectives open out from him, one backwards—his precursors—and the other forwards—his followers or opponents, either total or partial.

As a doctor, Freud was first interested in dreams when he realized that the enigmatic symptoms of neurotics had a secret meaning, to be found in earlier experiences, which the patient could not voluntarily recall, but which were faithfully registered and stored in the depths of the psyche. These depths were manifested chiefly in dreams. As Freud himself recognized, psychoanalysis owed its origins essentially to the Viennese Catholic doctor Josef Breuer. The decisive experiment was made between 1880 and 1882. Breuer was trying to cure a patient who for some weeks had been unable to drink, feeling an invincible repugnance every time she raised a glass to her lips. Nobody could see why, since she had always been able to drink easily enough. In certain absent-minded states, she mumbled allusions to some story. Breuer collected as many odd phrases of this as he could, hypnotized the patient—this was the heyday of hypnosis—and softly repeated the phrases to her, to see if this would make her tell the whole story. It did. It was an early childhood experience. She had once gone into her English governess's room—she did not like her—and seen a nasty little dog belonging to the governess drinking out of a glass. This disgusted her, but being rather afraid of the governess, she said nothing. The years passed by with no apparent development, and the scene was gradually buried in deep oblivion. But recently, exhaustion and a series of mental shocks had led to a nervous condition, manifesting itself in the strange symptom of hydrophobia. Several weeks of treatment had not been able to overcome her repugnance to the thought of drinking. Eventually Breuer made her relate the story under hypnosis and at once the indignation and disgust repressed since childhood disappeared, and after this relief (what psychoanalysis was later to call "abreaction") she at once asked for a glass of water. Freud, then a younger doctor, learnt of this case directly from Breuer, and the lessons it contained made a profound impression on him: apparently absurd neurotic symptoms could have a plausible explanation which must be sought in the unconscious depths of the psyche; these contain deposits of experience which continue to influence conduct, without the person's awareness: they have sunk down to the unconscious either through being spontaneously forgotten or through active repression; direct recollection will never bring them out; they have to be dug out by indirect means.

The most effective method of plumbing the unconscious then used was hypnosis. Great use, and misuse, of it was made in Nancy and the Salpetrière in Paris; Freud gained experience in both places, from Bernheim and Chavcot respectively. As it turned out, he had no hypnotic powers and had to abandon this method. But he would not abandon his attempts to explore the unconscious levels of the psyche, levels beyond the reach of memory. So he looked for other ways in which they might be manifested, and with great acumen concentrated on a number of psychic phenomena then ignored by official psychology (psychology of consciousness): involuntary slips of the tongue, incomplete actions, lapses of memory, fortuitous ideas, spontaneous gestures and movements, products of the imagination, and above all, dreams. All these phenomena, he said, are produced without conscious control and so must be manifestations of the unconscious and guides to its contents. He wrote two books about them, *The Psychopathology of Everyday Life* and *The Interpretation of Dreams*.

He was soon convinced that for "natural spontaneity" nothing could compare with dreams. He called them the "royal road to the unconscious", and made a study of them involving not only the books mentioned, but his whole life's work. Since then, psychoanalysis has developed chiefly on the basis of the interpretation of dreams.

38. *Facts to be borne in mind for the understanding of dreams*

It is time to examine the general lines of Freudian oneirology. He at once criticized "scientific" psychologists for reducing dreams exclusively or mainly to mere reconstructions of past or present sensations, internal or external. In this they missed the essential originality of dreams. Many writers had glimpsed something more, but their work needed to be completed and systematized. Dreams, he said—challenging the experimental science of his day—are a figurative language, a hieroglyphic alphabet. Once we can read it, we shall see that they are linked in a meaningful way to human life. They can be read with sufficient scientific accuracy, according to the peculiarity of the psychic word. This peculiarity was just what positivist rationalism, then at its height, would not accept. Academic circles did not even deign to reply. But Freud knew that he had found the key to dreams, and that time would prove him right.

For an understanding of dreams, one must know their origin, finality, theme, elements and manner of elaboration. Their *origin* lies in the instinctual life, whose instincts may be either primitive or derived. Their *finality* is pleasure, and also the protection of sleep, which is a pleasure in itself. Their *theme* is wish-fulfilment. Here Freud is categorical. Various critics opposed dreams of fear (nightmares) to this, but Freud always maintained that from one angle they would always appear as wish-fulfilment. Nightmares might satisfy a masochistic desire for punishment, or merely fulfil their vital function of waking the dreamer suddenly, in order to change his position or for some other reason. Towards the end of his life, however, Freud admitted merely repetitive dreams that did not fulfil a wish.

Their manner of elaboration is unconscious: the dreamer finds himself *post factum* with an already elaborated dream. The equally unconscious function which makes this elaboration possible is "psychic causality", as opposed to "physical causality", the fact that certain psychic states produce others; the phenomenon which can be seen at work in "association of ideas". It is a connection between some mental states and others, or a subjective interdependence, based on the actuation and particular direction of psychic forces, tendencies and emotions. Nature establishes circuits and connecting networks between these forces and their objects, through links produced by the individual's successive subjective experiences, in the manner of conditioned reflexes.

G

It is precisely this that makes the method of association of ideas the main instrument of psychoanalysis in understanding the meaning of dreams, when this is not obvious and straightforward intuition is not sufficient. These more complex dreams present a *manifest content*, which is perplexing, and also have a *latent content*, which has to be discovered.

39.   *Tendencies and their interaction, the framework of dreams*

In order to realize what dreams mean, one must understand their matter, their tendencies, and the incidents they produce by their mode of action. There are three common cases to be distinguished in this field.

1. A single wish appears for fulfilment without contradiction (no inhibition).

2. Two or more wishes of varying incompatibility demand fulfilment and reach a compromise (partial inhibition).

3. Two or more wishes struggle, and one wins to the exclusion of the others (total inhibition).

Naturally, there are numerous degrees and combinations of these three. For one tendency to eliminate another, or restrain it, is common experience, daily taking place in full consciousness. It was Freud's distinction to insist on the not unknown but largely unappreciated fact that this struggle among tendencies also occurs before we awake to full consciousness, without our realizing it. We only know its outcome. This unconscious inhibition is the famous "repression", one of the pillars of psychoanalytical theory, which considers it an automatic play of forces, of great consequence in the elaboration of dreams.

Freud groups human tendencies into three well-known categories: the *Id*, the *Ego* and the *Super-ego* (which he originally called the "censor", this being one of its functions). The *Id*, which Baudouin calls "the primitive", comprises the instincts, strongly physical in their orientation, fiercely obstinate, grossly selfish; the primary sources of psychic energy, the libido. According to Freud, this libido is predominantly sexual in character, taking the word in a wide sense, but without losing its essential meaning.

The *Ego* is for Freud, who did not recognize the existence of a spiritual sphere, a differentiation of the Id in its relations with the outside world. It can be called the equivalent of consciousness, with its sensory, imaginative, rational and affective-volitional aspects. Its field is the conscious, but it can also reach the neighbouring zone whose contents can be evoked at will, which Freud calls the pre-conscious. The Ego, situated between the individual and the world around him, tries to act in such a way that both spheres will be satisfied. Its resulting decision, according to Freud, is an effect, not of free choice, which he denied, but of an equilibrium of forces, depending on the different pressures put on the Ego at a given moment.

The *Super-ego* is an ideal in the unconscious built up by early experiences, on the basis mainly of the child's relations to persons and objects around him. It is formed mainly by assimilation of himself to certain people who occupy a privileged position in his vital outlook, and who are models, examples of progress in life for him. They are normally his parents first of all, and certain other people who feature in the child's life. Norms of judgement and action, embodied in these people, are "introjected" or unconsciously inserted into the child's mind, and form a system of standards by which he tries to judge, and as far as possible regulate, his whole conduct. This category exercises a steadying influence on the amorphous vital urges of the Id, and through trying to induce stability, clings too much to the past, is too conservative, and so can easily lose contact with the demands of the present. Notice here that Freud does not deduce moral norms from the concepts of good and evil, perceived by the soul as objective requirements made by God or objective reason, for a right ordering of conduct, but sees them as an empirical structure originating in society, an adaptation to one's surroundings, just as a shellfish or a plant adapts itself to its own. This ideal of oneself, or ego-ideal, watches over the conscious self and automatically, unconsciously, exercises the most important and dramatic censory and repressive function in mental life;

each tendency obviously produces its own lesser censorship and repressions. It is this Super-ego that produces anxiety, guilt, and a desire for self-punishment. In neurosis, its cruelty and vigour can go to inconceivable extremes.

The tendencies that most frequently come under the ban of this censorship are the cruder forms of sexuality, which cannot be fitted into the social framework and so are outlawed by it. Being outlawed, however, does not leave them any less vigorous or insatiable. One can imagine their power of intrigue: perpetually on the lookout for satisfaction in any shape or form, open or secret, through the proper object or a related substitute (intrinsically or extrinsically related), libidinizing apparently alien spheres, with an infinite capacity for metamorphoses that will bring indirect satisfaction, if forced to do so by the vigilance of the Super-ego. In dreams libido has a free hand to disguise itself in any form in order to deceive the censor.

This popular and dramatic manner of presenting psychological facts has contributed largely to Freud's widespread renown. Despite hostile scientific criticism of this theory as "mytho-psychology", there is no doubt that most people see a basis of truth in it.

All these categories intervene in dreams. The Id sometimes overflows with consummate impudence, but usually the censor controls it even in dreams, forcing it to have recourse to its disguises, in which it shows quite incredible subtlety. When psychoanalysis snatches off the mask, the uninitiated may sneer or rage, depending on their attitude. However, this virtuosity in disguising itself has been proved true in countless cases. Although the Super-ego is active in dreams, it is definitely less effective than in waking life; in general dreams show a weakening of the critical faculties of consciousness, which means that they have more natural spontaneity; the unconscious manifests itself more readily. This is why Freud called dreams the "royal road to the unconscious".

40.   *Mechanisms of dream elaboration*

All these tendencies, which form the psychic side of life, are at once the motors and the manifest or latent theme of dreams. In other words: the situations created by these tendencies, more or less co-ordinated, or anarchic and looking for satisfaction, are expressed as images in dreams. This enables us to understand the picture of forces in action and their mutual interference. These images become signs of ineffable psychic entities, retaining sufficient similarity to them to be recognizable. Freud calls these images "symbols" although outside psychoanalysis the word means something rather different. So he calls this primitive process by which psychic realities clothe themselves in images the *mechanism of symbolization*. Vast numbers of these images are stored in the warehouse of memory, ready to be called out by a dream. They are willing slaves, swift and elastic, and can be moulded into an infinite variety of forms.

The mechanism of *dramatization* must be added to that of *symbolization*. This means that the images are not static, which would severely limit their expressive capacity, but are actions in continuous progress, with a host of actors and scenes, like a film. This successive dramatic movement is a far more adequate representation of the original dynamism of psychic facts with their extreme intricacy and richness, and of their projection in time.

A third mechanism is that of *condensation*, by which elements of different origins can be fused into a single image to fulfil a complex expressive function. For example, a person can appear with his own features, but with another's hair, another's clothes, behaving like someone else in someone else's place. Analysis can decipher the meaning behind this fusion of so many disparate elements into a single image. However subtle or grotesque the condensation may appear at first sight, it turns out to be surprisingly accurate—within the limits of the dream's expression—in manifesting the relations between all the different elements, and the reason for bringing them together at that particular moment.

The mechanism of *displacement* is another of Freud's brilliant discoveries. Images remain inactive in the limbo of memory till they are moved by an affective charge, thereby entering as a means or a reflection, or by contamination, into the finalistic arrangement of some tendency in action. This affective charge can vary in intensity. It might be compared to a magnet drawing the images into an order corresponding to the main lines of a given psychic situation. It is a basic fact that these affective charges can change their sign, or transfer from one object to another, in accordance with very definite laws, which sometimes correspond to those that govern the association of ideas: likeness, contiguity, opposition, relation of a whole to a part and vice versa, of a cause to an effect and vice versa, etc. This is all conditioned by previous individual experience. For instance, a particular kitchen smell aroused a feeling of anxiety in one man; for a time he could not think why, but an analysis revealed that he had once noticed the same smell while undergoing an experience that had every right to cause him anxiety. These links or associations which permit later evocation and the displacement of the affective charge are continually being produced in us, with or without our knowledge, in the manner of conditioned reflexes. Affective affinity between two situations is sufficient for them to be elicited together. Affectivity is the queen of dreams, and since she is blind her rule allows the most fantastic combinations in space and time. But from the affective point of view, which is her own, her meaning is always coherently expressed. This fact is generally not known.

The censor is responsible for many of these displacements. If the proper object required by an instinct for its satisfaction cannot appear because the Super-ego with its ideal of decency has suppressed it, then it has to be represented by a substitute object, which, thanks to some connection or resemblance to the original object, can receive the affective charge destined for the original. As is well known, Freudianism, with its resulting near pan-sexualism, which in theory it denies, has given itself a free hand in seeking and finding substitutes for sexual objects. Any orthodox Freudian text-book can show examples, often unfortunate ones, of these excesses.[1]

---

1. For example Angel Garma's book, *Psicoanálisis de los sueños* (3rd edn, Buenos Aires, 1956).

These mechanisms can lead to an understanding of a large part of dream contents, but not all. Hence Freud makes a certain allowance for what he calls "secondary elaboration", that is, a readjustment to round off the story by introducing "padding" material to avoid loss of continuity, gaps, or too sudden faults of logic—understanding logic with the latitude proper to its dream expression. It has been noticed that this demand for logic is greater in dreams immediately preceding waking.

41. *The psychoanalytical method of interpreting dreams*

We have considered Freud's conception of the motor, materials, mechanisms and finality of dreams. We know that deep psychic life is manifested in dream fantasies with far more sincerity than the hypocrisy and ingenuity of waking consciousness allow. Everyone possesses this psychic life, but does not always want to give it conscious recognition. So an appeal to the conscious memory, to reveal the centre of disturbance which is producing neurotic symptoms from its undiscovered origin, is useless. Conscious memory will not and cannot remember. Various forces, such as active forgetting or "unconscious repression", prevent it. Freud invented the psychoanalytical method precisely in order to uncover these centres which produce disturbances.

The mainspring of the psychoanalytical method is, as we have seen, the interpretation of dreams. Very briefly, this method consists in placing the subject in a position of muscular and mental relaxation, inhibiting all voluntary control of ideas, imagination and feeling, as far as possible. In this state of passivity which allows the psychic current to flow, the analyst mentions various elements of the patient's dream, previously related, to him, and asks him to say, with complete sincerity and accuracy, all that occurs to him spontaneously: this is the famous method of "free association". These word-reactions are like hooks lowered into the pool of the unconscious, which fish out more and more tangled material, which in its turn becomes a new hook for bringing up more. So more and more new areas of the psychic life, formerly in shadow, are brought into the light and little by little the enigma of the dream is clarified, with a clinical certainty which deserves respect. These are not mathematical certitudes, but then neither is much of the evidence that we usually accept, such as historical arguments based on mutually corroborative pieces of evidence. Well used, this is a scientific method, and it is Freud's lasting glory to have discovered and developed it.

But, besides adequate competence, the analyst who uses this method must possess a *sound psychology*. And Freudian psychology, though it contains a great deal of truth, is not by any means complete or acceptable. Hence the failure of many dream interpretations made by Freud and his successors.

The analyst must have a *feeling for psychic reality*, which is indescribable and *sui generis*. Many criticisms of the Freudian method of interpretation point to its failure to focus correctly on psychic realities.

It has been objected that this method leads to many fantasies. Perhaps its nature, imposed by its material, makes it somewhat prone to fantasy; but then which method is not? Like any other, it must be used legitimately. When so used it is undoubtedly effective and valuable, even though still incomplete. It has been greatly developed by later writers, of whom the most important is Carl Gustav Jung.

II.   ONEIROLOGY OF CARL GUSTAV JUNG

42.   *His criticism of Freudian psychoanalysis*

Jung criticized, improved and completed Freudian oneirology more shrewdly than anyone else. He criticized its fundamental premises, among them the concept of the *libido*. For him this is not something sexual, as it was for Freud. He retains the word, but gives it a meaning of "psychic energy", which is eventually identified with the "vital impulse". Freud regarded the unconscious as a sort of dungeon of the

Id, overrun with desires repressed by the Super-ego. Hence he considered dreams—manifestations of the unconscious—as ways of escape and satisfaction of these desires, disguised in symbols so as to deceive the "censor". Jung considers the unconscious as vast as nature herself, containing anything that is not actually conscious, be it acquired or innate, memorable or beyond recall. The ideas he calls "innate" are not ideas in concrete form, but rather a certain selectivity and propensity to group concrete impressions received through the senses. So unconscious impulses are not always, as they were for Freud, infantile, animal, coarse. . . . They can also be noble and generous, because nature has a light as well as a dark side. Among other things, Jung criticizes Freud's idea of the mechanism of dream elaboration, and his analysis for its abuse of free associations, for defining certain images as sex symbols beforehand, and finally for its concentration on a retrospective, reductive and causal outlook, excluding the progressive, finalistic approach so necessary with vital, particularly psychic, functions.

43. *Jung's personal contributions*

A typical feature of Jung's theory is the distinction between the *personal* and *collective* unconscious. The latter comprises all that is inherited, the results of humanity's previous experience in the shape of cerebral dispositions towards the formation of certain set symbols, the *archetypes of the collective unconscious*, which crystallize fundamental vital realities of great importance. These are the symbols that appear in the dreams and phantasies of all men, primitive and civilized, and in all cultures, however distant in time and space. Experience, he claims, shows that many myths and religious dogmas belong to this category. This is Jung's most characteristic contribution and has been much criticized on practically every count. These archetypes, the critics say, are no more than abstractions which Jung has converted into causes. Again, the hereditary transmission of these entities contradicts experience, as it is understood today. However, one can retain the essentials from a psychotherapeutic point of view, because these symbols, referring to fundamental realities and experiences of life, find a deep emotional response in man. This in itself explains why they are found everywhere from earliest times, since basically human nature does not change.

44. *Nature and functions of dreams*

For Jung, dreaming is a *spontaneous and symbolic auto-representation of the actual situation of the unconscious*, that vast unconscious whose origins are confused with life itself. So it is not surprising that *auto-regulation*, one of the primary qualities of life, should be manifested in dreams. This quality, so evident in physiological life, is no less prominent in psychic life. This auto-regulation automatically proceeds to restore equilibrium when, for one reason or another, it has been lost.

The reason might be an act of fate, or misgovernment by the conscious, which is easily blinded with one-sided ideas and then imposes imprudent behaviour that leaves vital possibilities out of account, creating dangerous tensions or perhaps leading to breakdown. This anti-natural behaviour imposes itself progressively and induces progressive reaction. But the conscious is bound by its nature to repress the protest, so the reaction is unconscious and can only express itself in ways beyond conscious control: significant errors, failures, apparently inexplicable states of mind, various psychosomatic symptoms, headaches, organic disorders, spontaneous fantasies, etc. Above all, however, it shows itself in dreams.

The unconscious can also disturb the equilibrium, as when some force gets out of control (passion, physiological disorder, glandular failure, etc.). Then the conscious has to react to restore equilibrium with its own resources, understanding and will, and here, if necessary, it invokes the aid of a doctor or spiritual director.

So there is a constant relation of *compensation* between the conscious and the unconscious. This psychic law is fundamental to Jungian theory.

The *compensatory function* is active in all dreams: without exception according to Jung, who opposed this universal theory to Freud's equally universal one that all dreams are wish-fulfilment. Sometimes this compensation is obvious, but it can sometimes assume extremely subtle and deceptive forms. When the conscious and the unconscious agree on one particular case, but differ in the degree of enthusiasm felt for it, the compensation may only appear at the level of enthusiasm, and nowhere else.

There is also compensation when, if the conscious is too absorbed by one particular matter, attention is diverted from it by dreams that bear no relation to that matter. With our incomplete knowledge of the psyche, we can only say that such dreams have the function of producing beneficial relaxation: the so-called *playful function*. They may quite probably have another function, as yet unknown.

The *informative function* is also compensatory, in that it corrects the tendentious ignorance of the conscious with respect to certain realities.

Dreams fulfil a *reductory function* when an individual who has too high an opinion of himself in his conscious life, sees himself in a thoroughly unfavourable light, which can take the form of exaggerating his opinion of himself so as to hold his vanity up to ridicule. The opposite also happens: a person who is too pessimistic or timid can be consoled by heartening visions in dreams.

The *prospective function* is one of those most energetically affirmed by Moeder and then by Jung in opposition to Freud, who was too retrospective, though in his very retrospection he did admit the teleology inherent in every vital act. This function probes the future, stimulates progress, seeks solutions to current problems, points out obstacles to be avoided, shows ways out of difficulties, or dissuades one from following a wrong course.

The *reactive function* appears as a mechanical repetition of certain traumatic experiences: actions in war, a difficult examination, painful scenes, etc. The scene is repeated, always in the same way, a greater or lesser number of times. In these cases perception followed by abreaction does not have the purgative effect it has in other cases. This obstinate repetition seems to have the purpose of allowing the echo of the experience to wear itself out through repetition.

Other functions could also be mentioned, but these are the most important of those discussed by Jung. The compensatory function is fundamental to them all, fulfilled in a different way in each.

45.   *Dream structure*

So far we have considered the nature of dreams and their main functions; the primordial energy which instigates and institutes them; and the basic law of compensation which regulates them. The next question is their *general structure*. This can vary from the simplicity of a fleeting picture to the plot of a fairly long story, with every intermediate grade. Dreams normally contain four dramatic acts, as it were. There is first the *presentation* of scene and person: "I am in a street; it is an avenue. In the distance a car appears." Second act, *complication*: "The car is coming rapidly towards me, swaying from side to side. I think, 'The driver must be drunk'." Third act, *culmination*: "Suddenly I see that I am the driver, and so I am the drunk. But I am not drunk, only strangely uncertain and perplexed. I cannot control the car, which heads straight towards a wall and hits it with a colossal crash." Fourth and last act (unless the story is cut short before then), *conclusion*: "I see that the bonnet is crumpled. It is an unknown car, and not mine. I myself am not injured. I am left reflecting with some anxiety on my responsibility."[2]

46.   *Jung's method of interpretation*

Jung's interpretative method, like that of all the other schools, is developed on the basis of Freud's free association. But he disagrees with the Freudian tendencies to assign a fixed meaning to each symbol, and to see everything as a sex symbol while sexual images are never symbolic of anything else, contrary to the lessons of experience. Sexual experience, being among the most primitive, can most easily be used to express non-sexual ideas: there is ample linguistic evidence

2. C. G. Jung, "De la nature des rêves", *Revue Ciba*, 46 (Sept. 1945), p. 1611.

for this. Jung regards the long-established practice of assigning a fixed meaning to every dream image as the greatest danger. The autonomy of the unconscious and the changing course of psychic situations preclude any preconceptions. Each dream is something original which must be approached with a completely open mind. "The understanding of dreams", he says, "is so difficult that I have long since trained myself, when asked for my opinion on one, to tell myself that I know nothing whatever about its meaning. Only then do I begin to examine it."[3]

Jung's procedure begins with what he calls the *verbal trial of context.* This consists in comparing each detail of the dream with the ideas and feelings it suggests to the dreamer, making careful notes of the shades of real and affective meaning it has for him. Since, as has been seen, the unconscious is in direct relationship with the conscious, it would be absurd to attempt an interpretation without the dreamer's collabora-tion, since he alone can give the context and meaning of the symbols. This preliminary labour does not always succeed in deciphering the dream, but the material collected, together with more elicited by further associations, can clear the way for an interpretative synthesis.

This is the critical moment which makes the greatest demands on the analyst in the way of preparation and focusing: he must have psycho-logical understanding, a faculty for putting ideas together, intuition, knowledge of the world and of men, sufficient training and a specific knowledge of psychic manifestations in different cultures. He also needs an aptitude for what is called "empathy", with a special feeling for the affective life and its complications—"intelligence of the heart".

Without these gifts, and without possessing sure anthropological and psychological knowledge, he will not be able to use the method of free association by itself. Jung has continually drawn attention to the ambiguity of simple association. In fact, everything in us is related to everything else. A certain number of associations can lead to any result from any point of departure. Jung made the experiment of discovering a person's complexes from the text of a municipal by-law, which shows

3. Jung, "De la nature des rêves", *loc. cit.*, p. 1603.

how unconvincing is the deduction of the latent meaning of dreams from their sexual, or any other, nature, despite the continuous insistence of orthodox psychoanalysis. By the same method Adler always arrived at the "will to power". If one puts something into a dream in accordance with a preconceived theory, clearly free association can always find it there. Hence the absolute necessity of using this method with a due appreciation of its nature and limitations, and of handling it with extreme care. Only in this way can it be of value in psychological investigation. What is important is the overall picture.

Since interpretation can be made on different levels, or with different orientations, it is important to decide which is most suitable to the case in hand. In the first place, much has been said of *causal* or *reductive interpretation*, and of *finalistic* or *constructive interpretation*. The causal approach is usually attributed to Freud, as belonging more properly to his method, not because he denies teleology, but because his whole psychological theory centres on the Id, both conceptually (instincts) and chronologically (infancy). For Freud, all the adult material he studied stemmed from these sources, and his favourite method of understanding them was to reduce them to their primitive, early meaning; consequently he applied this principle to dreams. Experimental psychology also proceeds by assigning causes, reducing oneiric phenomena to their antecedents or sensorial concomitants. Jung knows, and expressly states, that the reductive explanation can be, at least partially, correct in many cases. But for him the ideal method should combine the retrospective, causalist and reductive approach with the finalist, prospective and constructive one.

The distinction between *objective* and *subjective* interpretation is also important. In the former, to dream of a person or thing implies a positive reference to that person or thing. In the latter the person or thing is used as a symbol for something personal to the dreamer, with some justifying connection. So in approaching a dream, the analyst must decide which method is required, or whether some things in it must be explained one way and some the other. Each dream is a separate entity. After all, the dream must reflect what is in the psyche.

And the psyche contains representations of objects, and personal experiences expressed as object-symbols.

Finally, there is a distinction to be made between dreams of an individual nature and dreams of a collective nature, and consequently the analyst must decide whether a *personal* or a *collective* interpretation is required. This is a typically Jungian distinction, corresponding to the differentiation between the personal unconscious and the collective unconscious. Personal dreams refer to strictly individual problems arising from the circumstances of the dreamer's life. Collective dreams refer to the perennial problems of humanity. Naturally, both meanings can be superimposed, and this is what normally happens. It is precisely those personal situations that take on a transcendent nature which provoke the appearance of general problems. The dreamer's age influences the type of problem posed. In the first half of life, orientation is more objective and problems more egocentric, as befits someone trying to make a place for himself in society, who needs to measure reality carefully so as not to fail. In the latter half, on the other hand, when these tensions have given place to the problems of a future life, the atmosphere is more propitious for an examination of problems relating to the philosophy of existence. The type of person also makes a difference: some people have an introverted theoretical outlook from their youth, others are extrovert and practical all through their lives. Education and the hazards of fortune also leave their mark on a person's outlook, and so on his dreams.

In each case, then, the analyst must decide which line of interpretation—causal, reductive or finalist; constructive, subjective or collective —is best suited to the particular dream. There are not many rules governing this decision. Given adequate knowledge, experience is the best guide. For people with strong instinctual tensions, who are unsatisfied and repressed, lacking balanced integration in a higher ideal, the reductive method, which uncovers the primitive forces underlying the state, may be best. On the whole, Jung considers the reductive method suitable for absurd, sickly or unintelligible psychic superstructures, where the symptoms need to be reduced to something more primitive and comprehensible. This is the Freudian method: such and such a symptom is "nothing but. . . ". For people who are developing, passing normally through progressive stages, and accepting the responsibilities of each, a finalist and constructive approach is normally indicated. But there are no set rules: each case must be treated on its merits.

47.   The Jungian "process of individuation" in dreams

These considerations lead to a necessarily brief discussion of what Jung calls the *process of individuation*. An isolated dream can only give an indication of a particular moment of mental life. For an understanding of its evolution—which is essential—a series of dreams must be studied. Psychoanalysis realizes this: hence the long course of treatment. Jung says the same. He lays particular stress on the importance of keeping a diary of dreams. Only a study of hundreds of dreams will give a clear picture of the compensatory function of the unconscious, particularly of its development according to a "scheme". The scheme is a natural, spontaneous process of maturation and development which passes through certain phases or seasons throughout life. Interference caused by conscious control or social relationships can interfere with this process and hasten or retard it, but Jung regards its uninterrupted flow as the course of theoretically normal mental development. This is his most important discovery. Once this process has been discovered, it can naturally be helped by psychotherapy.

Extensive knowledge and great skill are needed to discern this scheme or process of individuation in each case. This is far more difficult than being able to appreciate the compensatory aspects of particular dreams, for which a reasonable amount of theoretical and practical training will suffice. But wide and varied knowledge in fields which, prior to Jung, were not considered to be connected with psychology (though anything human is in a sense its concern), as well as deep psychological knowledge and understanding, are necessary for an understanding of the import of transcendental symbols which express

the process of individuation. With psychology, Jung has connected
certain branches of anthropology, and the study of civilization in
particular, as being guardians of collective symbols or *archetypes of the
collective unconscious.* Mythology; manuals of wisdom and initiation,
particularly in the Orient; folklore; the psychology of surviving
primitive peoples; comparative religious history; alchemy; certain
poems which are particularly representative of a culture and therefore
rooted in universal interest; religious and heroic iconography, liturgy,
etc.; all these, according to Jung, reveal the hidden depths of the
collective unconscious to the man who knows how to decipher and
read them.

All this knowledge is needed to be able to evaluate the symbols that
sometimes appear in dreams. The dreams containing them are *important*
and stand out from the ordinary run of trivial dreams. They leave a
deep impression and are not easy to forget. Some occur in childhood
and are remembered with emotion throughout one's life. They usually
occur at decisive moments and mark the stages in the process of
individuation. Here are two examples of archetypal dreams:

When N. was about fifteen, and had recently arrived in the city of
X. with her mother, two brothers and two sisters, she found herself
in great difficulty trying to support the family. Her mother and she,
the eldest, were seamstresses. The woman who ran the shop where
she worked was jealous of her, and she lost her job. She was plunged
into the depths of despair at being unable to help her family, and in
this state she had a dream. She was at the top of a very steep street,
looking down. Coming up it was a venerable old man in a white
cloak reaching to the ground, with a white beard, like a popular
picture of God the Father. A lady was with him, also elderly, dressed
in blue. She felt a tremendous respect for them. They came up to her
and asked, "What's the matter?" She told them her trouble, and the
old man said, "Show me your hands". She held them out, palms
upward. The old man and woman put a sort of iron rod into them,
saying to her, "With those hands you can do what you like". The
dream faded. Two days later she found work, better paid than by

H

the woman who had dismissed her, and from then onwards her hands always enabled her to do what work she liked. The dream made a tremendous impression on and remained deeply engraved on her memory.

In the next example, the dreamer was a young student:

> I was in a sort of temple or sacristy. At the end was a grey archway reaching up to the ceiling. There was a small carpet, on which stood a table covered with a cloth reaching down to the ground. On the left of the table, a high leather chair, covered in velvet. On the right, a saint appeared, not like an apparition, but like someone walking normally into a room. By his habit I at once recognized him as St Dominic. I knelt down and kissed his hands, which he held out to me, thanking God for such a great favour. But suddenly I felt a great struggle within me. I felt unworthy to kiss his hand, and felt a physical, satanic force inside me which would not allow me to approach him. While I was in this confusion, another saint came in on the left (the scene was like a canvas, but full of life); I immediately recognized him as St Francis. He was short, and sat down at once, while St Dominic asked him, smiling, referring to me, "What do you think of him?" I could not take my eyes off St Francis and thought, to myself, that he was not very impressive and even rather ugly to look at, while at the same time I felt ashamed at finding myself, a sinner, between those saints. St Francis smiled and I think he stroked my head. My confusion and struggle increased enormously when St Dominic, taking me by the hands and turning me aside, took his heart out of his breast and gave it to me to bite. Then I felt my spiritual anguish and physical revulsion disappear, and my whole being, body and soul, steeped in infinite happiness and peace. Then I woke up, still keeping this feeling of physical and spiritual well-being.

Jung affirmed that a comparison between the symbols in important dreams and the symbols that have played an important part in the history of mankind will show them to be the same. The dreamer is not aware that his particular dream is repeating an outstanding dream which has excited countless generations, or that it is giving particular expression to mankind's perennial problems, and so energizing man's very nature in transcendent purpose. The dreamer does not suspect all this; the truly expert analyst, according to Jung, thanks to the material for comparison at his disposal, can see its meaning and realize its significance. He is alerted by perceiving a particular symbol accompanied by an urgency and depth of feeling inexplicable on purely personal grounds. The collective nature of this feeling is revealed by studying the degree of influence of the symbol in question on the panorama of the human mind. This type of comparative work absorbed Jung during the latter part of his life with greater intensity than ever, though it always interested him, as witness his famous work *Transformations and Symbols of the Libido* (Vienna, 1921). The man-animal, the evil witch, the old man of the mountains, the great mother, the hero who kills the dragon who guards a treasure, the hero who dies and returns to life, the mysterious fountain, the enchanted cave, the magic tree . . . these are some archetypal symbols. Some are propitious and some are hostile. The whole of ancient mythology can be seen as a dramatized and exteriorized form of psychology.

These symbols appear in the individuation process in the following order: first, the *Shadow*, or unpropitious and unfavourable aspects of oneself; which must be recognized if *all* that we are is to be integrated into the personality. This can take many different forms. Then the *Anima* in men, and the *Animus* in women, the feminine principle in man and the masculine principle in woman, which must also be integrated. They can also take many forms. Then come symbols of wisdom, the *unifying symbols*, the symbols of "the Self", that is, the harmonized totality of one's being. These symbols take a special form, which Jung calls *mandala*, after the static, symmetrical, circular or concentric polygonal figures expressing energy in equilibrium, used in contemplation by Buddhist monks and others. Each one of these symbols produces energy and marks a stage in the process of individuation, each stage having its own purpose. In discussing dreams all these vital values can be assimilated by the conscious. This leads to knowledge of life and maturity.

There is much to be said about this individuation process, about its general direction, details, universality and authenticity. Jung has undoubtedly used it to express many real psychic facts observed by him. The whole idea shows deep human knowledge. Explicitly or implicitly, it also contains a philosophy. What judgement it merits is difficult to say in a few words. Its philosophy tends towards a vitalist naturalism that does not always agree with Christian philosophy. But the psychological facts are well worth careful consideration; even if they are not all acceptable as expressed by Jung, their substance should be observed and compared with the other forms in which these facts have been expressed in the long course of their observation by mankind. Approached in this way, the study of Jung's works, which may be difficult and dangerous, should prove a fruitful source of knowledge of man's psychic life.

IV

TELEPATHIC, PROPHETIC AND MYSTIC DREAMS

Our examination of dreams in history showed that they were not always considered important for the light they threw on the personality, as they are today, but mainly for their relation to the realm of mystery. They were considered a source of knowledge about occult phenomena (cryptaesthesia), distant happenings (telepathy), the future (precognition or prognosis) and the other world—the dead, spirits, and gods. No discussion of dreams can omit questions so interesting in themselves and which have intrigued mankind for so long.

48. *A necessary corrective*

Positivist science, in its objection to all mystery, relegated all these phenomena to the domain of occultism, the source of all deception. It thereby discarded an enormous weight of material which had accumulated through the centuries in every country. These facts—or fancies—(that must be decided), clashed so openly with rationalist dependence on "scientific" methods that most people did not even trouble to ask whether knowledge without the intervention of the senses might be possible. Admittedly spiritualist and occultist sessions (divination, horoscopes, fortune-telling, apparitions, materialization of spirits, telekinesis . . .) acquired, and retain, such a well-deserved reputation for being psychopathic, ridiculous, fraudulent and mercenary that a sensible person can hardly give credit to them. Admittedly, too, the morbid attraction exercised by the whole of this subject has made fools of even academic scientists of proved distinction, such as, amongst others, William Crookes and Charles Richet. Many honest attempts at serious investigation, either with a medium (the person who produces or provokes many of these phenomena) or without, have been made in the hope of establishing a basis for a future science of these strange phenomena. Some call this science metapsychics and some parapsychology. But these attempts have always been so exploited and spoilt by spiritualists and occultists in their proselytizing campaigns that even the least suspicious have been put on their guard. Consequently, none of this material can be discussed without discriminating between what is legitimate and what is not. The Spanish Jesuit Fr Palmés has written his *Metapsychics and Spiritualism* as a denunciation of the cunning of some people and the candour of others;[1] so let it be said here that I have no intention of becoming involved with anything suspect.

49.   Historical summary

Such well-attested phenomena cannot, however, be left out of account in an honest attempt to make a scientific examination of man as he is. This attitude is not new. In 1882, in the heyday of rationalism, an "advanced" group in London founded the best-known society for such studies, the Society for Psychical Research. With such a subject, it is not surprising that people of little scientific integrity should have become involved, as they did from time to time, but today its two publications, the *Proceedings* and the *Journal*, are the most important organs dealing with this subject. The laws formulated to govern the observation of psychic phenomena were as critically sound as the subject-matter and date allowed, though some questionable cases have been admitted. Today, they need to be rather more strict. The founders, Henry Sidgwick and Frederic Myers, were concerned chiefly with collecting unimpeachable data so as to put an end to the stereotyped

1. Fernando María Palmés, s.j., *Metapsíquica y Espiritismo* (Barcelona, 1950).

scientific reaction, which was simply to deny the facts. A glance through a book like Gurney, Myers and Podmore's *Phantasms of the Living* (2 vols.), 1886, which gives thousands of cases, is enough to convince one that even if only a hundredth part is true, it is still sufficient to justify and show the importance of such investigations. A branch was soon founded in the United States, the American Society for Psychical Research, and similar institutions followed in many countries, the best-known being the *Institut métapsychique international* in Paris, which has numbered Richet and Osty, names well-known in controversies on the subject, among its presidents. The value of the experiments made in these early years is very varied. Between 1892 and 1894 the Italian G. B. Ermacora conducted meticulous telepathic experiments.[2] But many others, including people who should have known better, were fooled by mediums and went to extremes. During the last twenty-five years, though spiritualist quackery has continued on its course, parapsychology has found its way into universities, with men such as Driesch, Rhine and Bender. Hans Driesch, the biologist and philosopher of vitalism, has established a basis for a rigorous method of investigation.[3] Rhine, working at Duke University, N. Carolina, U.S.A., has used statistical methods on a large scale to establish the existence, or non-existence, of telepathy and other phenomena.[4] Hans Bender, lecturer at Freiburg, follows Driesch's approach. Many people today cultivate these studies with seriousness and every type of precaution. There are serious specialist reviews and the bibliography is rapidly growing. The subject is still frankly in the experimental stage, though, more than any other, it requires observation of spontaneous cases, since the necessary faculties, at least in sufficient numbers, are very rare. The science is still only in its infancy, but as far as the obscurity of its object allows, its investigations have begun with promising results. Man is becoming more complicated than late

2. G. B. Ermacora, *La Telepatia* (Padua, 1898). For the history of the movement, see G. M. N. Tyrrell, *The Personality of Man* (London, 1947), pp. 47 and ff.

3. Hans Driesch, *Parapsychologie. Methodik und Theorik* (Zürich, 1943).

4. J. B. Rhine, *Extra-Sensory Perception*, 1934; *New Frontiers of the Mind*, 1938; *Extra-Sensory Perception after Sixty Years*, 1940; *New World of the Mind* (London, 1954).

nineteenth-century scientific optimism thought possible. Today, without renouncing the exactitude of the heroic age of "science", our horizons are broader, we have a more immediate sense of the mystery that surrounds us, and can adapt ourselves more readily to the demands of each branch of knowledge.

I. PSYCHIC VERSUS SPATIAL

50. *Terminological note*

This note will serve as an outline of the matters to be discussed. I am not concerned with telepathy and prophecy as such, but with their manifestation in dreams, which must, however, be seen in its general context. Etymologically, the word "telepathy" means "experience from a distance" ("experience" and not "suffering" here being the correct translation of the Greek *pathein*) and is used as a general term covering several activities which should be distinguished. The "telepathizer" and the "telepathized", or *active* and *passive* telepathy must be considered. The sender of the message is also known as the *agent* and its receiver as the *percipient*. The name of telepathy should properly be confined to the percipient, who acts like a radio receiver. The agent (transmitter) should be designated by a word such as *telesuggestion* or *telergy*.

Telepathic phenomena also include telaesthesia and cryptaesthesia. Telaesthesia is the active reading or perception of something distant, another person's thought or general state of mind, or an inert physical fact (a written message, an object, a scene, a situation). Cryptaesthesia is the same process when the object is close at hand, but there is some obstacle that prevents it from reaching the senses directly. All these phenomena, including precognition, which I shall discuss in due course, have in common the fact that they take place without the intervention of the senses; hence they are generally known as E.S.P. (extra-sensory perception) phenomena. I shall first give some examples and then outline the theories that have been produced in attempts to explain them.

I am taking for granted the fact that these are all natural phenomena, with no suspicion of preternatural intervention.

51. *Telaesthesia and cryptaesthesia*

These two can be taken together as meaning practically the same thing.

The first case is from the most amazing dreamer of all time, St John Bosco.

When he was a student, on two occasions he dreamt of the dictation that his teacher was giving the next day. The first time, realizing what had happened, he jumped out of bed and wrote down everything he had dreamt, but since it was in Latin, and he was not sure of the spelling, he took it to a priest to be corrected. So he went to class with the dictation copied out beforehand, and it did in fact coincide with that day's Latin exercise. The second time, an amusing and significant circumstance took place. The teacher prepared his lesson the preceding day and wrote out the passage for dictation in a notebook. John Bosco dreamt that night that he was reading it, and immediately got up and wrote it out from beginning to end, as he had done the previous time. But in class, the teacher found himself short of time, and only dictated half the passage. So when he corrected the dictations, he was puzzled and amazed to see that John Bosco had handed in not only the half he had dictated, but the other half as well. Could the boy have taken his notebook and copied it? Yet his conduct did not suggest this as likely. Summoned to give an explanation, the boy replied that he had dreamt it.

This is a clear case of both telaesthesia and cryptaesthesia, or perception of a hidden or distant physical object as opposed to the psychic content of another person. One might say that the boy had perceived not the page in the notebook but the teacher's mind, but then it is not likely that the teacher would have learnt the whole dictation by heart. There is no need to have recourse to supernatural intervention in such a case, since it is after all only a minor incident in a schoolboy's career, even if that schoolboy was later to be a great saint. It merely shows outstanding telepathic sensibility, which he showed later on other occasions.

The other case I want to quote is told by John W. Dunne, to whom it happened, in his book *An Experiment with Time.*

> In the spring of 1902, I was encamped with the 6th Mounted Infantry near the ruins of Lindley, in the (then) Orange Free State. We had just come off *trek*, and mails and newspapers arrived but rarely.
>
> There, one night, I had an unusually vivid and rather unpleasant dream.
>
> I seemed to be standing on some high ground—the upper slopes of some spur of a hill or mountain. The ground was of a curious white formation. Here and there in this were little fissures, and from these jets of vapour were spouting upward. In my dream, I recognized the place as an island of which I had dreamed before—an island which was in imminent peril from a volcano. And, when I saw the vapour spouting from the ground, I gasped: "It's the island! Good Lord, the whole thing is going to *blow up.*" For I had memories of reading about Krakatoa, where the sea, making its way into the heart of the volcano through a submarine crevice, flushed into steam, and blew the whole mountain to pieces. Forthwith I was seized with a frantic desire to save the four thousand (I knew the number) unsuspecting inhabitants. Obviously there was only one way of doing this and that was to take them off in ships. There followed a most distressing nightmare, in which I was at a neighbouring island, trying to get the incredulous *French* authorities to dispatch vessels of every and any description to remove the inhabitants of the threatened island. I was sent from one official to another; and finally woke myself by my own dream exertions. . . . All through the dream the *number* of people in danger obsessed my mind. . . . At the moment of waking, I was shouting to the *Maire*, "Listen! Four thousand people will be killed unless. . . ."
>
> I am not certain now when we received our next batch of papers, but when they did come, the *Daily Telegraph* was amongst them, and, on opening the centre sheet, this is what met my eyes: "Volcano disaster in Martinique—Town swept away—An Avalanche of Flame—Probable loss of over 40,000 Lives—British Steamer Burnt—One of the most terrible disasters in the annals of the world has befallen

the once prosperous town of St Pierre, the commercial capital of the French Island of Martinique in the West Indies. At eight o'clock on Thursday morning the volcano Mont Pelée which had been quiescent for a century. . . ."

But there is no need to go over the story of the worst eruption in modern history. In another column of the same paper was the following, the headlines being somewhat smaller: "A Mountain Explodes".[5]

He then copies other extracts from the paper.

Here certain peculiarities must be noted. In the first place, subsequent editions of the paper made it clear that the number of victims was not 40,000, but much less. But when Dunne read the paper quickly for the first time, he read 4,000 by mistake, and the figure 4,000 remained in his mind till he came to copy the article exactly, years later, and found that it said 40,000. That is, he read 4,000 by mistake both in his dream and awake. This fact, the time that had elapsed since the disaster, and other coincidences of detail between the dream and the newspaper report, not the reality, indicate the nature of his dream: it was not telepathy or telaesthesia of the actual event, but of the newspaper report, a reading of the report anticipated by telaesthesia and then dramatized by dream mechanisms. Unless the telaesthesia is held to be of the mind of the newspaper reporter, but this is not possible since, among other things, he dreamt 4,000 instead of 40,000. So it is a case of telaesthesia of written content, not of words as in the case of St John Bosco. How and why he had telaesthesia of that particular newspaper's account and not another's, of that event and not others, are problems which remain wrapped in complete mystery.

Here is another case of telaesthesia, taken directly from experience. It was told me by a companion of mine.

Father N. was being sheltered in a house in Madrid during the Spanish Civil War. One day there was one of those fateful searches and the householder, a young married man, was taken away.

5. John W. Dunne, *An Experiment with Time* (London, 1927), pp. 34-6.

They all felt that he was going to be shot, but did not know it for certain. In fact many people who were taken away escaped with their lives. In any case, they decided to call his father, who was living in a nearby town. He arrived, and as he came into the house he said, "I know why you called me. You needn't pretend: they have shot my son. I saw him shot in a dream, with five others, and he was the only one who had a coffin." No one in the house knew anything of this, but they eventually found out that he had in fact been shot with five others, and that he was the only one lying in a coffin, thanks to an uncle of his who had heard of it and had a coffin made for him.

This could conceivably be taken as a case of telaesthesia of the content of the uncle's mind, if in fact he had gone there himself and seen the six bodies on the ground, with only his nephew in a coffin; or if not of the uncle's mind, of the mind of someone who saw the scene. But all the indications are that it was direct telaesthesia of the actual event.

The next example is of telaesthesia of another person's thoughts. It is told by César Camargo in his strange book *Psychoanalysis of the Prophetic Dream*, which I shall discuss later.

Mr and Mrs N. lived in Caxorla, and had a servant whom they called *Antonia the Minister*. They were in mourning for the husband's father, who had died in Jaen some six months previously. There was some quarrel about the will and an important document, without which they would fare very badly, could not be found.

One night, at two in the morning, the servant, asleep, felt someone touch her feet, and woke up. She opened her eyes and saw a man standing at the foot of the bed, wearing a morning coat, top hat and white trousers. He said: "Don't be afraid, girl, I'm not going to do you any harm. Tell your master, my son, that the missing document is under the ninth tile, on the right as you go in, in the drawing-room in the house in Jaen." The vision disappeared and the girl fainted.

When she came to her senses she went to the next room, where her master and mistress were sleeping, and, frightened and trembling, told them the story. The husband asked her to describe his father very carefully: since she was new in the house she had neither seen him nor heard about him, but her description fitted so closely that there was no room for doubt.

The next morning, Mr N. went to Jaen, to his parents' house, into the drawing-room, counted the tiles, and under the ninth on the right as he went in, which was loose, he found the missing document.[6]

There can be no doubt about the truth of this story, since Mr N. himself told it to Camargo, while the servant was living. It could be called hallucination: some people will doubtless consider it an authentic vision. It probably involves, according to Camargo, a case of cryptamnesia in the husband, who had probably known his father's hiding-place a long time ago and then forgotten it. Under the stress of the urgent necessity to remember it, the memory was reviving in his subconscious. The servant, by telaesthesia of her master's subconscious mental process, had dramatized it in a dream, or perhaps in an hallucination.

I should also like to quote the following, the most conclusive case of telaesthesia of mental contents that anyone could ask for:

The girl Ilga K. of Trapene (Lithuania), of healthy parents, physically developed in a normal manner, was very backward mentally. At the age of seven or eight she had the vocabulary of a child of two. At school she managed to learn her letters, but was unable to make any progress beyond that point. At the age of nine, this child, unable to read or do sums, could read anything in any language, including Latin, and do the most difficult mathematical problems, provided that someone near the girl was reading the passage or doing the problems in *thought*. The local doctor, Dr Kleinberger, confirmed the case and reported it to Ferdinand von Neureiter, professor of forensic medicine in Riga. The girl was taken there to be examined by Dr Neureiter and his colleagues at the University. Ilga's mother was made to play the part of the agent and

6. César Camargo, *Psicoanálisis del sueño profético* (Madrid, 1929), p. 186.

was given lists of numbers. While she was going over them in her mind, Ilga in the next room was repeating them out loud.

On one occasion she said 12 instead of 42, but Dr Neureiter's handwriting revealed the cause of the slip: her mother had made the same mistake, which indicates that the child was not reading the paper telaesthetically, but the agent's mind. Dr Neureiter, concentrating hard on transmitting, read a passage from a Lithuanian poem, but the child did not respond. But when he was about to close the book "and break off the experiment with some disappointment, my eye is caught by the word *Bonte* (bride). . . . And at that very moment the child, situated in the adjoining room, produced the word. This was apparently the best way to promote the telepathic transmission, although—or rather because—I refrained from intentional sending." Another significant detail: Dr Kleinberger hid his watch under one of the cushions on a couch while Ilga was staying in the adjoining room. On entering, she exclaimed at once: 'The watch is under the cushions". On this occasion she had to turn up every cushion to produce the watch. Which means that she had not seen the *action of putting it in a certain place*, but had perceived Dr Kleinberger's thought, "I am going to hide the watch under a cushion". An extraordinary case of inability to read written words coupled with ability to read *thought* words.[7]

I wanted to quote this case, even though it does not concern dreams, because it is very illustrative. The girl Ilga would certainly have had the same faculty in dreams as she had awake. A few years ago there was a mentally backward boy in the North of Spain who could solve, at incredible speed, mathematical and other problems, such as, for example, what day of the week the 16th of September 1963 would fall on. Perhaps those who asked the question already knew the answers, as a check, and the boy read their thoughts. The same sort of thing can even happen with animals, since they, particularly those who live closest to man, cats, dogs and horses, are very capable of telepathy. Those calculating horses which are sometimes exhibited lose the

7. Jan Ehrenwald, *Telepathy and Medical Psychology* (London, 1947), pp. 47 and ff.

facility when their masters are not with them. There is no need to
think that the master always cheats by making some sign to the animal:
there may quite possibly be telepathic communication in these cases.

52.   Telepathy

In all the preceding examples the salient feature is the interceptory
power of the individual who receives the message, even when the
transmitter is inactive (only a physical object), or has no intention or
knowledge of transmitting. This is why I have called them telaesthesia
(or cryptaesthesia). The following cases show the part played by the
agent as well as by the percipient, at least in the sense that between
them there is some link, more or less explicit, but real, such as a special
affection or interest, or a definite intention to transmit. Here is one
example:

> Dr Ehrenwald had a patient, whom we shall call Miss N., suffering
> from various distressing nervous symptoms. As she did not react to
> normal treatment, the doctor was somewhat concerned about her
> condition and on the night of the 10th July 1941 . . . "I decided to
> try 'something new'. In previous years I had been advocating the
> method of histamine ionization . . . a procedure to which I was
> unable, to my great regret, to attract the attention of my British
> colleagues. For the sake of the non-medical reader, I may remark
> that histamine ionization is a method of physiotherapy which aims
> at producing a local irritation of the skin, resembling a nettle-rash.
> Why should I not try the method in her case. . . ? The erythema of
> the skin might have a beneficial effect. . . . These were my delibera-
> tions before I fell asleep. Next morning I entered the patient's ward
> with my small portable ionization equipment: 'I have something
> new for you, Miss N.' The patient seemed apprehensive. 'I hope no
> injections, doctor, I am so afraid. I had a strange dream. You came
> into this room, just as you are coming now, and I had a rash on my
> abdomen, a red itchy rash with small spots and weals. You looked at
> it gravely and then came Miss S. and said, "Well, this is cancer, I
> am sure".' I asked the patient to show me the place where she had

seen the rash. She pointed to her abdomen, precisely to the right hypochondric region where I was going to apply the electrodes soaked with the solution of histamine. . . . The patient herself was greatly amazed by the visible local effects of the treatment. It had produced the very same spots and weals, on the same place as she had seen them in the dream, she declared. I may add here that Miss N. had no previous knowledge whatsoever of the treatment", and no idea that it was to be used on her. Hence her idea that it was an injection.[8]

As Dr Ehrenwald goes on to say: "It is to be noted that Miss N. had not shown much aptitude for study, but had got on in life through her ability to 'handle' people in which she had been greatly assisted by an intuitive assessment of personalities. 'I feel at once what kind of people I have to deal with . . . whether they are good or bad, whether they like me or hate me. I get a picture of the whole person in a flash and my first impression has never deceived me.' " This indicates a telepathically sensitive condition. Many animals are said to "guess" how people feel towards them, just as they "know" which grasses in a field are good for them, and which are bad, though they also know how to use the "bad" ones as medicine if they feel ill. But the field of animal instincts, and insect instincts particularly, is too vast to discuss here. They have innumerable ways of perceiving objects hidden from us. All this is relative. A deaf man cannot realize that there is a tap running in the next room, but a normal man can hear the water running without seeing it. Nowadays, with wireless and radar, we are growing used to possibilities of communication which seemed incredible before. Bats have been shown to use a sort of radar to guide themselves at night, more sensitive than any man-made instrument. I heard of someone who had had metal false teeth screwed into his jaws, or something like that. The result was that his jaw became a wireless receiver and all day and all night he heard music and talking inside it. This was enough to drive him mad, and he had to go back to the dentist to have the extra-

8. Ehrenwald, pp. 77-80.

ordinary contraption removed. Another person told me that some-times, when he was on form, he could see two people in the distance talking and feel a sort of fluid between them and him. He understood what they were saying without knowing how. He had verified this by going up to them and telling them, much to their amazement, what they had been saying. He also said that when a parcel, which he was not expecting, was on its way, he could feel it coming. Primitive tribes everywhere always have their witch-doctor or priest, and travellers and missionaries never tire of relating their extraordinary powers of non-sensory perception. They will understand a conversation in a foreign language, when the speakers are using that language precisely so that the natives will not understand; or know what is happening at a hunt a day's journey away, with a fantastic wealth of detail. They know mis-fortunes, in particular, with great sureness and accuracy. They see all this in dreams or in trances induced by eating herbs or by secret rites.

Among all the circumstances in which telepathy is produced, one is outstandingly favourable: the agony and moment of death. We do not know what intensity of feeling, what reaching-out to loved ones, nostalgia, or vibrations or enlarged scope of the psychic faculties, can cause telepathy in these moments; but we do know that they account for more recorded cases of telepathy than anything else. Practically everyone must have heard cases which have happened to people they know. Here are some specimen examples. The first is double, since both agent and percipient were dying: General Serrano and Alfonso XII of Spain.

The general was exhausted by a long illness. He was paralysed, in an armchair from which he had to be helped up. One morning, however, to the astonishment of those present, he leapt up by himself and, standing to attention, shouted: "Ready! An adjutant, on horseback, to the Prado! The king is dead!" They thought he was delirious and tried to calm him; he fell back into the chair in a faint, but a few moments later, he again got up and said in a weak voice, "My uniform, my sword! The king is dead." These were his last words and he died a few seconds later. That morning it

J

was learnt that the king had in fact just died: his illness had been kept secret.[9]

Miss Jones, a nurse on night duty, was asleep one day when she very distinctly heard someone in her room call her by her first name, "Margaret, Margaret!" The impression was so real that she jumped up and ran into the corridor to see who it was. There was no one there. She looked at her watch: it was exactly half-past five. At dinner she asked so insistently whether anyone had called her at half-past five that her friends began to tease her about it. That night she received a telegram saying that a niece of hers called Margaret, of whom she was particularly fond, had died, at half-past five that afternoon. She went to her brother's house, and they told her that the child had called "Margaret" just before she died, which made her parents wonder whether she was calling her own name or her favourite aunt.[10]

In 1882, Stanley, famous for finding Livingstone, was a soldier in America; on April 16th he was playing cards with some companions. At one moment he lost consciousness and fell into a sort of sleep, in which he felt himself transported to England, to a room where his aunt Mary was lying in a bed, obviously about to die. He spoke to her, and begged her pardon for certain things he had done. She told him not to worry and gave him her hand. With this he woke up. Seeing everything around him unchanged, he asked: "What's all this?" His companions were surprised, so he said: "I thought I had been asleep a long time." He learnt later that his aunt had died the day after this experience.[11]

The next case is one in which a dying person took the initiative and "went to visit" relatives living far away.

Señora Raes, fifteen minutes before she died, told her husband that she was going to her native country, 1,400 miles away. She fell into a coma, and five minutes later regained consciousness and said:

9. Camargo, pp. 118-19.
10. Ehrenwald, pp. 85-6.
11. Georg Siegmund, *Der Traum* (Fulda, 1949), pp. 88-9.

"I have seen my brother". Some days later a letter came from her brother saying that his sister had appeared to him and he had seen her quite clearly.[12]

In my opinion there is no need here to talk of an excursion of Señora Raes's "astral body". It is a case of dream telepathy.

Finally, a very strange case which shows more conclusively that these are purely natural phenomena.

The Italian airman Mario Galli had a greyhound he was particularly fond of, called "Wamar". During the war in Ethiopia, he left the dog in his house in Turin. Nothing happened for some while; but one day the dog became very nervous, and went about sniffing anxiously. Then he went into his master's bedroom and curled up at the foot of the bed. Nothing would make him move or eat. The vet. was called, but to no avail. The dog died there of inanition and melancholia. When the news came that Captain Galli had been killed in action on June 27th, 1936, it was realized that this was the day his dog became anxious and began to die. The case was examined and Professor Rosa Gaggero made a report to the Italian equivalent of the R.S.P.C.A.[13]

Although these are not all cases of telepathy in dreams, they serve to show the different forms it can take; if these telepathic experiences can take place in waking states affected in some degree by trances and absences, there should be no difficulty in admitting them in dreams. The cases quoted so far have been spontaneous and observed. The next examples are some of the varying results that have been produced by direct experiment.

Between 1892 and 1893 the Italian G. B. Ermacora organized a series of experiments in dream telepathy, taking all the precautions necessary to ensure that the results should be scientifically demonstrable.

12. Camargo, pp. 115-16.
13. Réginald-Omez, o.p.: *Peut-on communiquer avec les morts?* (Paris, 1955), p. 94.

He tried to suggest certain dreams to a sleeping five-year-old child, without success. Apparently he lacked the necessary qualities. So he got hold of a woman, ill and confined to bed, who had a strong subconscious life (with sleep-walking and automatic writing). He asked her to transmit the following dream: The child was to be a goatherd, taking his goats out to graze on a hillside. He would lose three of them. On his way back, a lady, dressed in blue, carrying a parasol in her hand, would tell him that they had fallen into the river. The agent's room and the child's were closed and sealed, sufficiently far apart to make verbal communication impossible. The agent concentrated on the dream with the intention of transmitting it to the child. Success was complete. The child, who did not know that he was being submitted to an experiment, woke up and said that he had dreamt that he was in a high place, with a stick in his hand, among a lot of dogs with horns. The person to whom he was telling the dream, who did not know of the experiment either, asked, "Dogs with horns? Are you sure they weren't ears?" "No", the child answered, "they were real horns." It is a significant detail that the child said "dogs" and not "sheep", since he knew dogs but not sheep. Which once again shows that percipients translate the message into their own personal language, as usually happens in dreams.

Of a hundred experiments, fifty-four were positive successes, twenty-one half-successes, and twenty-five failures, but twenty-one of these failures could have been due to the particularly unfavourable circumstances in which the experiments were made.[14]

Since such experiments are relatively easy to carry out, they have naturally been made elsewhere. The *Proceedings of the Society for Psychical Research* have published the results of experiments organized and carried out with scientific care on various occasions. In 1881-2, in the Creery family, ninety-five successes, when only twenty-seven could be expected from mere luck, were recorded, out of 497 attempts. In 1883-5 Dr Malcolm Guthrie experimented with drawings as a basis,

14. Quoted by Siegmund, *Der Traum*, pp. 67-8.

also with good results. In 1888-90 Dr Alfred Backman carried out a series of experiments in Kalmar (Sweden), in which people under a sort of hypnosis had to describe distant scenes. The number of successes was also far higher than could be expected from sheer chance. Professor Henry Sidgwick made two series of experiments with colours and figures which also proved the existence of telepathy. In 1912 Dr Blair Thaw, of New York, obtained similar confirmation.[15] Different investigations have been made with varying degrees of success in several countries, some using mathematics to calculate probabilities; the best known names are Rhine, Carington and Soal.[16] Rhine has distinguished himself particularly, as I mentioned at the beginning of this chapter, by his use of large-scale statistical methods.

Dr Wilfred Daim has recently experimented particularly with dream telepathy, noting exactly the conditions of time, distance, emission, reception, object of the emission, faultless reception of phenomena, etc. His results not only confirm the existence of telepathy, but show various kinds and conditions of its reception in dreams. For example, telepathic contents occur simultaneously in agent and percipient; the dreaming percipient clothes the message in forms chosen from his own store of images, as was to be expected; when the telepathic message surprises a dream in the middle, it is incorporated into it; the dreamer seems to feel something strange in the telepathic intrusion.[17]

53. *Theories of telepathy*

In all telepathic manifestations the psyche escapes from the normal spatial conditions governing the sensory processes and the other cognitive processes dependent on them in one form or another. Since "each soul is tied to its body", the existence of these excursions of the

15. Tyrrell, *The Personality of Man*, pp. 106 ff.

16. Whately Carington, *Telepathy* (London, 1945). S. G. Soal, *Proceedings of the S.P.R.*, Vol. 40, pp. 165 and ff; Vol. 46, pp. 152 and ff.; Vol. 47, pp. 21 and ff.

17. Wilfred Daim, "Uber experimentelle Traumtelepathie", in *Neue Wissenschaft*, Zürich, Jhg. III, Heft 14-15 (Nov.-Dec. 1953), pp. 430-43.

soul outside the body is apparently highly disconcerting. It is very difficult to produce explanatory theories that can be proved correct. But man must have some explanation, good or bad, and various theories have been produced.

Doubling theory.—This is a favourite occultist theory: that one can double oneself, and be two selves. Many people claim that besides our earthly body, we have another more subtle one, which has been called "ethereal body", "perispirit", "astral body", and other names. It acts as a link between body and soul. Certain ascetic disciplines, they say, aim at freeing this body from matter so that it can perform various functions. These escapes and filtrations through obstacles to knowledge of hidden objects are in many cases simply the excursions of this subtle body. In support of this, they point out that the Catholic Church admits bilocation—in the life of St Anthony of Padua, for example. At the hour of death and in certain ill-defined states, the subtle body is freer and escapes with greater ease. Dreams provide one such favourable state. These states can be permanent in the case of certain people: mediums.

What can one say about this theory? In the first place, the bilocation attested in the lives of some saints has nothing to do with this doubling of natural components. The Church regards it as a miracle, the result of supernatural intervention. The explanation is that God produces the necessary visual and acoustic stimuli to give the impression of physical presence (external stimuli), or, if one prefers, stimulates the senses of those present so as to produce the physical impression (subjective modifications). So this type of bilocation is a very different matter. Natural bilocation, claimed by the doubling theory, is very far from being proved. Most in need of proof are those fantastic evolutions of the human soul, as the "astral body", and its activities, separated from the individual to whom they belong. As soon as the same telepathic phenomena are known—if only partly and by their results, not in their mechanism—the "doubling" theory becomes too far-fetched and gratuitous. Scientific principles state that what is capable of explanation by the lesser should not be explained by the greater; what can be explained by the more familiar should not be explained by the less familiar or the simple by the more complex. We say that something is explained when it can be fitted into a meaningful whole, a series of causes and effects, or of known laws. The doubling hypothesis does not fulfil these conditions, and instead of solving a problem, merely poses a greater one, the constitution of the human being.[18]

Irradiation theory.—This is another theory put forward by some people, according to which the emissory psyche radiates waves which are picked up by the recipient. At first it seemed simple and plausible, but now that everyone is familiar with all sorts of waves crossing space, it will not withstand analysis. In telaesthesia of natural objects it explains nothing in any case, since the emissive agent is inert; to claim that all inanimate objects give off radiations would produce an inextricable tangle and would make nonsense of any distinction between telaesthesia on the part of the agent and on the part of the percipient.

Cases of transmission and reception of the same object—the imaginary representation of a green triangle by both agent and percipient, for example—are the best examples for the application of this theory. Yet even here the idea of the transformation of the transmitted image into waves, and their stimulation of the receiving brain with the consequent production of the same image, runs into insuperable difficulties. Television is not a valid parallel, since it transmits luminous dots of varying intensity which rush across the screen at enormous speed, giving the impression of an image through their persistence in the retina.

Telepathic contents, however, are generally complex experiences, not identical in agent and percipient, but only corresponding. So, a dying man may think intensely of his wife, if she is far away: the image transmitted should be of the wife herself; the wife who receives the message should see an image of herself, just as her husband is seeing her,

18. On this question of the perispirit see Palmés, *Metapsíquica y Espiritismo*, Ch. XXXIII: "Absurdities and contradictions in the arbitrary doctrine of the perispirit". The Catholic philosopher Gabriel Marcel recently surprised people with a preface admitting a sort of perispirit (see p. 158). The book has been placed on the Index.

which may be a memory many years old. However, what she would normally see in such a case would be an image of the dying man, or a black catafalque, the sad face of someone else or any other augury of death which is at once, without the percipient knowing why, interpreted as signifying the death of the person in question.

This irradiation theory would be more acceptable if the hypothesis of psychophysical parallelism could be proved correct, but this is so full of manifest absurdities that it has long since been withdrawn from circulation. However, the very obscurity of this matter means that the hypothesis of human radiations *sui generis*, whether or not they can be combined with the physical radiations of nature for their movement, is still tenable, at least on heuristic grounds.[19]

In these two theories, telepathy is understood as being produced by a physical cause and through a physical field: the "doubling" of the person or physical radiations. The other theories introduce us to new worlds, whose originality takes a little getting used to, and where physical causality is not accepted as an explanation.

The psychic field.—Some writes postulate an atmosphere different from physical space—a psychic field, to give it a name—in which direct communication between souls is possible. This is hard to imagine, but is common to several theories. Just as there is a physical space in which the various operations of physical causality can take place, so there is this psychic space which we can only know by its effects (its defenders say) which maintains some souls in communication, or in possibility of communication, with others. I must confess that I see no difference between saying that some souls influence others directly and postulating this "psychic field" as a medium. Its only achievement is to tempt many people to think of it as something like physical space and so rob the latter of its unique qualities.

Cosmic consciousness.—Others say that this psychic space is a sort of universal consciousness, where everything, past, present and future,

19. See Hans Driesch, *Parapsychologie*, p. 98. For human radiations see J. de Tonquédec, "A propos des radiations humaines", in *Merveilleux métaphysique et miracle chrétien* (Paris, 1955), p. 123.

can be read: a sort of cosmic omniscience, or a living, omniscient cosmos with which individual consciousness can communicate; they do not explain how they would find the knowledge they seek in it. Mediums, or *metagnomes*, as Driesch calls them, are persons who have easy access to this universal filing cabinet, or, as E. von Hartmann says, are "on the 'phone to the absolute". The pantheistic consequences of this conception are obvious.

Animism.—Pure animism holds that parapsychological phenomena can be explained by the very nature of the soul since, among other qualities, it possesses the power of direct communication with other souls. Driesch holds that for souls to communicate with each other, a medium is necessary, through which contact is established—and this would be the "psychic field", without which any animist theory seems to him incomplete. Animists include spiritualists among their number, and there is no need here to recall the many abuses, stupidities and tricks that characterize their seances. But as they admit the perispirit and "ectoplasm" as well as spirituality, they can hardly be called pure spiritualists. Furthermore, the existence of animal telepathy excludes the spirituality of the soul as a cause.

Angelism-demonism.—The most prominent, but not the only, theory among Catholics has been angelism-demonism, which is an extrinsic explanation of parapsychic phenomena. It works like this: there is sufficient proof of the existence of extraordinary facts that seem to exceed the capacity of the normal forces of human nature. When these are justified on grounds not unworthy of God, they are either attributed directly to him, or to angels working on his orders or by his permission as pure servant spirits, or to the souls of the dead, spirits separated from their bodies, though naturally destined to form one substantial unity with them. In cases where there is no suitable justification, extraordinary happenings are attributed to the intervention of demons or the souls of the damned, with some mysterious permission from God. These evil spirits, whose intervention in human affairs must theologically be admitted, are responsible for many of the phenomena studied by parapsychology.

An enormous amount of abuse has been made of the use of angelic and demonaic intervention, particularly the latter, to explain not only marvellous phenomena, but also natural pathological states, as a sort of *Deus ex machina*. The Church during the past few centuries has made determined efforts to avoid these abuses, and the tendency is to restrict attribution to angels or demons as much as possible. Proof of this is the rule followed in the examination of supposed miracles in the process of canonization: when a natural cause can be found, preter-natural intervention should not be supposed.

Theory of original spirituality.—This attitude on the part of the Church, above all recently, has led Catholics to look for natural explanations wherever possible. In this, as always happens, some people use stricter criteria than others. Special mention should be made here of what might be called the *theory of original spirituality*. Its principal representative is Fr Alois Wiesinger, late Abbot of the Cistercian monastery of Schlierbach (Austria).[20] Basing his theory on the innumerable theological discussions on man's privileged state before the Fall, and using them as a basis of enquiry into the absolute possibilities of human nature, he applies the knowledge gained to the facts proposed by parapsychology. Faced with the evidence of marvellous facts ranging from parapsychology to mysticism, the Catholic psychologist is in a stronger position than the materialist or the purely animist parapsychologist: his examination of them can be more fundamental. For a materialist to accept the fact that thoughts and images can be transmitted from one mind to another without the intervention of physical media such as voice or gesture, requires a fundamental revision of his concept of science. But for a Catholic the existence of such facts is not an irreparable break, or anything of the sort, in the continuity of his scientific system.

The theory is this: the human soul, though united to the body, is simple, spiritual and immortal, even if dependent on the senses and brain for its actions while united to the body; parapsychic facts justify

20. Alois Wiesinger, *Occult Phenomena in the Light of Theology* (London, 1957).

the assertion that in certain states, in which this union with the body can be said to be relaxed or modified in some unknown way, the soul can perform acts more proper to a separate spirit, or, if one prefers, to that privileged situation which theologians assign to unfallen human nature, as it was when first created.

Theological circles at present regard this theory with a certain amount of reserve. Several theologians have attacked it. The author has replied to his critics in the prologue to the second edition of his book. Some explanation must certainly be sought: there are many facts which after so many centuries of testimony and experience cannot be rejected as unproved; they seem to have no religious colouring and so do not justify any recourse to God or the Devil as an explanation.

54. *Value of these parapsychological theories*

Do any of these theories amount to an explanation of parapsychic phenomena? If by explanation one means their reduction to laws previously understood in other contexts, then the answer must be "No". If one means an intrinsic explanation of a phenomenon by its manner of production, though this may be unique and not reducible to other known manners, then the answer is still "No". So what is gained from, for instance, the last theory, the only one that can be accepted, though at present it must be considered only as a theory? Simply, I think, recognition of the originality of a class of events whose existence must be accepted, just as the influence of the soul on the body must, as when the will says, "I want the body to shut its eyes", and we shut our eyes without further ado. This active contact between soul and body is a primordial fact, like feeling, imagination, etc.: these are primary data. To claim that the human soul can communicate without the agency of the senses and without regard for distance or obstacles is merely to recognize as a primary fact that the soul can perform such actions under certain conditions. The next step is to increase our knowledge of those conditions.

55. Conditioning of parapsychic activity

One can imagine the conscious as the centre of the person, as a scene brightly or less brightly lit by the degree of attention paid to reality at a given moment, surrounded by different fringes from which contents about to enter the zone of visibility proceed. The closest fringe is the pre-conscious, containing material almost on a conscious level, easily evoked. The unconscious (that is "unconscious psyche") is made up of a whole world of latent contents: spiritual memory and the functional constants of the spirit, physiological movements and their psychic concomitants, various mixed ideas and elements which can become conscious in the same form or camouflaged by recently extracted figurations. These are all farther from the conscious than the pre-conscious, measuring "distance" by the difficulty of voluntary evocation, but many of them approach spontaneously and appear on the surface when least expected. These two fringes are *autopsychic*, belonging to the individual psyche. The next are *physical* (own body and other bodies), either perceptible by the senses or not, which I am not going to discuss here, and *psychic*, belonging to another psyche, or *heteropsychic*: these reach the consciousness directly from outside, from the psychic regions of another being, from another psyche. This is what concerns us here in connection with telepathy.

Assuming this psychic topography, it has been observed that in "under-functioning" states, communication between the various zones is easier. A healthy man usually maintains a fairly rigorous, largely automatic, censorship or Customs check on the contents trying to reach his consciousness, and will normally keep fairly effective control of them. To deal with everyday life, he needs to be insured against the obscure rearguard action of his subconscious. This is so true that it can be used as a definition of mental health: silence of the subconscious, just as physical health might be called "silence of the organs". It is only when they are not functioning properly that one is conscious of having a stomach or kidneys. Similarly, when the mental flow is not under control, but imposes itself, the psychic functions are out of order. This can occur through fatigue, emotional shock, intoxication, distraction, sleep, illness, personal crisis, or many other causes: the result is always a diminution of the Ego and an aggrandizement of the Id, understood as the psychic forces in us, de-personalized. When the personal synthesis, the psychophysical integrity, is weakened, the membranes, so to speak, which divide the different autopsychic zones become more permeable than normal: the unconscious seeps through them into consciousness.

Neuroses show this phenomenon in all degrees from the mildest to the most severe—nervous tics, ob essions, amnesia, thought-blocking, voices, presences, etc., tending more and more towards real madness. These manifestations draw their substance from the depths of the unconscious, where these forces dwell, in the deposit of innate ideas and ideas accumulated during development in accordance with the laws of p ychic forces and many other laws, known or unknown to psychology. In all cases of vital diminut on, and many others that could be mentioned, there is a regression from what is personal, evolved, educated and disciplined, to what is natural, primitive, disorderly and uncontrolled, to a stage at which the rationalism and volition characteristic of full consciousness give way to intuition, feelings, and instincts.

Going back beyond neurosis along the line leading to disintegration into madness, this invasion of the conscious by the unconscious becomes progressively greater until de-personalization is complete, there is no critical faculty and no control over the psychic flow: this is the stage reached in states such as paranoia and schizophrenia. By now it should be clear that the states favourable to the reception of the auto-psychic unconscious are also those that favour heteropsychic reception, or telepathy. Primitive peoples (elemental, backward life) make far greater use of intuition, instinct and even telaesthesia and telepathy, than more civilized peoples. Children, particularly if they are sickly or backward, are often more receptive to parapsychic phenomena.[21] Women, especially if they have "delicate" nerves, or if they have rare and mysterious illnesses, that is, if they are living in a diminished state

21. Remember Aristotle's remarks, near the end of Section 5.

more open to primitive and unconscious influences, are "sensitive" persons (this term is used so as to avoid the word "medium") more often than men. Transitory stages of diminution, such as sleep, are also favourable to these phenomena. States of strong emotion, more so if allied to suffering, as in the death agony in particular, are also very favourable to this para-normal sensitivity. Mystic states deserve separate consideration.

So all the indications are that the development of these parapsychic faculties is not a gain in the process of complete human development, but a loss; this loss is compensated through primitive ways of life progressively abandoned by human nature in its normal progress toward fulfilment. This should not be stated as a rigid general rule, however, as there are exceptions and other contributory factors. On some occasions, the possibility of these phenomena is a gain. The ground here all seems very unsure. Telepathy, for instance, often does not take place when all these conditions are present, which evidently means that we do not know the exact conditions necessary. When telepathy does take place, its object is not always an important psychic content of the agent, but may be a marginal or unconscious one. The impact of certain interventions of grace, or of an evil spirit, can create a para-psychic situation. The irregularity with which cases occur makes a complete study of their mode of operation and the conditions governing them impossible. What is clear is that at certain moments man makes use of extraordinary cognitive faculties, not subject to the limitations of space and the senses. From the point of view of knowledge of human nature, this must have far-reaching consequences, which have not yet been discovered, because the problem has never been fundamentally posed. More time is needed for the study of these phenomena and the conditions governing them.

II.   PSYCHIC VERSUS TEMPORAL

Telaesthetic and telepathic phenomena move in space, at one particular moment; their peculiarity is to violate the laws of space, not those of time. The problems of time are far more arduous: can man have *direct*—that is the point—knowledge of the past and the future? Dr Rhine, the best-known modern parapsychologist, has said that with regard to the psychic conditioning of extra-sensory perceptions, there is no difference, at least no fundamental difference, between telepathy, precognition, post-cognition and telaesthesia.[22] This is a very considerable assertion. The history of humanity is as full of prophecies, particularly of prophetic dreams, as it is of cases of telepathy and telaesthesia.

56. Does post-cognition exist?

Ordinary and original human means of communication are bound to the present moment: those that are not are derived means. When we see or hear something, specific stimuli are reaching the retina or ear, here and now. The retarded means of communications which we continually use, are not free from the demands of actuality. We can listen to a speech made a year ago, but only through a recording, which offers us actual stimuli. We can see a scene which happened, or read a letter written six months previously, but only by actually seeing the film or reading the letter. So much for the external senses. The internal senses (imagination) are in much the same case. The human brain is the most wonderful of all tape-recorders or film libraries: it stores myriad sounds and forms for its own use. Auditive memory is an amazing device for recording and reproducing even the most complex sounds. When we remember a concert, our understanding tells us that the sounds are localized at some point in the past, but our memory of them has, inevitably, to pass through the present moment. There is always a connecting link between past and present: in this case the memory traces left on the brain and the images in the memory. We cannot conceive the possibility of direct "retro-sight" or "retro-hearing" of something past. Post-cognition is as much a violation of time as precognition; the jump backwards is as hard to make as the jump forwards, though in fact the future does present an

22. Quoted by Ehrenwald, p. 203.

added complication—free causes, since an action is by definition undetermined in the moment preceding it, given all the necessary prerequisites. So acts to be produced by free will in the future are understandably harder to know than past acts, which are determined once and for all: they had concrete existence at a given historical moment. Necessary future actions occupy an intermediate position: they do not yet exist in fact, but their causes already trace the line that must be followed by their realization, and the form they must take: an eclipse, for example. And between necessary actions and free actions come all the degrees of probability.

To be precise, we can either know things absolutely in themselves, or through some means. To know something in the past, present or future by the mere fact of its existence, future existence or possibility, belongs to the infinite knowledge of God. This tends to be overlooked by non-Catholic parapsychologists, whose philosophy has gone astray on this point. Man requires some "means", or a series of means, the last of which is his own idea. One of the means by which he can know something is the psyche of another person, as we saw in connection with telepathy. This should be borne in mind with regard to knowledge of the hidden past, or the past with no apparent sensory link with the percipient. The girl Ilga, who read certain things in the minds of other people, is a case in point: she had knowledge of the past actualized in an intermediary. This is possible, but it is not pure post-cognition, which I consider impossible, for reasons I shall discuss in my examination of pure precognition.

57.   *The problem of precognition*

It is easy to see that if post-cognition is sometimes extremely important, precognition could be even more so. As there have always been historians to investigate the past, so there have always been men intent on exploring the future. In ancient times nothing of importance was undertaken without consulting soothsayers, auguries, oracles or other forms of prediction. Dreams have always held a prominent place in this incessant quest. Books of oneiromancy deal almost exclusively with this aspect of dreams. And the fact is that among the millions of dreams which have failed in this undertaking, many are reported as having apparently succeeded. Cicero, we saw, examined these reputed cases at some length and decided against them. Aristotle examines them in his treatise *On Prophecy in Sleep*, and gives natural explanations: casual coincidence, the persuasiveness of dreams which lead to the performance of an action and so predict it in this sense, the fact that we dream of things we want to do and then do because we want to, or the vagueness of the dream message which can be applied to any one of a number of future actions, one of which takes place, giving the dream the appearance of successful prediction. St Augustine also cites many cases and gives various explanations, but never that of direct and immediate precognition without supernatural intervention.

58. *Pseudo-prophetic dreams*

Great care must be taken not to confuse genuinely prophetic dreams with pseudo-prophetic ones. These fall into several categories. *Symptomatic dreams* are based on hyper-sensitive perception of signs announcing illness or death, our own or other people's, and present an image, symbolic or direct, of that illness or death, thereby giving an impression of precognition. They can do the same for social, political and even physical events. I shall in due course examine the case of the Brussels greengrocer discussed by Fr Martín del Río; her predictions were, at first sight, fantastic, and aroused a great deal of discussion, but when the case is examined more carefully, human perspicacity is seen to have provided sufficient data to predict the course of events with a fair degree of certainty.

The case adduced by César Camargo as an irrefutable proof of dream prophecy both can and should be interpreted in the same way. He regards it as the most extraordinary premonitory dream in his experience, and considers that it would be difficult to find another to rival it. Here, then, is the *ne plus ultra* of prophetic dreams and *pièce de résistance* of his book:

K

A judge who had just been instructing the trial of a crime confessed himself obsessed by the matter: day and night, waking and asleep, for weeks on end, he could only think of corpses, blood and murders. He went to a village for a rest. Walking through the outskirts one evening, very tired, he reached a house standing by itself near a road through a wood, with a sign, *The Friends' Meeting-Place,* announcing it to be an inn. He went and asked for a room, and received an extremely unfavourable impression of the innkeeper, the whole place and the strange room they gave him. Examining it carefully, he found a hidden door, with a ladder on the other side leading down to the stable. He took the precaution of blocking it up as best he could, putting the table and the washstand in front of it. With these sinister forebodings, he went to bed. Before going to sleep he thought the door was being pushed open and that he could see a chink of light under it. He shouted, "Who's there?" but there was no answer. Despite this, he was so tired that he fell asleep. What could be more natural than the dream he had then? He dreamt that the innkeeper came in with a knife in his hand, plunged it into the sleeping man's chest (whether himself or someone else he was not sure), and then his wife helped him to take the body down into the stable. He left this sinister place at dawn.

Three years later, a certain Mr Arnaud disappeared. One of the few clues was that on the day of his disappearance he had been seen at *The Friends' Meeting-Place.* The judge read this in the papers, and felt a shiver as he remembered his nightmare there that night. What could be more probable? The same papers mentioned that another traveller had disappeared in the same place six years before. This was enough to convince him that he held the key to the mystery. As judge-instructor this was precisely his task. He went to the police station where the innkeeper and his wife were being held for questioning and asked if he could listen to the interrogation. The wife was questioned first, by herself. She said that the night Mr Arnaud had disappeared he had in fact asked for a room, but they had not been able to give him one because the only two they had were let.

"What about the third room, the one over the stable?" interrupted the judge.

The woman jumped.

"Mr Arnaud", the judge went on, with sudden inspiration, "slept in that room. You and your husband came up the ladder from the stable and through the hidden door. Your husband killed him and you helped him to take the body down into the stable to bury it."

Terrified, the woman exclaimed, "Did you see it all happen?"

When her husband's turn came, he was told the same story. Furious, he rounded on his wife, thinking that she had confessed the whole affair. He could not have condemned himself more completely.[23]

It is surprising that Camargo, who is so ready to affirm his rigorous criticism, should be dazzled by this case to the extent of making it the keystone of his "proof" of the precognitive power of certain dreams. He believes that the judge dreamt Mr Arnaud's murder three years before it was committed and at the same time dreamt the other murder that had taken place there three years before. So for him this is a case of conjoint precognition and post-cognition, the night of the dream being the vortex of a temporal angle, the arms of which lead out to two facts situated at an equal distance, one in the future and one in the past. The nice balance of this theoretical construction has dazzled Camargo. It fits in with his time theory which I shall consider later.

A cool consideration of the case, however, seems to show no difficulty in explaining it without recourse to precognitive faculties. We have a man preoccupied with the idea of murder, temperamentally nervous and suspicious, professionally trained to unravel enigmatic crimes and to seize any detail that might be a clue; he comes to a house outside the village, he is received by an innkeeper who looks a suspicious character, taken to a lonely room in which he finds a hidden door giving on to a stable. Before going to sleep, but long enough after he has gone to bed for the innkeeper to suppose him asleep, he hears a noise and sees a light behind the door. What else was he likely to dream under such conditions?

23. Camargo, pp. 210 and ff.

This is the most obvious and most useful explanation, but if Camargo did not want to accept it, he could still have explained the dream as telaesthesia of the innkeeper's thoughts. It is quite probable that the innkeeper that night remembered the crime he had committed three years before, and it is also quite probable that he thought of doing the same thing to the judge, and even tried to. These contents of the innkeeper's conscious, preconscious or subconscious might well have been read by the judge in his dreams. His state of mind, his fatigue and his being asleep are all factors that would favour telaesthetic sensitivity, as we saw when discussing conditioning factors. The fact that a similar crime was in fact committed three years later merely confirms that such people were almost bound to commit another sooner or later. The symmetry of three years before the dream and three years after is pure chance.

Here I have touched on another cause of many pseudo-prophetic dreams, *thought-reading*. As for perception of unpredictable signs announcing physical phenomena, we know that some people can "feel" rain coming. Many insects and animals are sensitive to electric and other changes which make them behave in certain ways, which men can interpret as foretelling some meteorological change. One occasionally reads of horses who have saved people's lives by becoming so nervous that their masters have had to take them out of their stables, and shortly afterwards the house has collapsed. Animals can also feel the approach of earthquakes. All the infinitesimal sensations which precede some cataclysm can be felt by "sensitive" people and induce them to have dreams which later seem prophetic: this is knowledge of the future in its necessary, or highly probable, causes.

These causes of pseudo-prophetic dreams do not quite cover the whole range of recorded cases of so-called natural precognitive dreams. They do give enormous scope for apparent prophecy, especially thought-reading, but there may be other causes, not yet investigated and perhaps impossible to know at present, which would account for another section of these dreams, before having to fall back on a natural precognitive faculty. I recognize the fact that there are cases which, if they did happen as they are told, are truly astonishing. Diabolic or angelic or directly divine intervention must of course not be left out of account as possible explanations.

What is certain, according to Catholic doctrine, is that only God can know future events with absolute certainty. Spirits superior to man, whose understanding enormously surpasses ours, can know, if not purely free acts, at least those acts which men will in all probability perform. There are so many contributory causes in a free act that when the moment of decision arrives men usually do what is indicated by the sum of attendant circumstances, objective and subjective. Absolutely free acts, independent of this psychic proclivity, are, according to all the evidence, very rare. If men, especially some men who have a gift for it, can often foresee what people they know well are going to do, the higher spirits must be able to see far more. The extent to which they intervene in the formation of human premonitory dreams has yet to be determined. I shall discuss this question too, but not before examining the different theories of natural precognition.

59. *Theories of natural precognition*

These theories all have one basic fault in common. They start from the assumption that natural precognition exists. Instead of saying, "We do not know how it happens, or that it really exists, in the sense of pure and simple knowledge of the future in itself", they start out with the most fantastic hypotheses. One of the most famous of these theorists is J. W. Dunne. He has written several books, of which the first, and the one that provoked most discussion, was *An Experiment with Time*, from which I have already quoted. His interest in precognition was apparently awakened by the fact that he had several dreams which he interpreted as prophetic, though from his own account of them they do not seem to be anything of the sort: they can more plausibly be interpreted as telaesthetic. The case of the Martinique earthquake, which I have quoted as an example of telaesthesia, is one of them. Dunne, with unparalleled audacity, theorizes beyond all reasonable limits until he leaves common sense far behind.

He starts from the idea of a fourth dimension, which has been a matter of mathematical speculation for a long time. Just as a straight line is a succession of points, surface a succession of straight lines, and volume a succession of surfaces, so time, for Dunne, is a succession of volumes, or rather of moments at which the psyche (the observer's attention) meets the volumes. This succession of moments is in fact a series of conscious acts of attention. This series gives us the feeling of duration, just as the successive images on a film, thanks to their persistence in the retina, give the feeling of movement. But since this successive transference of attention is itself a temporal process, a "time", which evidently cannot be explained by the illusory time of the afore-mentioned subjective impression, Dunne is obliged to postulate a fifth dimension, also temporal, consisting of a process identical to the fourth, with its corresponding progressive displacement of attention. This leads him to postulate a sixth dimension for the same reasons, and so on indefinitely. So that we are left with an observer who is never fixed, since by definition he is always an ulterior postulate *in infinitum*. For Dunne, the world is an enormous conglomeration of these series. So time is always made up of "illusory impressions", an unreal observer. Everything always exists simultaneously, and so the problem of precognition is nothing of the sort, but merely the problem of cognition. He supports all this with mathematical formulas. Critics have on the whole attacked his system as inconsistent, but each from his own point of view. So C. D. Broad refutes him saying that he cannot conceive the existence of this unending series of dimensions, nor how there can be an observer at the end of a series which is by definition unending; he thinks, however, that the theory can be saved by restricting the number of spatial dimensions to five.[24]

Camargo also quotes Maeterlinck's criticism, that Dunne's extravagances are untenable and that the final result is more words than reality. He then recognizes that there is some truth in it and selects concepts he considers acceptable, which, with others from other places, he proceeds to build up into a theory of his own. Briefly,

24. See Camargo, p. 225. Also Tyrrell, *The Personality of Man*, p. 93.

Camargo considers that time is the fourth dimension, to which he attributes the same qualities as Euclidian three-dimensional space: so he claims that time has angles. Following his cyclic concept of the Universe he suggests that time is curved and accepts the possibility that it may be only one aspect of a higher five-dimensional entity. He also involves himself in other Hindu and occultist eccentricities, which need not detain us. This fourth dimension, he says, overlooks the two slopes of time, the past and the future. In the "astral vehicle" (the borderline between the spiritual and the physical world), the spirit climbs to the "eternal and unchangeable essence of time", where everything exists. This it can only do under certain circumstances—in sleep or in drugged or hypnotic states, or when the "sensitive" quality is present—which condition the parapsychic moment. Hence his fascination with the symmetry in the judge's dream, the moment of synthesis between the crime committed three years before and the one to be committed three years later. This was an angle in the fourth dimension (time). The whole structure was too attractive for him not to have enthused over what he considered the obviously precognitive character of the dream. With this theory, he considered that he had explained precognitive dreams.

What can one say about all these ideas? They all have such manifest absurdities that there is no point in spending too long on refuting them. In the first place, to add a fourth dimension, time, to the three dimensions of Euclidean space is to leap from calculus to ontology. Points, lines, surfaces and volumes have a real homogeneity which enables them to be easily added to each other. Time is something ontologically very different. If mathematicians introduce the time variant into their calculations this does not mean that the two things are in fact homogeneous, since these calculations are by their nature complex and abstract. So, if one is calculating the rentable value of a building, one does not only take the number of cubic feet (space) into account, but also how long the premises will be used (time); if one establishes an ascending scale of values of situation, outlook, perfection of construction (solidity, heating, telephone, décor, etc.), or of financial arrangements, or of payments and other such conceptual lines, there will be a series of values in which each can be made to influence the amount of the rent. But no one would attempt to call them all spatial dimensions. They are all very different, but all the same in that they represent values along the abstract line of human utility, the price of which is calculated as the rent of the building. To attempt to introduce time as a spatial element in which one can situate oneself *really and geometrically* at a point from which one can observe the past and the future directly, is sheer nonsense.

Another affirmation made by many of these authors in support of their theses is that "time does not operate in dreams", just as space does not: we can be children at one moment and adults at the next, or both together, two beings somehow amalgamated; we can jump from one point to another and be in different places at the same time: a-temporality and a-spatiality. If "time does not operate" means that the dream flow of images does not respect objective historical reality, just as we can by-pass it in our waking phantasies, this does not mean very much. This is not the purpose of dreams; their purpose is to express, in their own particular language of images, the dreamer's mental state or manner of appreciating certain realities. But from this it is a very long way indeed to the claim that during sleep the human mind climbs to an observation-post astride the course of time, a sort of drawing-room in eternity, from which it can contemplate the closed cycle of immovable time, seeing the whole past and the whole future as though they were both taking place at the same time, with the present, on a sort of super-panoramic screen. This is fantasy run riot. It is in fact nothing less than equating the human animal with God. God can indeed, from his eternity, incapable of change, see everything in himself and in the direct essence of things. The fact that these authors so easily confuse the human situation with the divine is not entirely fortuitous, since many occultists and people who have dabbled uncritically in esoteric occultist practices have in fact fallen into the trap of pantheism.

60. *Precognition and Catholic theology*

Finally, I want to make the Catholic position on these matters clear. Catholics admit all manner of precognition through deduction or intuition of causes, including telepathy and reading the thoughts of someone who has the intention of doing something or knows that someone else has the intention; thus they retain all the aspects of man's parapsychic powers that can be validly proved. They do not admit direct vision of past or future events *in themselves* and still less of free future acts: this belongs to God alone. However, having made this point, Catholics admit that God can grant this knowledge to creatures. This is the case of authentic prophecy, which is not natural precognition, but supernatural, miraculous. This is why the gift of prophecy bears a divine stamp and is one of the signs of a divine mission. The angels, according to Catholic theology, can know created beings and their acts in a far vaster and more penetrating way than men, but they cannot know free future acts. God can use angels to communicate certain knowledge beyond reach of man. The souls of the dead in themselves know no more than the knowledge they acquired in this world, but God can communicate all classes of knowledge to them. The souls of the blessed and the angels see all that it is their nature to see, in the divine essence. Their intervention in human affairs cannot take place without divine command.

These are the natural and supernatural explanations on the basis of which Catholics examine all supposed cases of precognition. Fundamental to the whole question is an extremely rigorous critical verification of the facts. Many so-called prophecies will not stand up to methodical examination: they are pseudo-prophecies.

III.   APPARITIONS OF THE DEAD IN DREAMS

61. *Do spirits appear?*

This is another perennial question about the dream world. The fact that dead people appear in dreams as they were when alive is not in the least startling: memory draws on old and new images and some of these images are almost bound to be of dead people. But this is not the question; even though some of these dreams can be extremely vivid, they remain dreams. What we want to know is whether, on certain occasions, the dead person appears in the form of a ghost or hallucination, or in a dream with real presence and in direct communication with the dreamer.

In the first place, what are these presences? Mystics speak of invisible presences, felt as one feels the presence of another person in the dark, without seeing him: there is simply the certainty that he is there. Spiritualists also talk continually of "presences"; so do lunatics, just as they talk of people reading or stealing their thoughts. These are feelings that people have. Sometimes they can be true—when there are good reasons for thinking like this—but sometimes they are no more than subjective impressions.

The dead are spirits. How can spirits appear? Physical presence is that which is commensurate with a space, and this is proper to bodies. God, Uncreated Spirit, is present everywhere by his nature, since he fills everything; by his knowledge, since he sees everything; by his power, since he conserves and actuates everything and can produce effects wherever he wishes. Angels and human souls separated from their bodies (during the interval between death and resurrection of the body) can make themselves present through their own substance, that is by transferring their substance from one place to another. Angels, but not human souls, can also be present by their action, according to their natural powers. Separated human souls, according to Catholic theologians, *of themselves* only know those things of which they acquired knowledge in the world, and perhaps not all of them, so they cannot know what happens outside themselves. And since they cannot know anything new, they evidently cannot love it. Nor can they act on human bodies, since they are destined by nature to affect the body they inhabited, and none other directly; they can only act on others through the medium of their body. From which it follows that separated souls, *by virtue of their own powers alone*, cannot communicate with other beings. Only by the power of God can they know new things—God infusing the image into them—and so love them. Divine power also enables them to take on appearances as ghosts and simply appear, or exercise some influence and, of course, communicate.[25] All this, however, is not natural, but supernatural. So there is no foundation for the claims made in occultist writings, that spirits of the dead can be obliged by enchantments and formulas to appear at definite times and places, which would mean that a natural process could influence and force these ultra-terrestrial beings independently of the will of God.

The angels in their glory and the souls in heaven also see in God all those things that God in his generosity has destined for them, which in the first place are those naturally related to them so that they will not feel frustrated in that blessed state where there can be no frustration. So it is clear that in God the souls in heaven know everything that might interest them, either because they knew those things here below, or because they have been invoked by human beings, or for any other reason. We cannot doubt that they are aware of the vicissitudes and longings of people who were dear to them on earth.

Before attaining the beatific vision, these souls pass through purgatory. These souls in purgatory are those to whom the majority of apparitions, strange noises, moving furniture, gusts of wind, banging doors and what not are attributed. Religious people interpret these signs either as a pleading for prayers or as a forecast of some event for which they themselves must prepare, death in particular.

Such apparitions do, of course, take place in dreams, but these are supernatural manifestations. Many lives of saints (and others) are full of cases too well-known to need quoting here. To decide when a dream is natural and when it contains a supernatural apparition is a question that must be examined with the utmost care, taking all the

---

25. On separated souls and their powers see Suárez, *Tractatus de Anima, Liber VI, De statu animae separatae.* Ed. Vives, Vol. III, p. 781 and ff. Theological opinion varies somewhat on the activities and knowledge of separated souls. See Antonio Royo Marín, O.P., *Teología de la Salvación* (B.A.C., Madrid, 1956), p. 181 and ff.

circumstances into account. Then it must be decided whether the supernatural visitation has occurred by the wish or merely with the permission of God—the latter category being actions of the devil. We know that God, in his hidden wisdom, allows evil spirits to intervene in human affairs to a certain extent. But each case requires definite proof, since many natural mental illnesses produce very convincing imitations of diabolic manifestations.[26]

62. *Provoked apparitions*

What I have to say on this subject apparently contradicts the evocation of Samuel by the witch of Endor, as recounted in the First Book of Samuel (Kings):

> And the Philistines were gathered together, and came and camped in Suram: and Saul also gathered together all Israel and came to Gelboe.
> And Saul saw the army of the Philistines, and was afraid, and his heart was very much dismayed.
> And he consulted the Lord, and he answered him not, neither by dreams, nor by priests, nor by prophets.
> And Saul said to his servants: Seek me a woman that hath a divining spirit, and I will go to her, and inquire by her. And his servants said to him: There is a woman that hath a divining spirit at Endor. Then he disguised himself: and put on other clothes, and he went, and two men with him, and they came to the woman by night, and he said to her: Divine to me by thy divining spirit and bring up him whom I shall tell thee.
> And the woman said to him: Behold thou knowest all that Saul hath done, and how he hath rooted out the magicians and soothsayers from the land: why then dost thou lay a snare for my life, to cause me to be put to death?

26. See J. de Tonquédec, s.j. *Les maladies nerveuses ou mentales et les manifestations diaboliques* (Paris, 1938). On apparitions see Karl Rahner, *Visionen und Prophezeiungen* (Innsbruck, 1952). Also Pierre Lorson, *L'avenir mystérieux des âmes et du monde* (Paris).

And Saul swore unto her by the Lord, saying: As the Lord liveth, there shall no evil happen to thee for this thing.

And the woman said to him: Whom shall I bring up to thee? And he said: Bring me up Samuel.

And when the woman saw Samuel, she cried out with a loud voice, and said to Saul: Why hast thou deceived me? for thou art Saul.

And the king said to her: Fear not: what hast thou seen? And the woman said to Saul: I saw gods ascending from the earth.

And he said to her: What form is he of? And she said: An old man cometh up, and he is covered with a mantle. And Saul understood that it was Samuel, and he bowed himself with his face to the ground, and adored.

And Samuel said to Saul: Why hast thou disturbed my rest, that I should be brought up? And Saul said: I am in great distress: for the Philistines fight against me, and God is departed from me, and would not hear me, neither by the hand of prophets, nor by dreams: therefore I have called thee, that thou mayest shew me what I shall do.

And Samuel said: Why askest thou me, seeing the Lord has departed from thee and is gone over to thy rivals? (I Samuel 28. 4-16.)

(Samuel goes on to tell him that for his sins he will be defeated and killed, and that the kingdom will pass to the House of David.)

At first sight it seems that the spells of the divining woman were more powerful than God or Samuel, since the impression is that God has refused to speak to Saul and that Samuel was "brought up" (from the world of the dead) annoyed, but powerless to resist. However, as the commentators explain, God, who had previously "gone away" from Saul, wanted to halt him in his evil ways, and so permitted the unorthodox circumstances of the scene, commanding Samuel to announce to Saul his forthcoming defeat and divine punishment.

Since this book is about dreams, I am not going to examine spiritualist claims to have brought up souls of the dead in their séances. Leaving aside the question of materializations, which have lent themselves to so much trickery, the most serious-minded modern spiritualists have recourse to messages, either through automatic writing by the medium acting as the passive instrument of the dead person(?), or through boards or glasses which indicate successive letters of an alphabet placed on the table and so form messages. All this is clearly far removed from authentic divine revelations.

As Catholic writers who have examined this question say, diabolic intervention in these cases must not be left out of account; on the contrary, it seems very likely to take a hand in them, in order to corrupt many people with the marvellous effects sometimes undoubtedly produced. Here is an example:

> During one session to which I had gone as observer, to reclaim those who let themselves be taken there in the hope of conversing with dead relatives, in the middle of a prediction which interested one of those present, there was a sudden stop, with the prompt disappearance of the supposed dead person. This happened when I, without letting anyone see, called on our Lady, placing my hand on a miraculous medal hidden under my jacket, asking her to cover up the evil spirit. The medium came out of his trance and said, "I don't know what's happened: I suddenly saw 'him' covered with medals, and now he's gone."[27]

In France and some other places there was recently a movement among Catholics in favour of a sort of Catholic neo-spiritualism, trying to console those who had lost people they loved by evocations similar to those of the spiritualists. This movement did not hold the extravagant and heterodox theories of true spiritualism, but respected the Gospel and dogmas, and even tried to help people to lead a better life, in the true tradition of Catholic spirituality. It was given a great boost by Gabriel Marcel's famous preface to Marcelle de Jouvenel's *Au diapason du ciel*. The Church stepped in and placed it on the Index. It may be well to recall here that according to Catholic moral teaching, any communication, real, pretended or attempted, with spirits or separated souls, is a grave sin. So communication with the dead is not a

27. Réginald-Omez, o.p. *Peut-on communiquer avec les morts?* p. 171.

show to which Catholics can go with impunity if they intend to take part.[28]

To end this section, I think it would be appropriate to quote one of the many cases from the life of St John Bosco, which has the advantage of indicating Catholic teaching on the subject of communication with the dead. The Count and Countess de Colle-Fleury, great patrons of his works, lost their son Louis in the flower of his youth. Their grief was tremendous, and John Bosco did what he could to console them. The boy had been "an angel" during his life and had regarded the saint as a father. After his death he continued to communicate with him for some time. In one dream he appeared to him and took him on a long journey to America, showing him the missionary fields his followers were to tread, and telling him many things that were to happen to those missions in the future. On other occasions he appeared in other forms and gave him messages for his parents. John Bosco had many strange conversations with him. Here is one of them:

"Dear Louis, are you happy?"
"Very happy."
"Are you alive or dead?"
"Alive!"
"But you died . . ."
"My body is buried, but I am alive."
"Is this not your body that I see?"
"No, it is not my body."
"Is it your spirit?"
"Nor my spirit."
"Is it your soul?"
"Nor my soul."
"What is it then that I see?"
"It is my shadow."
"But how can I be talking to a shadow?"
"Thanks to the grace of God."

28. Besides Fr Palmés' book, already mentioned, on Spiritualism and Metaphysics, see the recent work by Fr Giovanni Arrighi, *Spiriti e spiritismo moderno* (Turin, 1954).

"And where is your soul?"

"My soul is near God, with God, and you cannot see it."

"And how can you see me?"

"In God all things are seen; past, present and future can be seen in him as in a glass."

"What do you do in heaven?"

"I say continually: 'Glory to God! Thanks be to God! Thanks be to our Creator, the Lord of life and death, the Beginning of all things! Thanks! Praise be to him! Alleluia, alleluia!'"

"Have you any message for your parents?"

"Tell them I pray for them constantly and so repay them. I am waiting for them in heaven!"[29]

IV.   DREAMS AS VEHICLES OF DIVINE COMMUNICATION

63.   *History, Scripture and the Catholic tradition*

In the historical survey at the beginning of this book, we saw that old religions considered dreams, or many of them, to be the work of the gods. In Catholic theology it is made clear that God, who made man capable of dreaming, can communicate with him in his dreams. In fact Scripture contains a whole series of examples in which dreams appear as a means of communication between God and man. Perhaps the best example of theophany in dreams is Jacob's ladder:

But, Jacob being departed from Bersabee, went on to Haran. And when he was come to a certain place and would rest in it after sunset, he took of the stones that lay there, and putting them under his head, slept in the same place.

And he saw in his sleep a ladder standing upon the earth, and the top thereof touching heaven: the angels also of God ascending and descending by it:

And the Lord leaning upon the ladder, saying to him: I am the

29. Rodolfo Fierro, s.d.b., *Biografía y escritos de San Juan Bosco* (Madrid, B.A.C., 1954), p. 57.

Lord God of Abraham thy father, and the God of Isaac; the land, wherein thou sleepest, I will give to thee and to thy seed.

And thy seed shall be as the dust of the earth: thou shalt spread abroad to the west and to the east, and to the north and to the south: and in thee and thy seed all the tribes of the earth shall be blessed.

And I will be thy keeper whithersoever thou goest, and will bring thee back into this land: neither will I leave thee, till I shall have accomplished all that I have said.

And when Jacob awaked out of sleep, he said: Indeed the Lord is in this place, and I knew it not. (Genesis 28. 10-16.)

Solomon's dream is equally well known. This is how it is told in the First Book of Kings:

He went therefore to Gabaon to sacrifice there: for that was the great high place: a thousand victims for holocausts did Solomon offer upon that altar in Gabaon.

And the Lord appeared to Solomon in a dream by night, saying: Ask what thou wilt that I should give thee.

And Solomon said: Thou hast shown great mercy to thy servant David my father. . . . And now, O Lord God, thou hast made thy servant king instead of David. . . . Give therefore to thy servant an understanding heart, to judge thy people, and discern between good and evil. . . .

And the word was pleasing to the Lord that Solomon had asked such a thing.

And the Lord said to Solomon: Because thou hast asked for this thing, and hast not asked for thyself long life or riches, nor the lives of thy enemies, but hast asked for thyself wisdom to discern judgement,

Behold I have done for thee according to thy words. . . .

And Solomon awaked and perceived that it was a dream. . . . (I [III] Kings 3. 4-15.)

Throughout the Old Testament there are texts in which dreams are something sacred. A very explicit text from the book of Job will be discussed in the next chapter. I have already discussed Joseph's dreams, and am not going to discuss the prophets here.

L

In the New Testament there are the warnings given to St Joseph in a dream, telling him that Herod was seeking to kill the child Jesus, the dreams sent to the Magi, and those given to St Joseph on the return from Egypt. The text, "Your old men will dream dreams", is applied to the descent of the Holy Ghost on the Apostles.

Religious dreams in all their aspects abound in the Catholic tradition. This is a subject that offers no difficulties, and which I am going to deal with in the next chapter.

V

DREAMS AND SPIRITUAL DIRECTION

64. *The relationship between dreams and the spiritual life*

Most serious writers are agreed that one of the main causes of the perpetual anxiety in which modern man lives is his separation from the basic principles of existence, his apostasy from religion. All religion, says Jung, is a psychotherapy; besides being a sufficient reason for its own existence, it fulfils a psychotherapeutic function. So it is not strange that modern man should be in such need of psychotherapy.

The Fifth Catholic Congress of Psychotherapy and Clinical Psychology was held in April 1953, on the subject of *Psychotherapies and man in his present condition*. The fact that it was held in Rome, the centre of Catholicism, where the Supreme Pontiff has so often diagnosed the root of man's trouble, invited us to delve deeper and deeper into the relation between psychotherapy and religion. One of the principal aspects of this task is to try to christianize the whole movement of psychological and psychotherapeutic ideas which has developed from starting points that are, from a Catholic point of view, inadmissible or at least incomplete.

I chose *The possible relationship between dreams and the spiritual life* as one of the many points along this line of investigation which deserved attention, for obvious reasons. Dreams have come to occupy such a central place in modern psychotherapy; and in the domain of religion, spiritual direction affords the closest parallel to psychotherapy.

To connect dreams with spiritual direction is, I know, unusual.

163

Dreams are the playground of absurdity, it is generally thought, and there are sayings in every language to discredit dreams. The Bible has the following lines on the subject: "Where there are many dreams, there are many vanities, and words without number, but do thou fear God" (Eccles. 5. 6).

Writers on spiritual direction very seldom mention dreams, and when they do, it is generally to discuss supernatural dreams. Neither St Teresa nor St John of the Cross has a word to say on the subject. The only place I have seen them discussed is in the Italian review *Vita Christiana*, which published Fr Aurelio Floris's discourse on *Dreams and Spiritual Direction* (*Sogno e direzione spirituale*), delivered at the *Istituto di Studi Spirituali*, at the Minerva in Rome, in Spring 1948. He limits himself to a brief outline of the information that dreams can provide about the spiritual state. Rather than reaching conclusions, he says, his aim is to provide some notes towards the solution of the problem and to leave the question open. The editorial note justifying the publication of the article should be enough to frighten anyone off such dangerous ground.

The bad name dreams have had for centuries is largely due to the superstitious and occultist use made of them, and also to the fact that many apparent absurdities in them had not been explained as they have been recently. Depth psychology and its ideas applied to psychotherapy have now done much to rehabilitate the dream function, although their influence has perhaps been confined in this respect to fairly narrow circles. Theologians and spiritual writers have only been interested in prophetic dreams, or those that serve as vehicles for divine communication, or diabolic suggestions. Natural dreams have generally been treated with either complete silence or the gravest suspicion as a senseless or dangerous business.

That this is a particularly tricky question is undeniable. My own observations are put forward here as a stimulus to further study. I have reached certain conclusions, but I trust to criticism and discussion to bring study of the subject to the level it deserves.

Approaching the question directly, I consider that from the point of view of spiritual direction, dreams can be one of these things:

a temptation,

a question of moral responsibility,

a source of information about the state of the soul,

a source of instruction and guidance,

or, finally, a source of energy.

These categories apply to natural dreams alone, although others exist which are used by God as a means of bestowing ordinary or extraordinary favours.

I.   DREAMS AS A SOURCE OF TEMPTATION

65.   Why dreams can be a vehicle of temptation

Dreams are a natural phenomenon, reflecting every aspect of human nature, including the instincts. So temptations originating in the instincts, and in "nature" in general, can come through dreams, where there is the aggravating factor that the critical faculty and self-control are neutralized or diminished, very often giving instinctive movements a free hand.

Temptations of diabolic origin also find ample scope in dreams. Spiritual works provide abundant testimony of this. "This sense of the imagination or phantasy", says St John of the Cross, "is where the devil usually comes with his snares, sometimes natural, sometimes supernatural; because this is the door of entry to the soul, and here the understanding comes to take and leave what it will, as in a port or market" (*Ascent*, I, II, Ch. 16, n. 4). So the devil can arouse concupiscence, or produce fantasies leading to error, spiritual illusion, pride, vanity, etc.

This experience is so commonplace and universal that there is no need to insist on it. St Augustine in his works provides many pathetic accounts of these evil dreams. Those recounted by St Alphonsus Rodríguez are still more pathetic, and even terrifying.

66.   *Do virtuous people have bad dreams?*

Before going any further, I want to refer briefly to the question of whether morally bad, or tempting, dreams are commoner in virtuous people than in those who are vicious or "in-between". Jung has brought the matter up in several places in his works where he deals with the law of compensation, fundamental to the whole relationship of the unconscious to the conscious, and so to dreams. According to him, virtuous people very frequently have orgiastic dreams while, on the other hand, unabashed sinners commonly allow themselves the luxury, so to speak, of dreaming highly moral behaviour. If Jung is referring to outwardly virtuous people, or to those who are still struggling to attain virtue, this may well be true, although, as he himself says, the law of compensation must not be taken too literally. Compensation can be effected in many ways, and is not always a matter of going crudely to the other extreme. Reason and experience teach that those whose virtue has led them as near to peace as is possible in this world, do not have dreams in which the senses take their revenge. It has long been known that virtuous habits become second nature, in an inner atmosphere of harmonious integration; their discipline affecting even primary movements, the sources of dreams. One of the best authorities on asceticism and mysticism, Padre Alvárez de Paz, wrote this in the sixteenth century: *Est igitur somnus viri iusti, in hoc gradu (quinto) castitatis positi, quietus et purus et sanctorum operum et desideriorum quae in vigilia praecesserunt cogitatione formatus. Et si Deus aliis eius imagines aperiret, quas somnians evolvit, non aliquid obscaenum aut impurum, sed omnia munda et sapientiae plena conspicerent.*[1] ("So the sleep of the just man, who has reached this (fifth) grade of chastity, is tranquil and pure, formed by thought from the holy works and desires preceding it in waking. And if God were to let others see the images of his dreams, they would see nothing obscene or impure, but everything clean and full of wisdom.") I shall deal in due course with the reasons for this, also with the exceptions, and the reasons for them.

Just as dreams can provide temptations, so they can of course provide

1. Alvárez de Paz: *De exterminatione mali et promotione boni.* Book V, part II, Ch. 9.

resistance to temptation. The same principles and experience indicate this, and there are numerous examples of it. It is said of St Francis Xavier that one occasion a dream he had set up such strong resistance to temptation that it made him vomit blood. This case obviously requires further examination; I quote it here only because it is very well-known.

67. *After dreaming*

Temptation through dreams means chiefly that the dreamer experiences temptations after waking, from the memory of the dream images; these are often particularly troublesome on account of their diabolical originality, their suggestive force, and their persistence. The remedies against them are no different from those usually prescribed against other temptations of this nature. A devout person must feel saddened and humiliated after certain dreams, since, although it is true that like many waking temptations, they happen in us without our consent, they still show us the misery of our condition and the dangers that surround us. After dreams that tend to lead us to sin, we should make an explicit rejection on waking, or rather in many cases make our rejection implicit in forgetting them as soon as possible, since it is common knowledge that in matters of sexuality flight is a better form of defence than attack.

II. THE QUESTION OF MORAL RESPONSIBILITY IN DREAMS

68. *A curious letter by Caramuel*

The question of responsibility in dreams arises from time to time. Freud deals with it in his *Traumdeutung*, and Grünewald has recently devoted an article to it.[2] A curious letter by the theologian and

2. E. Grünewald, "Traum und Verantwortung" in *Wiener Zeitschrift für aktischepr Psychologie.* July 1950, p. 117.

philosopher Caramuel has recently come to light; it is dated Wurzburg
1645, and addressed to the great contemporary scientist Fr Kircher, of
the Gregorian University.[3] In it, the author displays his anxiety to
know if he is morally responsible for his dreams. He wants a scientific
answer, because, as he says, "judgement depends on experience; and so
since some people have, or think they have, some experiences, and
others have others, they form different judgements. Examining my
own experiences closely, I have come to suspect that what is generally
said about the sleeping state is false, and that it cannot be proved that
the sleeper lacks the use of reason and will while he is asleep." To
support his theory he continues: "Examining many dreams, my own
and other peoples', I find circumstances in them which not only
cannot be perceived by the imagination or fantasy, but which must
be perceived by the mind and even by a fairly cultivated and keen
mind." He recounts a dream he had the previous day about a formal
academic disputation, in which, invited to attack the thesis moved, he
did so with great vigour and extremely subtle and original arguments.
He woke up, profoundly impressed, and examined the arguments to
see if they were valid; to his astonishment, they were, and his letter
continues: "so that man's mind does not rest when he sleeps, but
carries on working, sometimes with great brilliance: even, at times,
more brilliantly than when he is awake. . . . If all this, as would appear,
is true, why should the will not also be active in dreams? Here I
hesitate. To affirm this would be to occasion endless scruples of conscience; to deny it appears to contradict the evidence of reason." He
again repeats that he does not want to hear authorities quoted, but facts
proved by experience, since he has lost confidence in the general
opinion, which denies dreams the use of intelligence (the basis of free
will), while his own experience tells him that reason functions in
dreams and sometimes with great efficacy. In conclusion he says:
"Whoever would be so indulgent with himself that he would excuse
all his dreams as natural necessity, would appear to be very unwise".

3. R. Ceñal, s.j. "Juan Caramuel. Su epistolario con Atanasio Kircher, s.j.". Letter III.
In *Revista de Filosofía*, Madrid, Vol. XII, No. 44, pp. 101-147.

The terrible consequence of his theory is: "He who is asleep sometimes sins, not only through preceding free choice, as is well known, but through present free choice". This cruel doubt was tormenting him and he wrote to Fr Kircher to resolve it.

69. *St Thomas's solution*

Kircher's reply is not known, but if Caramuel, like a good Scholastic, had consulted the authority of St Thomas's *Summa Theologia* alone, he would have seen the problem better put, and its solution. In fact, for full and deliberate freedom of choice (which alone admits of full responsibility), any use of the reason is not sufficient in itself, as Caramuel supposes in his letter, but the fullness of judgement is needed, the capacity to form a synthesis of all elements and to make a proportional evaluation of them. St Thomas also concedes that dreams involve some use of the understanding, *secundum quod vires sensitivae interiores magis vel minus opprimuntur a somno, propter vaporum turbulentiam vel puritatem, secundum hoc usus rationis magis vel minus impeditur in dormiendo (S.T.,* IIa, IIae, q. 154, a. 5, ad 2) ("according as the interior sensitive forces are more or less oppressed by sleep, by the turbulence or purity of the vapours, so the use of reason is more or less hindered during sleep"). When organic disturbance is slight, he says elsewhere, not only do the images appear with greater harmony, but man *iudicat interdum in dormiendo ea quae videt somnia esse, quasi diiudicans inter res et rerum similitudines* ("sometimes judges that what he sees are dreams, as though distinguishing between objects and the appearances of objects"), that is, one is aware of the fact that one is dreaming and judges the dream as such, a faculty that would appear proper only to waking. However, St Thomas adds, *ex aliqua parte remanet sensus communis ligatus; et ideo licet aliquas similitudines discernat a rebus, tamen semper in aliquibus decipitur* (Ia, 84, 8, ad 2) ("common sense will always be tied in some way, so that it may be capable of distinguishing between some objects and their appearances, but will always be deceived in some things"). This could not be put better: in dreams one is "always deceived in some things". And this is why on waking one immediately realizes it has been a dream. Hence St Thomas, with most of the authorities, maintains that one cannot actually be held responsible for one's actions in dreams. If Caramuel had remembered those passages where St Thomas does not deny, by any means, a certain usage of reason in dreams, he would, I think, certainly not have worried about his moral responsibility.

So that in dreams we are actually, at the actual moment, not responsible; our use of reason is lacking in that degree of complete critical fullness which, together with a clear consciousness of oneself, is an indispensable premiss for the deliberate exercise of free choice. Does this mean that there is no problem of moral responsibility in dreams? Far from it.

70.   *Antecedent and consequent responsibility*

Responsibility, besides actual, can be divided into antecedent and consequent. Consequent responsibility is contracted on waking, when we take up a conscious attitude to the dream. If bad acts committed in dreams are complacently approved and remembered, this is obviously morally wrong; if they are rejected, this is clearly good. This is not contested by anyone and there is no need to discuss it further.

Antecedent responsibility is more complex. Dreams are not only products of nature, but also, in a way, of the person. The expression "everyone has the dreams he deserves" is not altogether true, but neither is it completely false. Jung insists that dreaming is a natural process, which means that it is necessary and autonomous. But this can be qualified: there are dreams, or elements in dreams, which are "merely natural", and there are dreams, or elements in dreams, which are "nature elaborated", and this elaboration, which is a life-long process, obviously contains many acts for which one is responsible. Referred to one particular dream, this responsibility is of course so diffuse and distant that for practical purposes it is non-existent. The case is somewhat similar to that of health and character, which are partly natural and partly the fruit of our free choice, besides also being partly dependent on atmosphere. Just as we can sometimes be held partly responsible for a particular state of health or for having a particular character, so it can be said that in a way we are partly responsible for the general trend of our dreams, even though we cannot be held responsible for any particular dream, since dreams are so largely autonomous. So the responsibility is remote and indirect. It can be assessed on the principle of *voluntario in causa*.

By this principle, an effect—here a wicked dream—does not influence the moral qualification of the acts which can be regarded as its cause, unless three conditions are fulfilled: foreknowledge of the effect, freedom to perform the cause or not, and obligation to prevent the effect. Dream psychology teaches that the contents of future dreams are highly unpredictable. The writers who have treated this question most fully declare that future dreams are so independent that they even seem to take a delight in fooling our conscious expectations. I know that Hervey de Saint-Denis called his famous book precisely *Les rêves et les moyens de les diriger*, and that, according to him, much can be achieved in this direction. Let us suppose, if only for the sake of argument, that one can achieve control over one's dreams: one's moral responsibility obviously increases. But I am sure that this control over dreams must be very relative and subject to many surprises. Nobody need consider himself obliged to learn this subtle and problematical art in order to prevent wicked dreams. "Day-dreams" or imaginings, if freely provoked and accepted, are of course another matter; they are far more controllable and very different from authentic dreams during sleep. If they are mere involuntary distraction, on the other hand, and as long as they remain so, one is not responsible for them.

The second condition, freedom to perform the cause or not, is not fulfilled either, because it is impossible to point to a single and exact cause. There will always be a mass of more or less remote and indirectly related acts, the *sum total of which* can produce an influence on dreams. So not only will the part corresponding to each act be infinitesimal, but the influence it exercises on tendentious dreaming and particularly on individual dreams will be indeterminate, for the same reason, and also because the relation of cause to effect will be doubtful. With such vague and remote matters, free will does not even bother to ask itself whether it should take action or not. Also, the terms of real free choices have their proximate causes; licit or illicit, these concern only the act they definitely cause, not the contingencies of an uncertain future.

Finally, the third condition is that we should be obliged to prevent the effect. This obligation corresponds to the moral law referring to the effects of acts. Now this law is based on the causal connection between act and effect, or at least the influence of the presumed cause on the presumed effect. We have seen that the influence of presumed causes is particularly uncertain: so with this basis lacking, the law cannot apply. So there is no obligation to prevent the presumed effects—dreams. Compare this with drunkenness: if one knows beforehand that when drunk one will perform a particular wrong action, and then gets drunk despite this foreknowledge, however confused it may be, one would be to a certain extent responsible for performing that wrong action. It would be voluntary *in causa*, even though one may have had no special intention of doing it: for something to be a bad effect, moralists teach, it need not have been positively intended, but only foreseen. All this shows that the main point which emerges from this question is the uncertainty of any complete link between dreams and their possible causes.

71. *Proximate causes and responsibility for them*

This uncertainty clearly applies to the remote causes so far discussed. It might be asked whether there may not be proximate causes more directly connected with dreams. The authorities all agree, and we all know from personal experience, that our sensations, feelings, preoccupations and physical state when we go to bed can all influence dreams. To be sure, this influence is not always, by any means, certain or foreseeable, but it is probable in one way or another. It cannot be called an influence on the details of any particular dream, but it certainly acts on a certain type of dream: if this type is completely immoral, that is sufficient for the present argument. So anyone who deliberately went to sleep under the influence of excessive stimulants, such as aphrodisiacs, or tried to excite the sexual instincts through sensual sensations, desires or imaginings, this with the direct intention of provoking dreams of this nature, would clearly not only be sinning in actually committing these acts, but would also be morally responsible for the dreams that would most probably result. It is different if the cause produced is permissible in itself, but by its nature likely to provoke immoral dreams. As long as one neither delights in the thought of wrong dreams in advance, nor in the fact of them afterwards such causes can be produced with a clear conscience. This is because there is no direct or indirect intention of producing an eventual effect; it would be unbearable, and a source of painful confusion, to have these uncertain future effects weighing so heavily on our conscious decisions. Also, these effects are, at the actual moment of dreaming, purely physical or material acts, and not fully human actions. So practically speaking, spiritual direction need not worry either about the dreams themselves or about their causes or occasions when these are permissible in themselves. We do not make dreams, we suffer them.

All this applies to responsibility, strictly speaking. From the point of view of prudence and the ideal of perfection, these dreams can obviously be very useful pointers to what can conveniently be done to make them better.

What is true of dreams is also true of sleep-walking, and of those quasi-hallucinations of certain drowsy states which produce such a strong sensation of reality that one can have a particularly bad conscience from imagining in one of them that one has done something wrong. But there is no need for this. One must be fully awake to be fully responsible. Finally, that other vague, diffuse, life-long responsibility which I mentioned certainly exists, but it is nothing more than the general responsibility we feel for not being better: in fact it is less.

III.   DREAMS AS A SOURCE OF INFORMATION ABOUT THE STATE OF THE SOUL

72.   *The impartiality of dreams*

One of the clearest revelations of modern psychology is the power of dreams to inform the dreamer of his overall mental state. They have been known to be an expression of physical states from the time of Hippocrates onwards. Ancient medical treatises recommend the observation of dreams to diagnose and forecast the course of illnesses. Mental states reflected in dreams are also mentioned, but they are not fully considered. The depth psychology of the last seventy years has really been responsible for all development on this point. The particular virtue of dreams as a source of information, compared to the conscious, is their greater degree of sincerity, a sort of physical sincerity. The conscious is often blinded by self-love, or fails to appreciate all the elements in a mental situation. If one has an interest in not knowing something, one can finish up by really not knowing it, though it remains active in the unconscious. This is the basic theory of repression and the dynamic unconscious which has been so abundantly demonstrated by psychoanalysis. I should like to see a term introduced into psychology to indicate "active forgetting" ("obliviation"?) and distinguish it from forgetting through passivity, extinction of the echo, spontaneous lack of interest, etc. Neuroses, states of inner conflict, are the most obvious manifestation of this *effort to hide*, which some instincts, struggling with others, are continually making. Hence the treatment of neurosis had to begin with a *method of revelation* independent of the conscious: failures, errors, free associations and above all, dreams. Dreams are largely, but not altogether, free from conscious control. Many tendencies originating in conscious life intervene in them besides unconscious urges, and their intervention, in so far as it restricts the free expression of opposing instincts, is what Freud called the "censor". Despite this, however, dreams have far more liberty than waking thought; even the "censor" often only succeeds in producing a disguise which a suitable analysis can remove. So the whole of unconscious life is shown on the dream screen in corresponding images. The fact that they correspond means that they somehow reveal psychic realities, especially instincts and affects. Dalbiez calls this *psychic expressivity*. Other writers, such as Vetter,[4] following the ideas of Klages, do not consider these symbols an *expression* as such, since the meaning of an expression must be clear and immediately intelligible, which dreams very often are not. Vetter says that dreams are more like the different forms which living beings—plants, animals and even human beings—take on during the course of their life, than a strict expression of the psyche, as tears and laughter are. It is a question of terminology. The concepts may be different, but they have a common basis which allows general linguistic usage to employ the term *expression*, and more particularly *psychic expression*, to designate these manifestations, even though they are not immediately intelligible, but require a certain amount of interpretation. By interpretation I mean referring each sign to an experience and so discovering its meaning and the meaning of the whole. Immediately or otherwise, dreams express psychic reality with automatic accuracy and so have a very high informative value. For the spiritual director, this is the essential point. The lucid consciousness can evidently achieve great sincerity in its expressions; with practice, it can come to have a great objectivity in its descriptions of even its deepest states. Certain natural qualities and acquired virtues facilitate this truthfulness, such as humility, which suppresses the principal enemy, pride—principal, but of course not the only enemy nor always the most powerful: this will depend on each person and each situation.

The people directed, however, will not always possess these qualities or virtues. They will often have traces of neurosis, and with the best will in the world hide or disguise many things that the director should know. Pinamonti devotes a substantial chapter in his book on spiritual direction to a warning to confessors against these unconscious deformations to which penitents subject their examinations. All other writers on the subject say the same. This is why they all insist on the need for a

4. *Erlebnisbedeutung der Phantasie* (Stuttgart, 1950), p. 118.

spiritual director, who, besides his knowledge and experience, has the advantage of viewing the questions impartially, as an outsider.

Dreams also possess a great degree of impartiality in their judgements on the state of the soul, in registering advances, failures, hesitations, impasses, and in general all the different vicissitudes of spiritual evolution.

73.   *The law of progressive impregnation*

All this presupposes a basic *law of impregnation of nature by spirit*. At the outset of life, everything is unconscious. As development progresses, this chaos is seen not to be completely amorphous, but to contain certain directions, which form patterns. The conscious gradually emerges, tenuous at first, but becoming more distinct and active. This conscious, with its attributes and resources, centralized in a being with understanding and will, is situated between the external world of objects and persons and the depths of the natural inner being. Drawn in both directions, it seeks to adapt itself to the two extremes. Environment influences its nature either consciously or unconsciously. The principal task of life, entrusted to this lucid, free and responsible faculty which we call the self, or consciousness, is to build an integrated personality, well balanced between its material, spiritual and mixed elements, and well attuned to man's transcendental demands and relationships, particularly towards God, as the ultimate end and point of reference for all the rest. But this task is a long and difficult process, an ascesis. We have obstacles in the way of accomplishing the task, but we also have natural and supernatural aids, the latter through the merits of Jesus Christ, many of which have been put into concrete forms by the Church he founded. Spiritual direction is one of them, supernatural and natural at once, since a combination of both aspects is a normal rule of Providence.

This whole task of adaptation and transformation, performed by our own efforts, but with the external aids mentioned, is a series of pressures put on human nature, obliging it to modify itself, at first superficially, and then, provided the necessary conditions are fulfilled, more and more deeply. The limiting case is reached when the "old man" (natural man) is transformed and fused into the "new man" (spiritual man) to such an extent that the two become one. Hence St Paul could say: "I live, now not I, but Christ lives in me". This Christian impregnation of man means that the objective Christian law becomes an inner law and natural to man. Distances between objective rules of conduct and spontaneous inclinations are reduced, until the two generally coincide. The *law of grace* becomes *second nature*, so that virtuous acts become as easy and delightful to follow as the promptings of human nature. The progress of this progressive impregnation can be measured. One can see it oneself by a sincere and thorough examination of conscience, and verbal communication and conduct can make it apparent to the spiritual director: "By their fruits you shall know them". If the person directed is humble and sincere, his confessions will generally be sufficient guide to his confessor. But eventually it will happen, or at least it theoretically could happen, that his information will have to be supplemented by observation and apt interpretation of dreams.

Natural spontaneity (of the "first" or "second" natures) is dominant in dreams. For just this reason, the way we behave in dreams can sometimes be an indication of the degree to which the Christian law has been assimilated. The first phases in spiritual life will obviously show consciously correct behaviour, but this will naturally still be something of a struggle; it is imposed by conscience and maintained by continuous endeavour. At this stage it is not surprising if the person behaves less correctly in dreams than he does in waking life. This shows that the Christian impregnation is still superficial (unless other factors intervene, such as diabolic temptations of the good man in dreams, or a particular physical condition). In these cases, the conscious by itself can give an inadequate idea of the state of the soul. As virtue becomes firmer, habits stronger, and the feelings more disciplined, so the unconscious will be informed by this discipline and in dreams will gradually come to act in accordance with the new law. St Thomas says, *virtuosi nanciscuntur in dormiendo meliora theoremata prae aliis non virtuosis*

M

("the virtuous come to have better visions in dreams than those who are not virtuous"), and quotes Aristotle in support.[5]

74. *Dreams and chastity*

There is one particular field in which the truth of all this can be proved, since all the difficulties come together in it: chastity. Sexuality, with its strong organic basis, which makes it follow its own amoral biological course, and its immense affective power in the psyche, is the strongest enemy of spirituality. In dreams, according to popular belief, man's animal nature gains the upper hand, and humours, instincts and effects are all-powerful. So if it can be shown that real chastity can have the power to correct and spiritualize dreams, it should not be difficult to admit this spiritual impregnation in other domains of the subconscious. Experience must decide this, and from early Christian times experience has said that love of purity can be great enough to reach the very intimacy of dreams, that is, the unconscious.

St John Climacus (seventh century), the great disciple of St Gregory Nazianzen, says: "The chaste man is he who even in dreams always remains perfectly insensible to physical difference and beauty: this rule is the ultimate of perfect and consummate chastity".[6] St Laurence Justinian, Patriarch of Venice (1381-1455), following the fifth-century ascetic writer John Cassian, says: "The final degree of chastity is not to see lubricious phantasies of women even in sleep. For although these illusions cannot be considered sinful, they are nevertheless an indication of concupiscence latent in the marrow. They may occur in several ways. As a man is accustomed to think and act while awake, so will he be tempted while he sleeps. This is the aim of continence, this is the height of chastity. . . ."[7] There are numerous other similar texts. Alvárez

---

5. Quaest. disp. *De veritate*, 28, 3 ad 7.

6. Climacus, gradus 15.

7. *Castimoniae gradus est ne illecebrosis phantasmatibus feminarum vel dormiens illudatur. Licet tamen hanc ludificationem peccato esse obnoxiam non sit credendum, concupiscentiae tamen latitantis medullitus indicium est. Quam tamen ludificationem diversis modis constat accidere. Nam secundum illum usum quem vigilans vel exercere vel cogitare consueverat etiam dormiens unusquisque tentatur. Hic est continentiae finis, haec pudicitiae consummatio . . .* (Inst., Lignum vitae, trat. De continentia. Ch. VI.)

de Paz, the ascetic and mystic writer already quoted, sums up the tradition thus: "This will show in what the fifth grade of chastity consists. The man who possesses it feels no lusts of the flesh when he is awake, and even in dreams suffers no illusions of impure phantasies."[8] He gives three reasons for this in that dreams are produced by three causes: physical constitution, the emotions, and previous occupations. The chaste man dominates his body through penitence, his feelings and heart are free from all carnal desires, and when he is awake, he neither speaks nor thinks of these matters.

These natural and supernatural means do not succeed in killing the roots of such deep-rooted human affects, but in containing them and quietening them. So the chaste man does not become *radically* less human and less sensitive (as some old texts, influenced by stoicism, would have), because without his effort concupiscence would reassert itself. The peace of chastity is armed and watchful, but through long practice and complete acquiescence in their use, this very vigilance and defence become natural—always supposing that God's grace is present. Above all, perfect chastity should not be regarded as an isolated and negative part of the personality, a sort of vacuum left by the expulsion of earthly love, motivated by a proud desire to be "angelic" (in the worst sense). It is one of the many elements that go to make up an overall, highly integrated situation, and far from being a vacuum, it is the greatest possible fullness and the highest possible exaltation of human love towards the highest possible object, God. Once possessed, God will in his turn possess the human soul with incredible strength. To be united to him is to reach the most positive situation possible; it corresponds to the integration of all loves at their proper level, when they are most purified and most extended in offering. Here more than ever it is important to repeat that nothing is suppressed, but that everything is outclassed and replaced: divine love takes the place of human

---

8. *Iam ex his intelligitur in quo consistat quintus gradus castitatis. Illum enimpossidet qui n on solum in vigilia nullas carnis impugnationes patitur verum et in somno nullis impuris phantasmatibus illuditur.* (Jacobi Alvárez de Paz, *De extermin. mali et promot. boni*, Book V, Pt II, *De Castitate*, Ch. IX.)

love. The nature of what we rather lamely call "Christian continence", in its fullest expression, should be viewed from these heights. The human being finds his happiness within the confines of a law that is most often contrary to the instincts of his senses, but which a sublime assimilation has made natural to him; he benefits from the most powerful dynamism known: that of perfect charity. How can a man who has known this long for the troubled ardours of sexuality, which seem so necessary to ordinary mortals? This final grade is no longer chastity militant, but chastity triumphant. It is, of course, impossible to achieve with our own natural resources alone: all spiritual authors rightly agree that it is a special gift of God, though, like any other gift, it requires our co-operation.

75. *Interfering factors*

This degree of Christian impregnation reaches the unconscious and is registered in dreams. But even when these heights of spiritual perfection are reached, the possibility of diabolic intervention, acting with divine permission to disturb the imagination, must not be left out of account. But cases of this are rare and require special proof. According to Alvarez de Paz, the Devil usually keeps a respectful distance from these holy souls. From the psychological point of view, these diabolic interventions, since they belong on another plane, cannot even be called exceptions, but preternatural interferences. Nor can the temptations which assail those who have reached this *pax carnalis*, through organic disease affecting the humours or the tissues connected with the genetic function, be called complete exceptions, though an outside observer might consider them such. Thomas à Kempis says, "Some are particularly tempted at the outset, some during the course, and others at the end". The reasons for this—one might add—can be either natural, supernatural or pathological. Spiritual manuals deal with the manner of recognizing and appreciating these interferences, and a prudent and experienced director will take all such factors into account.

76. Dreams, the mirror of the situation

It is important to bear in mind that dreams reflect the degree to which the unconscious has been impregnated in the states described. Consequently, they reflect the intermediary stages on the long road that leads to these states. This is traditional Catholic doctrine, inherited from the Greeks and their successors. It is summarized in the words of Alvárez de Paz, which I have already quoted: "So the sleep of the just man who has reached this fifth grade of chastity is tranquil and pure, formed by thought from the holy works and desires preceding it in waking. And if God were to let others see the images of his dreams, they would see nothing obscene or impure, but everything clean and full of wisdom."[9]

Modern psychology fully confirms this. The series of dreams published by Jung, Layard, Ania Teillard, and the deductions of many authors from unpublished or only partly published series, point to the same conclusion: that dreams hold up an impartial mirror to each stage of mental evolution. One class of dreams listed by the authorities is "dreams of situation", which merely manifest the actual state of the dreamer's mind. All this is more widely known, and there is no need to dwell on it. The testimony of spiritual writers is not so generally known.

77. Where the law of compensation comes in

All this can serve to show the degree of truth contained in Jung's affirmations that continent people have orgiastic dreams and debauchees have honourable ones, in virtue of the law of compensation. One can be sure that continent people who have lascivious dreams are not *perfectly* pure, but only apparently so, or at least not purified in their innermost affects. They may be sincerely continent, but they are still in the early stages of the fight for purity; they have at least not yet reached the final stages, unless they are victims of organic disease or diabolic intervention. Does this mean that the law of compensation

9. See Section 66.

between the conscious and the unconscious does not apply in the last stages of spiritual progress? This would be an exaggeration. The compensation may be there, but in keeping with the new configuration of the mental world of holy people, and so based on realities compatible with their state. The plasticity of human nature, naturally so great, is here in the omnipotent hands of God, and nobody can risk placing a limit to its possibilities of evolution.

78.   *Conclusion and confirmation*

I have taken chastity as an example because of its exceptional demonstrative power, but as much could clearly be said of any other line along which it is possible to trace the progress of Christian perfection. The trajectory from pride (in every form) towards humility could be another example; so could that from insatiable, aggressive egoism towards forgiveness, generosity and self-sacrifice, or that from profane criteria of conduct towards criteria based on faith. The progressive impregnation of the unconscious and its reflection in dreams would apply to these lines, and to any others. Someone who dreamt that he was being threatened with death unless he renounced God, and that he did not renounce him, preferring to accept death, might be showing that his religion was well rooted in his soul. It would be more prudent, however, not to trust one single dream, and to study the dreamer's overall situation before coming to a conclusion about such a dream: it might be a transference and not literal.

The man who knows how to observe dreams, then, will have at his disposal a highly impartial source of information about the state of the soul, on its deepest level as well as on the more superficial ones, which, if not the only essential factor, is at least an important one. Dreams exercise their informative function most fully at times of crisis, when the unconscious speaks to the conscious more fully and more clearly.

As a final note, before passing on to the next point, I should like to draw attention to the parallel between dreams as a source of information on the progress of virtue and the experiments made by Dr Delgado and

Dr Carillo in Lima on *narco-diagnosis of remission in psychosis*.[10] Patients who appeared outwardly cured, or were pretending to be, were drugged into an unconscious, or very relaxed, state; whilst in this state they were astutely questioned on their critical problems, giving them a chance to unburden themselves and show whether their recovery was in fact well-founded or not. The unconscious told the truth, which the conscious either could not or would not reveal. The same happens with the different "truth drugs", which have been so widely used and abused for clinical and other less legitimate purposes.

IV.   DREAMS AS A SOURCE OF INSTRUCTION AND GUIDANCE

79.   *The blind leading the blind?*

I have already said that reason and the fully lucid conscience are the basic instruments given us by God to organize our lives towards their ultimate end. But it may be useful to repeat it once more at this point, since the heading of this part may seem strange to many people, particularly in a chapter on spiritual direction. Dreams are usually synonymous with nonsense and caprice, so at first sight to expect them to act as a guide in such a serious matter seems a perfect example of asking the blind to lead the blind.

I am not of course referring to the supernatural dreams of which the Scriptures and the lives of the saints are full. These can obviously guide us, but they do not belong to the natural, spontaneous "oneiric function" which is the subject of this book. Between supernatural visions sent in dreams and everyday anodyne dreams without significance, there are a host of other special dreams which, while still natural, can rightly be considered gifts of God in the sense that "good thoughts" are often held to be sent by God or one's guardian angel, although, strictly speaking, they may not be. The Gospel tells us that every hair of our head is numbered, and God must take far more account of each

10. *Revista de Neuropsiquiatría* (Lima, 1946), pp. 355-68.

good thought. Because the normal run of secondary causes (psychic laws in this case) is very often sufficient to produce thoughts that seem "inspired", spiritual works contain so many rules for distinguishing true inspiration—St Ignatius, Cardinal Bona, Fr Scaramelli, etc. In the same way, many dreams seem inspired, and deserve to be referred to divine providence, if not directly, at least indirectly, through the nature God gave us and preserves in us.

Although natural dreams may not seem the natural function best suited to guide us, since their products are often so far removed from reason, this is not always the case. Saying that we can be guided by dreams does not mean by their lack of reason or opposition to reason, but by their reasonableness, which is often greater than one thinks, though it may not be clear at first sight. God has given us two forms of reason, one conscious and the other in the oneiric consciousness. This is a great blessing, because conscious reason cannot always act on our weak will with the efficacy easily achieved by oneiric reason. Numerous instances of this could be quoted. The more one studies dreams, the more one realizes that they are not "mere detritus excreted by the psyche", as one writer has called them; nor are they, as another has said, the sum of everything puerile, egotistical, animal and backward in human nature; nor again an automatic mechanism which overrides and supersedes reason.

80. *Dreams as direction*

Dreams are an extremely complex phenomenon: absolutely everything in human nature appears in them, from the lowest and most trivial elements to the most sublime. They fulfil a multiplicity of functions in our economy, understood in its widest sense, playing different parts on different occasions and in different situations and people. Those of interest here in relation to spiritual direction are those which show them as a source of instruction and guidance. They might be classed as: the religious function (on our relations with God); the ethical function (on the right ordering of our actions); the theoretic-didactic function (on truth and its assimilation and exposition); and the prospective function (which contains all the others, but is directed particularly towards the future, seeking solutions to further spiritual development).

81.   *The religious function*

Once one is convinced that there can be no fundamental opposition between psychology, philosophy and theology, one can start from any of the three to demonstrate that the unconscious is concerned with individual religious problems and that these problems are consequently reflected in dreams. Starting from philosophy and theology, one finds the great basic principle which St Ignatius puts at the beginning of the *Spiritual Exercises*: that God made man to know him, love him and serve him in this world so as to possess him in eternity; thanks to the Redemption, this process is realized in the bosom of the Church, leading through elevation to the divine order of things through grace to the contemplation of God in heaven *sicuti est*, as he is. As God does nothing without good reason, it follows that human nature must contain the disposition necessary for the attainment of that destiny. Man must be capable of knowing God, of adoring him and loving him above all things, of incorporating himself into the Church and finding himself at home there. From our psychological point of view one must consequently suppose, *a priori*, that man possesses a functional adaptation which renders the execution of this programme of life not only possible, but natural and free. Tertullian's succinct phrase, *anima naturaliter christiana*, means this, that everything in man is designed to blossom into Christianity. No less concise is St Augustine's famous sentence, *Fecisti nos Domine ad te et irrequietum est cor nostrum donec requiescat in te*, "Thou hast made us, O Lord, for thee, and our heart is troubled until it rest in thee". God is then, not only ontologically, but psychologically, the human soul's centre of gravity.

One could compile a wonderful anthology from these two Fathers down to our own times, showing in writings and particularly in the lives of saints the expression of this clamour for God, which springs from the depths of human nature. Theologians, philosophers, poets, architects, painters, sculptors, musicians, and above all saints and mystics have given utterance to the hymn of praise owed to God by all Nature. It has been interrupted by hatred, superstition and indifference, but none the less, an harmonious and powerful song, *vox tronitruum multorum*, has constantly arisen to heaven in praise of the Origin and Ultimate End of all creation. The same is shown by the anonymous myths and legends which crystallize collective ideas from earliest times and all corners of the globe.[11]

The *a priori* argument has led us to an *a posteriori* one, which has recently been studied by Jung as a simple matter of psychological experiment; it has led him to the conclusion that religion is a natural attitude of the human mind. The second part of his book *Psychology and Religion* deals, in his own words, "with those facts that demonstrate that a genuine religious function exists in the unconscious". From his subjective point of view, Otto says the same: "the *numinous* is a perceptible form *a priori*" (of human understanding). Religion, then, is not arbitrarily created by the individual from his experience, but a *general* condition to which man is subject independently of his will, embracing both his cognitive and emotive aspects; it is the preparation, capacity and nostalgia for the adoration and complete self-surrender due to a Supreme Being. The actual content of the religious functions will depend on many factors, but the very existence of the function implies an ultimate power, a Supreme Being, just as the existence of the eye implies light.

To Jung, despite the many blemishes in his works from a Catholic point of view, belongs the credit for giving depth psychology a religious direction, notably absent from its beginnings. His work should be very carefully, and constructively, revised by Catholics. He has certainly recently treated Catholicism with far more respect than he did previously. Although the professional obligations of

11. See Hugo Rahner, s.j., *Griechische Mythen in christlicher Deutung* (Zürich, 1947).

psychological science force him to maintain a strictly phenomenological point of view, we, from a human as well as a psychological point of view, must draw the ontological conclusions imposed by the facts adduced by him.

Victor Frankl, in all his works, but most particularly in *Der unbewusste Gott* (*The Hidden God*), deals at length with what he calls the "spiritual unconscious", as opposed not only to the "spiritual conscious", but more directly to the "instinctive unconscious"—the Freudian "Id". It is in this spiritual unconscious, he claims, that the source of neuroses is to be found, in repression of man's natural relationship with transcendent being. (One wonders what Freud, or even Jung, would say to this.) For him, one must start from God in order to understand man. St Augustine has said that God is more us than we ourselves. And, he says, every man has an unconscious faith, even if he is a conscious unbeliever: "existential analysis" should help to reveal this hidden faith.

Catholics have begun to take active notice of the work of Jung and others, seeking a sort of synthesis between depth psychology and theology. Theology, while particularly necessary to the present age and still flourishing within the Church, has undoubtedly been weakened to a significant degree by over-stressing rational elements—a fault of the age—to the detriment of other more hidden and indefinite forces in man. Yet these other forces can be dynamic and fruitful in the Church's aim of forming "Christ in us". To go to the other extreme of overstressing the irrational elements would of course have far more dangerous consequences; the ideal is an ordered and balanced synthesis of all the elements that should go to make up human personality.[12] As well as *homo libidinosus*, the unconscious must be held to contain

---

12. Among the Catholics who have contributed the most constructive criticism in this field, I should like to mention specially Fr Victor White, for his *God and the Unconscious*; Goldbrunner, for his account and criticism of Jung, *Individuation*; Wilfred Daim, for his important book *Umwertung der Psychoanalyse*; Caruso, for his very suggestive *Análisis psíquico y síntesis existencial*; Nuttin, *Psychanalyse et conception spiritualiste de l'homme*; Madame Choisy, *Psychanalyse et Catholicisme*; R. Hostie, *Du Mythe à la religion*; Henri Gratton, *Psychanalyses d'hier et d'aujourd'hui*; and other earlier writers of such distinction as Dalbiez, López-Ibor, Laín Entralgo, Maritain, Fr Gemelli, Fr César Vaca, etc.

homo religiosus, who belongs there with at least as much right. This is why religious problems occur so frequently in dreams, especially in later life. This is a wide subject, but it must suffice here to indicate its essentials.

Examples of religious dreams abound in works devoted to the subject. So as not to make this account too long, I shall only quote a few unpublished ones, from my own collection:

A man of about forty-five: "*I dreamt of a disturbance in a tunnel, without quite knowing what it was about. Finally a deer ran out of it. I followed it. It seemed to be looking for a spring to drink from and at the same time to be fleeing from hunters.* Spontaneously, as soon as I woke up, I thought that the deer represented something in the depths of the soul seeking God. It is the most common biblical symbol in literature and art. *It comes out of the tunnel* (the unconscious, the depths of the soul), *where there is some disturbance and a hint of persecution*: this is the trouble of the heart created by God, which, as St Augustine says, cannot repose until it rest in God; at the same time there are certain adverse forces in my nature, which seek objects incompatible with God. *It comes out of the tunnel*: desire for God reaches a conscious level. *I follow it*: hesitation again; I take it as a guide, but stay a little behind it, feeling something holding me back. The whole dream left me with a great longing for God."

A woman of about fifty: "First Friday. I don't want to ignore last night, or rather this morning's dream. It left me with pleasant, soul-comforting thoughts. *I dreamt of souls changed into bunches of grapes, on which many of the grapes were bad—these were sins. They were hanging in a muddy place through which I had to pass. I was sorry to see that the good grapes would be spoilt by the rotten ones. I wanted to prevent this, and began to cut the rotten ones out. This seemed a long task and took me several days. I cannot tell how long, but I finished my task and the bunches were left clean and succulent.* They moved me to exclaim: 'Almighty Lord, I thank thee for teaching me in such a simple manner to cleanse my soul of its sins'."

She adds: "Perhaps you don't think this is very important, but it is for me. It has made such a strong impression on me! I have had several other dreams which I have not written down and so cannot remember fully. Once, several years before the war, I saw our Lady appearing in a part of heaven. That was a wonderful thing. *And four days ago I dreamt of the Holy Ghost, not as a dove, but as a person in a white garment, like the usual statues of the Sacred Heart, standing in an opening circle of glory. He held out his hands and welcomed a soul from some deep place, and carried it up to heaven.* . . . . Nothing else, but it was all so lovely. . . . . I woke up so impressed, and have been thinking about it a lot."

Another woman, of about thirty-six: "I sometimes have terrible struggles in dreams: all my worries assume gigantic proportions. Let me tell you about one. . . . That dream I had two years ago, for example, in which *I saw a man from the telegraph office where I worked during the war; he was riding a bicycle along the street. 'Why aren't you at the office?' I asked. 'What are you doing as a delivery boy?' 'I'm dead.' 'Oh!' 'I'm delivering warnings to all the living.' 'What must we do?' I asked. He replied, 'That', pointing to the background, where the Blessed Sacrament was exposed, with two nuns kneeling in front of it. 'Of course', I thought in the dream, 'I must pray.'* "

Another of the same person's dreams: "I woke up and remembered that *I had been dreaming of a faded picture of our Lady at the foot of the Cross. I heard a voice say, 'She saw the victim die, and she had to love those who killed him.'* I had never meditated on this, nor do I think the thought had ever occurred to me, at least not so clearly. On another occasion I woke up with the impression that I had been repeating 'Thy kingdom come', to myself all night."

82. *The ethical function*

The ethical function of the oneiric consciousness is comparable to that of the waking consciousness; comparable, but with the difference that in dreams it is unconscious. Both innate and acquired tendencies operate from the unconscious and so are manifested in dreams. They can be either conceptual frameworks which direct thought, or impulses which control action. This is the basis of the so-called laws of psychic life, which are sources of phenomena predetermined to a greater or lesser extent. In the moral field, there are not only objective laws (norms), but subjective ones (forces). Moral perfection is achieved when one set is made to correspond exactly with the other. According to Catholic moral teaching, the root of natural moral laws is syndaeresis, which St Thomas defines as: *Lex intellectus nostri in quantum est habitus continens praecepta legis naturalis, quae sunt prima operum humanorum* ("A law of human understanding, insofar as it is a habit which contains the precepts of the natural law, which are the primary precepts of human behaviour"). (Ia, 94, 1 ad 2.) And elsewhere he says: . . . *synderesis dicitur instigare ad bonum et murmurare de malo, in quantum per prima principia [scil. operabilium] procedimus ad inveniendum et iudicamus inventa* . . . ("Syndaeresis is said to incite to good works and discourage from bad ones, insofar as by these primary principles [of behaviour] we proceed to find a thing and to judge it once we have found it.") (Ia, 76, 12, c.) It is the decision preceding and the remorse or satisfaction following an action. It is not only an authority who commands, but a supervisor who controls, and a judge who condemns or approves.

The part it has to play in the overall pattern of the vital functions is clear once life is seen as a progression, during which we must resolve each successive problem posed by new adaptations. As sensitive beings, we use sensitive means to progress towards a sensitive goal; as intellectual beings, we use intellectual means to progress towards an ultrasensitive goal. The same can be said of each facet of man, but they must be seen in proportion and as forming a whole. The ethical facet is the most specifically human of all, because it concerns the complete essence of human nature. Morality is rightly defined as the concordance between actions and human nature *as such*, taking every aspect of it into account. So the moral being naturally progresses towards morality, on his own impulse and with the adequate means of knowledge and instinct. If a being, as a principle of action, can be called a nature, then man has a moral nature.

This is the root of what is called the "ethic unconscious", the basic layer where the cognitive and instinctual demands which govern us are generated. The two fundamental acts in which its operation is manifested are, as St Thomas says, investigation, and evaluation of the results of this investigation, in the moral order. The natural law presents the initial nucleus of this dynamic "ethic unconscious" which makes practical moral reasoning possible. By this reasoning, we continually assimilate new norms of behaviour, progressively more derived and more complicated, till they reach those highly differentiated complex wholes which represent the highest point of development of the "moral personality". This process of moral assimilation is one of the most difficult problems posed by psychology. Psychoanalysis has given particular attention to it, and, together with psychology of form, has found new flanks on which to attack it.

The formation of the moral sense, as of all the other aspects of human development, is subject to innumerable vicissitudes and is often defective in its results. Hence the fact that so many men do not always have the right moral reactions, and the innumerable problems that this poses for spiritual direction. We know that in man everything tends towards integration in search of unity, and that all anarchy is therefore pathogenic. So in moral integration, none of man's component elements should be left aside: the whole man—affective-instinctive, imaginative, sensitive—should participate. The traditional upbringing given by many mothers to their children shows an instinctive grasp of this. Etienne de Greef has laid particular emphasis on the part played by the affects in concrete morality. The sort of contraction and expansion in moral integration discovered by Freud, which he calls projection and introjection (in the formation of the Super-ego), are known to be phenomena completely impregnated with affectivity. But it would be a great mistake to think that affectivity alone is enough, and Freud failed to see the importance of the spiritual element, cognitive and appetitive, direct and reflected, in the formation of a complete and solid moral feeling. Many rationalists, too, have failed in believing that morality is purely a question of reason: "education can make prisons unnecessary".

These influences all act on man from the time of his earliest infancy in the bosom of his family and society. His hereditary capacities, situation, and personal reactions all combine to form, for better or for worse, the deposit of moral reactivity which rules his conduct from the depths of his unconscious.

This whole complex network of forces which holds the ethic unconscious in place, by a fundamental law of vital teleology, makes its resources converge at any given moment on the point of central interest, which here is ethic interest: the line of conduct to adopt in such and such a circumstance. When a problem faces us, we tackle it spontaneously, and so the forces of the ethic unconscious act spontaneously when something concerns them. Our inner field is magnetized automatically and on several levels, in different forms, according to the dominant organic and mental conditions of the moment. If these conditions are those of waking, the action taken will be conscious; if they are diminished, but not quite those of sleep, it will be less conscious. In the last sleep before waking, when the organism is refreshed and the psychic functions less disturbed, it will show itself in fairly coherent dreams, in which reason plays a considerable part, in which reasonable elements seem to arrange and settle themselves, and in which the voice of judgement, quelling illegitimate or distracting interests of the waking consciousness, is heard reproaching, showing solutions, and commanding. If the organic conditions are those of deep sleep, or when the psychic functions are still insufficiently refreshed, there are either no dreams, or the dreams are more disconnected and nonsensical. On either level, waking or sleeping, with their different degrees, the behaviour of the psychic forces is basically the same: they converge on the solution of outstanding problems, with energy proportionate to their importance. Both waking and sleep provide surprises and exceptions to this, particularly sleep, since its laws are less well known.

All this should show how the ethical function works in dreams. It can be compared to the waking conscience, because conscience is usually defined by Catholics as "reason knowing the law". The ethic function will show itself in dreams with greater or lesser force depending on how deeply the law has been accepted, how strongly habits have been formed, and to what extent affectivity has organized itself in relation to the law—that is to say, how far the process of impregnation of the unconscious (discussed in the preceding section) has progressed. Given the initial natural nucleus, the unconscious gives back in dreams all that was originally put into it by the conscious or by more or less unknown or uncontrolled marginal perceptions.

Some writers, such as Jessen, quoted by Freud, have denied the existence of ethics in dreams. He says that in dreams conscience is silenced and one commits the worst crimes without caring or repenting.[13] Radestock, also quoted by Freud, claims that the series of dream images are connected and unconnected with no intervention at all on the part of reflection, intelligence, aesthetic taste or moral judgement. Such statements are unwarrantable generalizations of part of the truth, as are the opposing statements that in dreams we always behave as we do in waking life.

To answer both extremes, we must remember the principles I have explained: one is that there are different levels of oneiric consciousness, and the other is that there are different degrees of impregnation of the unconscious. Some writers treat dreams as though they were all exactly the same thing, or speak of conscience in relation to dreams as though its influence on the unconscious were always the same.

So these two principles can never be stressed too much. Nor should it be forgotten, with regard to the first, that the level of sleep is not always the same in all the organs at the same time. It has been clearly shown that not all parts of the brain sleep at the same time or to the same degree. This will vary according to the wear to which they have been subjected and the variable conditions under which they are refreshed. In sleepwalking, the motor area is awake and the imagination asleep (so the sleepwalker can walk along high cornices without giddiness), whereas in normal dreaming the motor is asleep and the

13. Freud, *The Interpretation of Dreams*, p. 77.

N

imagination very much awake. The same is true of the different functions. So even when someone is said to be in a light sleep, when manifestations of reason could more probably be expected, not all the concomitant functions of reason will necessarily appear. This is an extensive source of irregularities, or of what we call irregularities since we do not know the laws that govern them.

The second principle—impregnation of the unconscious—has been sufficiently explained in discussing the informative value of dreams. Two men whose outward conduct seems the same may be impregnated by the law to a very different extent in their unconscious, or may have assimilated it to a different degree, which is the interesting point in assessing dreams.

The laws of association, so active in dreams, provide other principles of explanation by which to make differing pieces of evidence agree. Here I want to mention only the law of contrast as it appears in certain neuroses, since although I am dealing with dreams and not neurosis, it is well known that comparison between dreams and neurosis and psychosis has often proved an excellent heuristic principle. So if, for example, a mother is obsessed with a desire to kill her children, to the point where she does not even dare to take hold of a knife, although she loves her children with all her heart, she is obviously suffering from an obsession by contrast with her very love. If she dreams that she is killing them, or that she wants to kill them, a good interpreter will not conclude that she hates them, but that she loves them madly and is obsessed with the fear of doing them harm. Also, in dreams or awake, heights which make us feel giddy can at the same time give us a desire to throw ourselves into space, not from any desire to commit suicide, but for precisely the opposite reason. Certain timorous souls feel an obsession to blaspheme in the same measure as they fear God, or feel tempted to impurity while hating it: the process is the same whether they are dreaming or awake. There may be other contributory factors, such as hunger or thirst, physical oppression, or pathological local disturbance.... It is most important to remember the recommendation of all the authorities on therapeutic dream interpretation: that dreams cannot be interpreted except in the light of fundamental knowledge of the dreamer *at the time of dreaming.*

After this, there is no need to insist too much on the help that the ethical function of dreams can afford to spiritual direction. The discussion of dreams that have an ethical content with the penitent can be an exceptionally good occasion to orientate or influence him, since these ethics are individualized, as it were, based on his own personal material, a sort of auto-vaccine, and not, as so often happens, based on abstract advice or external impositions, both usually fruitless. Even though dreams may not be remembered, they have some effect; if they are remembered, they have more, and still more if they are conscientiously analysed and assimilated.

83. *Theoretic-didactic function*

"Education through pictures" has often been a teachers' slogan. In this dreams can undeniably play a major part. The incredible virtuosity with which they give perceptible, dramatic form to the most intricate and subtle concepts is a never-failing source of wonder. They enable truths that are obscure, or disregarded through prejudice, to be assimilated. This is naturally also true on the spiritual plane—perhaps even more so, since spirituality is so closely bound up with psychology, and its shades, enigmas and seemingly calculated lack of precision accord well with the nature of symbols.

When Nathan told David the parable of the rich man who killed the poor man's sheep, David took it as the same sort of objective reality that we take our dream dramas to be, ingenuously giving way to the feelings the situation demands. But then comes the analysis: *Tu es ille vir,* "you are that man", as Nathan said. How would David have taken the story if it had been couched in personal terms from the start? Surely his pride and his love for Bethsabee would have hindered the salutary effects that God intended it to have? But while he thought of it as outside himself, he could listen to its lesson with an open mind. When the parable was explained, he could feel the full force of it, applied to himself. The same happens with dreams.

Our Lord explained the Kingdom of God in parables, an eminently oneiric procedure, to the extent that the interpretation is, as we have seen, the same or very similar in both cases. With dreams it is, of course, more difficult, since the meaning of their symbols is strictly personal, even if the theme is objective, whereas didactic parables addressed to a crowd presumably have a meaning that can be understood by all.

Many of the imaginary visions scattered throughout spiritual books are, purely and simply, dreams. Fr La Puente in his *Spiritual Guide*, discussing "supernatural contemplation through likenesses", has three examples which are obviously dreams, certainly very beautiful ones.

While this person was at prayer, our Lord showed him the struggle between the soul and the body described by St Paul, in this manner: With his mind's eye he saw a very beautiful and modest maiden, dressed in a rich, white robe; she was standing, a little way above the ground, and near her, to one side, a man was lying; he was dark and ugly, but his eyes were gentle and caressing. They both had an iron ring round their ankles, attached to a long chain, which held them bound and as it were imprisoned. The man tried to make the maiden look at him, but she would not, though this was obviously such a struggle that she could not help glancing at him from time to time, and as she did, sadness brought her down to the ground, while the man joyfully began to get up, until she looked at him too much and sank to the ground; at that moment the man jumped up and began to run mercilessly, dragging the poor maiden through mud and over rocks until he reached a cliff and threw himself off, so as to drag her with him. But she, seeing the danger, gained great strength, clung to the rocks, and began to climb gradually upwards, pulling the man after her on the chain, crying out to heaven and begging for help. Her cruel enemy kept clambering up the chain and throwing himself off with a jerk so as to pull her after him; but she held on firmly, pushing him away when he came near, and imploring God's mercy. At this point the vision vanished and he understood that this was the cruel struggle that the soul has to maintain with the body, to which she is united, which would drag her down and cast her into the depths when she looks at it with too much indulgence and gives credit to its flattering persuasions, which end in violent demands. . . .

Another time, the Lord showed him the state of the lukewarm soul, which tries to pray without mortification. In the middle of a vast field he saw some deep, strong, white foundations, seemingly of marble. A beautiful young man was walking among them, and calling to this person, said to him, "I am the son of a most powerful king, and I have laid these foundations to build a great palace upon them. There you will live and will receive me when I come to visit you, which I shall do often when you have a good room ready for me and open the door when I call, and a time will come when I shall live with you and you will be delighted with my company. You can see how big the palace will be from the size of the foundations. I shall build it, but you must bring the materials." His soul was afflicted, thinking it impossible to fetch so many materials, but seeing his distress, the young man said, "Yes, you can; start bringing something, and I shall help you." This Person began to go, and then stopped after a few steps; he looked at the young man, and found pleasure in the sight of him, but still did not trouble to please him; he felt great respect for him, and knew that he was being watched by him, but yet was not ashamed not to obey him. As he stood there, he saw dust settling on the beautiful foundations, and straw blown by the wind, and from time to time clouds of dust hid them from his sight. Rains also came, carrying filth in their waters, and the foundations were almost covered with mud, in which weeds began to grow; the foundations were eventually so overgrown that only the part on which the young man stood was clear, and then suddenly a dust-storm hid him, and everything was covered with dirt. Afraid at finding himself alone among the rocks and stones, he went down on his knees and wept for his laziness; thinking that the young man was inside the foundations, where the dirt could not touch him, he called out to him with a great cry, saying, "I am coming, Lord, with the materials you asked me to bring; come out so that we may build the palace, because I repent of my laziness which has made me delay so long." Then he was given to understand the vision: the foundations were the virtue of faith and the other virtues which Christ our Lord puts into the soul at Baptism, desiring that we build there a rich palace of the highest perfection, co-operating with him by bringing the materials, which are observance of his precepts and counsels, for the sake of the same Lord, who is the master-builder of the palace. . . .

Again, remembering that God our Lord, when he wished to speak to the prophet Jeremias, commanded him to go into a potter's house, he saw another vision: he went down a ladder into a very light room in which there was a large lump of clay, near which a very venerable old man, with a cloak reaching down to his feet, was walking; as he walked, he broke pieces of clay off the lump and formed them into pots, which he placed on a dresser which seemed to have been carved on his orders: this appeared to indicate that he wished to drink out of them. He saw that some of the pots broke, whereupon the old man threw them to one side, where there was a heap of them; he seemed sad that they should break when he could have prevented them; this person did not understand why he allowed them to break, nor did he dare to ask him, because his whole demeanour was so full of majesty that he could not be asked more than he intended to reveal. He continued to walk up and down the room, looking at all the pots, and when he reached the heap of broken ones, he sometimes reached out and took some, which he mended and put on the dresser; he did not seem to choose which to mend, but always took the ones in front; so the broken pots seemed to be in a continual struggle to get to the front so that they should be seen and taken. And since the Lord later revealed to this person the deep mysteries represented here, he regarded himself as one of these pots, formed from the clay of the human race, fashioned by the hand of God to be placed on the dresser of his glory, but through his own faults broken, losing the wholeness of his first justification. God, in his omnipotence, could have prevented the breakage, but his just designs prevented him from doing so, leaving every man his free will. Seeing himself such a broken vessel, he threw himself on the heap with the others, hoping that the venerable Lord would pass by and look upon him with mercy, and heal him, taking him from that abode of misery to place him among the whole vases, as he did with St Mary Magdalen. . . . (*Spiritual Guide*, Treatise III, Ch. VIII, Para. 2.)

The difference here made between our own imaginings and those we receive ready-made from God, granted that in the latter there is a more captivating liveliness and novelty, is only the difference between our conscious imagination and dreams. In past ages, the products of the unconscious have too readily been attributed to God or the Devil, since they seem to come from outside ourselves and to possess almost superhuman strength. Catholic writers, without going to the other extreme, freely admit the exaggerations made in this respect. The possibility of supernatural visions in dreams is of course not denied, but nowadays more rigorous proofs are needed. And some dreams that we call natural, since they do not seem to surpass natural possibilities, can and should be called gifts of God, and sometimes even special gifts, in the same way that good thoughts can be so called.

The correspondence between Blessed Diego de Cádiz and his confessor contains several accounts of dreams, generally accompanied by a spontaneous explanation of them, though he sometimes asks his confessor what they can mean. He presents a wide range of types of dream: informative, demonstrative, prospective, etc. His whole correspondence shows that he found them a most fruitful means of increasing his devotion and his understanding of dogmas. Here are two examples:

One morning in the Community I began to have a dream and my understanding was shown a sword in its scabbard, with no hilt, in the hands of a man who was both blind and deaf: I soon realized the meaning: *This is preaching without prayer.* Without seeing these things in their true form or through my senses, I understood the rebuke and instruction given me there; the rebuke was merited and the instruction most abundant, though I cannot explain it. I understood the sword to be the grace of preaching, given to me regardless of my merits, which like a sword is difficult to unsheathe and almost completely impossible to wield without a hilt, so I could not use it without praying or trying to pray, that is using the grace given to me for the right purpose. (*Life of Bd Diego José de Cádiz*, by the V. Rev. Sebastián de Ubrique, Seville, 1926, Vol. I, p. 190.)

On the night of the 31st last (Jan.) after a troublesome nightmare, in which I saw myself beset by the Enemy in different guises, defending myself with the *Gloria Patri*, the Holy Name of Jesus, etc., I again fell asleep and dreamt that after wandering along strange, rough tracks, as though on a journey to the Mission, I found myself, I know not how, on top of a very tall tower, set on one side of a gorge, in the depths of which flowed a river.

I was indescribably frightened, because I thought I would fall from the tower. Next to it was an even taller, beautiful building, in which there seemed to be monks. I called out to the Superior to help me in my danger by building scaffolding round the tower, across the gorge, etc. He seemed to reply, but I could not hear his words. Shortly after, I was inside the keep, which was like those the Moors left in some parts of Spain, but it had no staircase nor any other means of getting up or down, outside or inside. Being thus confused, I noticed a window on the side away from the precipice, but this looked over an abyss even deeper than the other, ending in steep gorges, through which the river flowed into the dark distance. To the left of this opening was a little wooden ladder, narrow, with two steps about half a hand wide and somewhat sloping; it moved easily when I touched it, and was held only by the rope which fastened it firmly to a little open terrace, which led to the big building. There were three steps to climb—the two extremely dangerous wooden ones, and a third to the firm terrace. This could evidently not be done without a miracle, but seeing that another Capuchin friar was calling me from the terrace, with someone else whom I could not make out clearly, though fearful of the danger, I decided to leave the weight I was carrying on my shoulders, since I could never climb the steps with it, and so I went back into the middle of the keep. It seemed like a great sack of sand, and I was so weak that I could not take it off until some unseen hand helped me. I returned to the little opening, ready to go up the steps, and at tha moment I awoke, with all my attention riveted on this dream. The bottom of the abyss on the side of the steps was full of corpses of people who had tried to climb them and slipped.

I know I should not investigate the meaning of such matters, but I cannot get out of my mind that the laying down of the sack is the necessary preparation for death by laying down the burden of one's sins, which cannot be accomplished without divine grace, and that death, the step into eternity, is so terrible that only with God's help can one set one's foot on the final safe step. Comparing this dream with the teachings of Faith, I find it corresponds very closely. Its effects are good: devout fear, humble hope, fervent prayer, particularly at Mass, when it made me search for an explanation. It is now my usual subject for meditation in prayer: only to think of putting my foot on the third step fills my whole soul with joy, and the thought of the first fills it with fear. I seem to see myself falling into the abyss, for lack of courage to put my foot on the second step, and so between fear and hope, devotion is always with me. (*Ibid.*, pp. 538 ff.)

Of all saints, or at least of all modern saints, St John Bosco must be the one in whose life dreams have played the largest part. In many of his dreams there is no need to see special divine intervention, but in some of them—the prophetic ones in particular—one must. Oneirically, he was evidently a particularly gifted person (a "good dreamer") and, whatever his destiny, would almost certainly have had abundant and interesting dreams, but here it is the religious functions of dreams that concern us, and their didactic function in particular.

The basis of the logical arrangements of thought that take place in the unconscious and emerge in dreams, sometimes in surprising and felicitous ways, must, to my mind, be sought in the *habitus primorum principiorum intelligibilium* ("habit of first intelligible principles"). These parallel that *judgement* discussed earlier, which is the *habitus primorum principiorum operabilium* ("habit of first practicable principles, or principles of what is practicable"). That is, there is a judgement applying to the cognitive world, as there is an ethical judgement applying to the operative world. These first principles, embedded in the very nature of our cognitive faculty, govern and uphold the reasoning processes by which we acquire many other derived principles which, like the first ones, also have power to organize, consciously or unconsciously, everything about which we can think, practical or theoretical.

There is one difficulty to be solved before going on: the theoretic-didactic function can often have an objective theme, but some writers maintain that the meaning of dreams is always subjective. Georg Siegmund says in his book *Der Traum*, "The true presupposition on which interpretation of dreams must be based is that the images that appear in them do not mean what they show, but are symbols of subjective realities" (p. 74). The answer to this is that it is often, and even generally, true, but not absolutely: experience can contradict it. For example, those dreams of which one hears so often, in which a scientific problem is solved, or a business worry resolved, surely have an objective content? And those great transcendental dreams about the origin of the world surely solve a problem as much as any others? There is quite a list of inventions that have been made in dreams. Poincaré, the mathematician, has related one example which happened to him. The philosopher Magnan used to write out his current problems and place them under his pillow, to see if his dreams could solve them, as he had found they sometimes did. Caramuel, we have seen, found new arguments in his dreams, and Jerónimo Gracián makes the same claim. The present writer once found the obvious explanation of strange symptoms in one of his patients in a dream. Generally speaking, the principle that dreams provide the same experiences as waking life has been found fundamental, singularly rewarding, and in agreement with experience: so one can have dreams of games, business, conscience, politics, geography and mathematics; theoretical and practical dreams, retrospective and prospective, profane and religious, physiological and spiritual dreams, etc. So there are also both objective and subjective dreams.

The universality of dream subjectivism can, however, be admitted in one respect: for something to emerge in a dream, it must obviously be already in us. The same is true of knowledge: it may have an objective content, but it always has the subjective condition of being a "knowing", that is, a vital act on the part of the subject. One can go further: for a dream to exist supposes not only a certain preparation or occasion for dealing with some problem on the part of the dreamer, but a preoccupation with it, or interest in it. So the way to make the unconscious speak about something is to be interested in that thing. This would appear to be the psychological basis of those ancient oracles in which the gods were consulted through dreams: incubation dreams. The mere fact of coming to the temple and lying down there to sleep, in expectation of the reply, was one way of provoking the oneiric function. But as dreams are by definition the realm of the unexpected, interest is far from being an infallible promoter. Dreams often appear as a result of the development of curious, insignificant germs of thought left forgotten in the marginal zones of waking consciousness, making us wonder how on earth we came to have that dream. Dreams, in fact, sometimes seem to take a delight in deceiving our conscious expectations.

84. *Prospective function*

The prospective function attempts to find solutions for the future. As such, it is nothing but an aspect of all the functions: those already discussed have been seen to have their prospective moments. But prospection must be considered apart here, for it has great practical importance. The unconscious, when it looks into the future, is only continuing the work of the conscious, and both are merely fulfilling one of life's primordial functions: teleology. When some part hurts, attention is concentrated on it; when something is loved or wanted, thoughts tend towards it; when something is feared, worries and energies converge on it. The conscious can become infatuated or over-distracted and fail to see dangers that threaten; the unconscious—the "heart"—will have a dark presentiment of them, without being able to make the conscious aware of this; during sleep, its fears will occupy the stage which the day's cares and distractions have vacated, and find means of expressing themselves. The dangers that the conscious fails to see, or refuses to recognize, are often inner dangers, of an affective nature (and so ignored by rationalistic, extroverted minds), and if the unconscious warning is not heeded in good time they can often produce profound mental disturbances and lead to great distress.

They may also be the dangers of nascent illness, spotted in some corner of our organism by the unconscious reception of signals so faint and ambiguous that the conscious cannot perceive them, and amplified under the calm mantle of sleep into ill-omened phantasmagoria. Classical and medieval authors recount numerous cases of such dreams, such as that of a man who, soon after dreaming that he was struck on the ear, went deaf. So from the time of Hippocrates onwards—and almost certainly earlier—dreams have been studied to diagnose illnesses.

Sometimes, if the conscious is set on one particular course, dreams tell it in a thousand different ways that it is the wrong one, as reality later proves. Marginal perceptions have realized its wrongness, but the conscious, concentrated on stronger perceptions, has not heeded their warning; the unconscious retains some trace of them, and this, sanctioned by the vital processes, emerges in dreams in the shape of some fantasy or other. Jung has produced many convincing examples of this, such as the man who dreamt that he was walking along a road, when he met a dragon in the shape of a huge crab blocking his path. Analysis revealed how opportune the dream had been.

This function naturally operates in spiritual life. Georg Siegmund quotes one case from early Christian times: In Constantinople, Evagrius was desperately in love with a married woman, and unconsciously repressed any conscious attempt to face up to the dangers of his situation. One night he dreamt he was in a dark prison, when an angel appeared to him and said: "You will die here, unless you leave Constantinople at once". The dream made such an impression on him that he immediately fled to Jerusalem. Later he realized that the prison was the disorderly passion to which he was enslaved, and the darkness the blindness of mind it produced in him. His conscious obviously wanted to show him this, but there is none so deaf as he who will not hear. But his oneiric function with its greater independence was able to give such a drastic exposé of his true situation that he was forced to take the necessary resolution.

It is worth pointing out that although prospective dreams generally refer to the dreamer, they occasionally relate to other people. It is possible to dream of some harm befalling someone one loves, or one's country. Martín del Río, in his *Disquisiciones Mágicas*, relates the apparently prophetic dreams of a good woman of Brussels at the end of the sixteenth century, which foretold disastrous ends for several people—ends they shortly met. People were astonished, and the author tells that Justus Lipsius discussed the case with him, inclining to the view that natural dreams can have the prophetic instinct attributed to them from earliest times. Martín del Río, on the other hand, was inclined to think that these were cases of natural foresight, for which the woman had in fact sufficient evidence. Except in her dreams, however, she could not combine and evaluate the different pieces of information she possessed. He also admits that the Devil, who cannot foretell actions involving man's free will, since only God can know them, can however, with his superior intelligence, make prognostications based on probability and communicate his predictions to certain people in dreams.

Jung's *Psychologie und Religion*, the memoirs of Frau Wackernagel, the lives of Bd Diego de Cádiz, Mother María de la Encarnación and above all of St John Bosco, all provide striking examples of how dreams indicate the stages reached in spiritual life. Many other saints, and of course many other people too, have had notable dreams. It is not in vain that the unconscious plays such an important part in religious life.

V.   DREAMS AS A SOURCE OF ENERGY

85.   *The cross of the spiritual director*

The spiritual director's most frequent lament must be the little result his advice seems to produce in his penitents. This does not come from

the penitent's lack of knowledge of what he ought to do, but his lack
of will-power to do it. Many people reach, as St Ignatius says, "a
certain degree of contentment of soul", and then stick there. They
reach a state of mediocrity, bordering on lukewarmness, if not actually
that. Or the confessor may find that despite their obvious good will,
clearly shown in many other ways, his penitents seem to suffer from a
physical inability to correct particular faults. These may be cases of mild
neurosis, or of declared obsessions (of which the much-discussed
"scruples" are a form), which can keep a grip on souls for years and
years. Or they may be hardened sinners, or people who lack the restless
spirit needed to pose their religious problems effectively, or who feel
themselves held back by a strange resistance or by an inadequate concept
of religion, or who have theoretical difficulties they cannot overcome.
In all these cases their process of religious maturation (which has still
to be fully confronted with Jung's process of individuation) is being
held back by an invisible force. They may reason with themselves, or
priests may exhort them, for as long as they please, but they remain in
their morass of apathy. Every confessor must have known many such
penitents.

It is all too easy to say, "Their time of grace has not yet come".
Grace is of course the basic ingredient in sanctification. But is this
always the real reason for their failure? Cannot mediocrity be prolonged despite abundant grace? And can one not be unfaithful to grace?
If one cannot, then there is no such thing as responsibility. The roots
of this spiritual laziness and apathy are very hard to find and cure, since
they are to be found at the same time in the heights of grace and in the
depths of the unconscious. But if the proverb "God helps those who
help themselves" is any guide to conduct, spiritual direction must
follow it too, and not only pray for divine help, but also investigate the
ways in which it can make use of the natural powers that God means
men to use in the task, common to God and man, which we call
"sanctification". *Facienti quod est in se Deus non denegat gratiam*, "God
will not refuse his grace to the man who does what is in him to do".
The problem is how to make the man do *as much* as is in him. Modern

psychotherapy can help here, since its function is precisely to remedy those extreme cases in which human endeavour is crumbling. Mental analysis has learnt how to penetrate into the depths of the psyche, to stimulate them and release energies (which are sometimes tremendous) confined there by the play of psychic conflicts. So it is often not a question of lack of energy, but of how to utilize existing energy, how to direct it towards a useful end, in this case personal sanctification. Charles Baudouin has hit the nail on the head in entitling two of his books *La mobilisation de l'énergie* and *La force en nous*. All Jung's works contain suggestive pages on this subject, particularly *Über die Energetik der Seele—On the Energy of the Soul*. This has in fact been the dominant idea behind all modern psychotherapy since the middle of the last century, and more so since Freud.

86. *The need for psychological knowledge*

One obviously cannot expect every spiritual director to be an expert psychotherapist, but it must be recognized that his professional know-ledge should, in fact must, include some psychological training. In fact, to fulfil its task completely, spiritual direction must be able to satisfy innumerable demands, and so there has long been a lack of good directors. Psychology, of course, is only one item here, but in one way or other, under one name or another, it is indispensable. The type of psychology most concerned with the problem we are discussing here —lack of will-power—is depth psychology. Its original clinical aim was to understand and alleviate mental problems, and a vast amount of study has led to conclusions which spiritual direction must assimilate if it is to be worthy of its task. Not that one must fall into the trap of equating spiritual direction with psychotherapy, although confessors have been called "doctors of the soul" for centuries, and were the chief exponents of what psychotherapy then was. Up to a certain point this is inevitable, since, as Jung says, all religion is a psychotherapy. But today the word denotes a more technical and specialized profession. Baudouin says that medicine acts on physical causes; education, spiritual direction and philosophy appeal to reason and the conscious will; while psychotherapy deals in the intermediate zone of involuntary psychic forces. So in its strictest sense it is a technical manipulation of psychic determinism. In practice, however, this division of man into zones must not be carried too far. There can be no doubt that education, spiritual direction, and any leadership of men, must often handle unconscious and determinist energies. Psychotherapy, too, must co-ordinate the resources of reason (Frankl's logotherapy is this and something more), and if necessary must apply physical medicines. *The whole man* must be taken into account.

87. *Instincts and images*

One of the central truths of depth psychology is that the primary instincts (higher and lower) and the tendencies derived from them, which form our stock of energy, find their way towards the under-standing and the will through the imagination. Theoretically this must be so, since the imagination occupies a border zone between sense and spirit. So *psychic forces are closely linked to images*. Sometimes these images have a primary, direct connection with them, as in the case of those that represent the natural objects of the instincts; then on top of this basic lot of connections between tendencies and images a very complex system is gradually built up, in accordance with the laws of displace-ment of psychic energy studied by psychoanalysis and by reflexology. Hence when a tendency becomes active, a hidden synergism produces certain images in the imagination. And vice versa: when certain images are formed in the imagination, the connected tendencies are invariably aroused. The play of conditioned reflexes and displacements of psychic energy can cause energies from different sources to converge on the same image, collecting there as though in a reservoir; it can also leave some images devoid of energy. Both types of image emerge in dreams, but when the conscious relinquishes its hold on the imaginative flow, the images charged with energy (and consequently with affectivity) will clearly benefit, and emerge either more often or in a more central position. To be precise, the inductor mechanism of images is not only that of laws of association, but also (or more) that of *affective homotonality*: images charged with the same affect attract each other. These images in which many tendencies combine are *symbols* (in the psychotherapeutic sense), representations of combinations or groups of tendencies.

88. *Symbols: nodes of energy*

When they express universal combinations, these symbols can be common to all mankind: these are the archetypes of the collective unconscious discovered and studied by Jung. But symbols are more commonly subjective. They are the strategic nodes that bind the individual system of energy together: that is, individual combinations. So one can see the importance of finding these privileged centres in order to stimulate energy in cases of spiritual apathy. Now the realm of dreams, as has just been shown, is a particularly favourable place in which to find them, if one is capable of making an adequate analysis. Clinical records of psychotherapeutic treatment show that during the course dreams reflect the movements of psychic energy, and even become the means whereby much of this energy is liberated and canalized. There is no need to stress the dynamic quality of symbols, since this is elementary knowledge in modern psychology. However, there is a passage from Aeppli, a disciple of Jung, that might well be quoted here:

Part of this liberated current of psychic energy has already been experienced by the dreamer, as the meaning of his dreams became gradually clearer during interpretation. We know where this torrent of energy comes from: it springs in the energetic field of the symbol and flows into us when our dreams acquire conscious status. We have already indicated that collective psychic energies have formed the general human symbol, and at the same time have poured themselves into the glass of these created images, which are and enclose concentrated psychic energy. Using a technical simile, we could compare this to a powerful accumulator, and say that the symbol is a

o

great transformer of these psychic energies, and that the connection energizes us. If the symbol is correctly interpreted, the archetype broken down into its component elements, the action of the dream completely explained in analysis, and if the oneiric meaning and the conscious are compared to each other, then the symbolic argument of the dream can no longer hold the forces that formed it together. Once dreams have been "solved", they set their psychic energy free, and it flows into the dreamer's conscious.[14]

And if it flows into his conscious then it flows into his will and into action. So what cannot be obtained from the conscious by the theoretically most convincing reason , can be procured by immobilizing energies that are irrational, but reconcilable with reason. As St Anselm said: *Non in dialectica complacuit sibi Deus salvos facere homines*, "God was not pleased to save men by dialectics". At least not always. Nor can imagination be said to be a help in difficulties; in mental prayer it can be used to form scenes externally comparable to those of dreams, but these do not touch the heart in the same way. The scenes must not be mere images, but symbols, images charged with psychic energy, like those that so often appear in dreams. This enables dreams to move us more easily, and they are helped by other characteristics: their intense impression of reality, the passive state in which we receive them, free from the adverse criticism that destroys so many conscious processes; the absolute concentration, free from all distractions, with which they are received; the shock of surprise produced by their unexpectedness; and the feeling of mystery and supernatural intervention produced by the prodigies they set before us. All these characteristics, added to the central fact of psychic energy, contribute to shake us out of our affective neutrality. Only a reasonable conscious assimilation after the dream is needed if we are to benefit from all these advantages, and this we can make by ourselves or under the guidance of a competent spiritual director.

14. E. Aeppli, *El lenguaje de los sueños*, Barcelona, 1946, p. 223.

VI. CONDITIONS AND LIMITATIONS

89. *Limitations on the part of the nature of dreams*

The first and most fundamental limitation is that the normal means of directing human life to its proper ends is the conscious mind, understanding and will, which occupies the responsible centre of our being and makes us persons. The invasion of the conscious by the unconscious eventually leads to madness, through intermediate states which become more morbid with the progressive invasion by the unconscious.

Since sleep is an unconscious state, Jackson and Moreau de Tours have been able to advance the hypothesis of a parallel between sleep and madness, distinguishing the different levels of dissolution in both states and thereby explaining the difference in behaviour they imply So sleep would be a physiologically normal, transitory period of madness. From which it follows that dreams, the typical product of this unconscious state, are not the function best qualified to regulate conscious conduct.

Jung has recently written a surprising confirmation of this point of view:

Many people with some, but insufficient, knowledge of dreams and their significance, are easily led by the sight of their refined and tendentious compensations to believe that the dream function does in fact pursue a moral end, that it warns, admonishes, consoles, preaches, etc. Believing in the omniscience of the unconscious, they willingly assign to their dreams the initiative for taking necessary decisions. So their disillusion is increased when they find that their dreams become progressively more insignificant. Experience has taught me that a little knowledge of dream psychology produces a tendency to exaggerate the importance of the unconscious, to the detriment of conscious decision. It should not be forgotten that the unconscious only functions satisfactorily when the conscious is fulfilling its role to the limits of its ability. Then dreams may perhaps add what is still lacking or lend a helping hand when our best efforts have failed.[15]

15. C. G. Jung, "De la nature des rêves", *Revue Ciba*, Sept., 1945, p. 1612.

Anyone familiar with Jung's works, and the frequently exaggerated importance he gives to the unconscious as opposed to the conscious, particularly in the realm of ordering behaviour, must feel surprised at some of the remarks in this passage. Its tone is harsh—perhaps too harsh, if I may be allowed to criticize so great an authority. Having read his works assiduously, I must confess to finding him extremely paradoxical and even self-contradictory in many places. I should say that his reduction of the dream function to such an extent must be a consequence of his earlier excessive attachment to a vitalist philosophy, according to which the last word on life must be sought in life itself, and particularly in its most uncontaminated manifestations, such as the unconscious and dreams. But if one prefers reason enlightened by faith as a guide to behaviour, and regards dreams as valuable only in so far as they assist reason in its guiding mission, Jung's disavowal of them here must still seem excessive. So I should take it as meaning this: dreams are not the final arbiter in the direction of life, but an occasional help to the conscious.

We have seen that reason is not absent from all dreams and that to look for what is reasonable in them, to sift and assimilate this by reason, is not a departure from the principle that the active conscious holds the central responsibility for the development of the personality and the attainment of the ultimate ends of life. So for ordinary spiritual direction the normal function is, by the very nature of things, the conscious. But to turn, under the guidance of reason, to the unconscious to see what it can give in exceptional cases, when all conscious resources have been exhausted, or for any other valid reason, is only to make reasonable use of the resources that God himself has given us. The conscious should aim at the maturation of the whole human being, external and internal, mental, affective and operative. The Church often gives examples of the use of a-rational (not anti-rational) ponderables and imponderables, since all these factors influence life, and religious life in particular. If dreams have not till recently been used as much as now seems feasible, this is because their study is a recent development.

These are the general limitations that can be deduced *a priori* from the nature of dreams. But in spiritual direction actual cases must decide and the most important factor is the penitent himself.

90. *Limitations on the part of the penitent*

These can also be decisive. For example, some people have a constitutionally excessive communication between their conscious and unconscious. They are on the way to a psychotic state, which is the end of this road. In such cases anyone who tried to cultivate an intensification of unconscious activity would be running a grave risk—of regression to a lower form of mental life. The correct course would be rather to stimulate the conscious, tactfully, and teach it to deal adequately with its hypertrophied unconscious; this will demand particular study and prudence. Other cases present the opposite: people who are habitually excessive extroverts, with very little sense of inner realities. Here the danger is less and, to begin with, dreams can even be a means of leading them to Christ, the ultimate goal of all. Many authorities agree that in dealing with children, one should not use dreams. Generally speaking, I think this should be extended to include young people. According to Jung, the disposition towards having valuable dreams increases in the second half of life. Of course many people are led to believe that they do not dream by an inveterate habit of despising and forgetting their dreams. Practice can make them see that this is not so. At a mature age, then, always bearing the person's habitual disposition in mind, his dreams may be useful, unless there are reasons indicating that they will not be.

To pass from *habitual dispositions* to *actual states* in particular: this activation of the intercommunication between the conscious and the unconscious—which is permanent only in a few people—may occur in others, who are otherwise quite normal, in times of illness or of moral crisis. They may then have striking dreams which they cannot forget, and which will make them meditate on hitherto neglected problems in their lives, or on death and the next world, or on a better approach to their religion. If the spiritual director finds his penitent of his own accord telling him a dream that has impressed him, he may, if he is adequately prepared, obtain surprising results. He would be wrong to oppose a preconceived idea that this way is useless; it can be a vehicle of divine grace, and many advantages can come through it. By refusing to consider the dream, he would be defrauding his penitent.

Up till now I have been speaking of spiritual direction in the strict sense, and not of psychotherapy. But as the same person can be at once penitent and mental patient, there is the problem of cases in which psychotherapeutic treatment should be considered, either concurrent with spiritual direction or not. Generally speaking, the priest should not dabble in psychotherapy. But in practice, and if all the necessary considerations have been taken into account: preparation, permission, aptitude, etc., there may sometimes be pressing reasons why he should. There might not be a sufficiently capable or sufficiently Christian psychotherapist in the district, for example; or the person might refuse to confide in anyone except the priest. In such cases the priest would be running a grave risk if he either left the patient without treatment or sent him to someone who might do him more harm than good.

In any of the cases so far mentioned, the special dangers that this "descent to the depths", giving as it does official recognition to dreams —though controlled by faith and reason—represents for the individual in question should not be forgotten. They are, for example, that attributing too much importance to dreams can produce a tendency to live in a world of fantasy; that violent temptations may be unleashed; or that he may become aware of instincts which, if he lacks the maturity to understand and direct them, were better kept from his knowledge. A certain mental limitation, or lack of psychological sense, involving the inability to appreciate these inner realities, should also be a warning to the spiritual director not to use dreams. In all cases, the dangers of switching from spiritual direction proper to psychotherapy should not be minimized, particularly with women whose mental balance is not perfect.

91. *Limitations on the part of the director*

The limitations on the part of the director are no less numerous. Here more than ever the distinction between *spiritual direction* proper (including a certain use of dreams) and *psychotherapeutic treatment* must be kept in mind. The latter obviously requires special ability, technical knowledge, and adequate professional training. It also requires that the spiritual director and the treating psychotherapist should not be the same person. Psychotherapeutic treatment is one of the most delicate of all operations, since it comes so close to religion and morals on one hand, and handles forces that can be devastating on the other. If only one person in a thousand will make a doctor, only one in ten thousand will make a psychotherapist. The type of treatment he gives will be influenced not only by his scientific and technical knowledge, but also by his personality and ideology.

This choice of a spiritual director is equally important, as the authorities are never tired of saying. If one adds the special require-ments needed to interpret dreams to the general requirements (already numerous enough), it follows that they can only be used in a limited number of cases. If every director needs spirituality, mature judgement and discernment, knowledge of asceticism and mysticism, experience, etc., then the director who can be trusted to handle such an ambiguous, dangerous and treacherous instrument as dreams needs even more than these qualities. As to whether the confessor should be expected to master the didactic analysis generally required to practise psycho-therapy, I should say definitely not, for reasons I shall explain.

92. *Limitations on the part of spiritual progress*

The final series of limitations in the use of dreams in spiritual direction consists of those imposed by the phase of spiritual development through which the penitent is passing. St John of the Cross continually insists on the need to free the soul from all attachments of the senses in order to arrive at spiritual union with God. The use of sensory images and the figures of the imagination are a step forward, and this should not be forgotten if one is not to slip backwards, but once their mission has been fulfilled, they should be abandoned in favour of a purely spiritual approach. In the *Ascent of Mount Carmel*, St John of the Cross explains the different steps and the moments at which they must be made. In the early stages it is as useful to concentrate on images that lead one forward as it is harmful to pay exclusive attention to them in the later stages, when their time is past. To those who object that it is God who sends imaginative visions even to those well advanced in spirituality, and that it seems wrong to want to correct God by regarding them as unimportant, he replies that they produce their effect in two ways: the mere fact of experiencing them gives them a direct, automatic effect, even without reflecting on them; and they can have an effect through conscious meditation and reasoned assimilation. So that even though one pays no conscious attention to them, they can still be effective. This distinction is also valid in the case of ordinary, natural dreams. A dream is completely used only when full memory, compression and integration into the whole personality are added to the immediate experience. But this only happens with a tiny fraction of all the dreams we have. Most of them are totally forgotten and their effect is limited to the immediate impression they make on the unconscious. This effect may be a mood, vague desire, relief or worry, etc., felt on waking, without our knowing where it comes from. These forgotten dreams come to act as a sort of internal psychic secretion, formed in the unconscious and flowing back into it. But there can be no doubt that they thereby perform an important function: auto-regulation of psychic equilibrium.

VII.   BASIS OF A PRACTICAL METHOD OF UTILIZING DREAMS IN SPIRITUAL
DIRECTION

93.   *Various possible methods*

In the use of dreams, I repeat, one must distinguish between the more or less empirical *educative method*, based on a sort of psychological common sense, and the technical *psychotherapeutic method*. Between the two there could be an *intermediate method*, using definite psychological knowledge for formative purposes. The educative methods are called "directives", and include spiritual direction. Strictly psychotherapeutic methods are called "non-directives", since their basic task is to handle psychic forces. I must also repeat that strict psychotherapeutic treatment of the mentally ill falls outside the scope of these considerations. I am dealing only with *educative* techniques, in the sense of developing, from the potentialities of the person being educated, by his own action in particular, the ideal forms to which one aspires. So educative technique must be the technique of helping the person to help himself, of stimulating his own inner life. It must not consist merely of commands, prohibitions, punishments, exhortations, explanations, advice, warnings, etc., but must try, by all the means at its disposal, to make use of all the potential good in the person being educated, to exclude the potential evil, and to lead the forces that exist in him towards a happy union between subjective impulses and the objective law.

In certain cases, we have seen, dreams can help to further this aim. What qualifications must the spiritual director possess? There is a very wide range of possibilities between the highly specialized qualifications the psychotherapist must possess, in view of the responsibility of his work, and the minimum capability needed to utilize dreams on an empirical educative basis. Prudence counsels one not to undertake any task for which one is not qualified. If the director lacks even this minimum knowledge, he should not use dreams at all. If he possesses the minimum, he could use it to give a sort of accommodating interpretation of dreams with a view to deriving spiritual benefit from them, provided that they offer sufficient basis for doing so. This practice has long been widespread, is so now, and always will be.

94. *Accommodating interpretation*

Does this idea seem intolerable in view of the present state of oneirology? That depends on how it is understood. I would compare this accommodating interpretation with its equivalent in biblical texts. All spiritual books are full of accommodating biblical considerations. Preaching and spiritual direction, prayer and contemplation, have made, and still make, extensive use of accommodating interpretations. This notwithstanding the fact that biblical studies have reached a very high standard and are capable of providing a far more truthful interpretation based on the real meaning of the texts. But in any sort of assimilation, and particularly in matters of religion and morals, the subjective factor is decisive: *Quidquid recipitur, ad modum recipientis recipitur,* "Whatever is received, is received in the manner of the recipient". If an accommodating interpretation is received with faith it will be effective, even though the original meaning may be something else. Our Lord will say to the soul, *Fides tua salvum te fecit,* "Thy faith has made thee whole". Naturally, the interpretation, based on an accommodated text, is supposed true and known from other sources.

This can be applied to dreams. The truths taught through a simple, unscientific interpretation of the dreams are—this is the hypothesis— truths based on faith or reason. So there is no need to be afraid of going astray in this respect. Whether they have a greater or lesser effect on the penitent, through the subjective forces latent in the dream, will depend on the success of the interpretation, and the extent to which it is practicable. So the more knowledge the director has in this respect, the better. If one thinks of the vast mass of psychological cultural, mythological, historical, religious, ritualistic, and alchemistic knowledge, not to mention general knowledge of anything that concerns the symbolizing activity of man, that Jung considers specifically necessary in order to interpret dreams, one might be tempted to condemn as too simple my requirements of a modest amount of psychological and, in particular, analogical sense, as all that is necessary for an effective interpretation of dreams on a spiritually formative level. But I am only putting these forward as minimum *initial* requirements.

95. *Multivalence of dreams*

Jung and others maintain another possible objection: that the uncon-

scious knows exactly what it means; hence, if its meaning is wrongly
interpreted, it will not accept the interpretation, and no energy is
mobilized. I would not deny this, but add the following observation:
that dreams can be interpreted in several different ways, is a well-
established psychological fact, but this does not mean that any interpretation will do. Not all dreams are the same, just as not all situations
or problems are the same. In some cases the unconscious wants only a
few things, or perhaps only one; in others it will want many, to fit its
many different levels, and whichever is offered will be absorbed into
the circuit or circuits of energy that the dream represents in its symbols.
Finally, it must be recognized that the psyche in general has a fluidity
and even ambiguity which often makes some instincts appear to take
the place of others. This fact, and the ease with which psychic energy is
transferred by analogy from one object to another, form the basis of a
very wide multivalence. It is just this that enables each school to find
what it wants in dreams—its own preconceived theory. It was Jung who
declared that this was the worst failing of Freudian analysis: that
starting with the associations suggested by elements in *one dream*, it
arrived at the combination X and took this as proof that this combination X was the true latent meaning of the dream, without considering
what the dream taken as a whole might mean. But this same combination would have been reached by associations beginning with anything,
since any point of departure can be made to furnish a chain of associations leading unfailingly to the required combination. Jung himself
proved this by "interpreting" a trivial municipal announcement. I am
not saying this to assert that dreams may mean anything, but to show
that they do leave the interpreter ample space in which to manoeuvre.[16]

96. *St Teresa's confessor on dreams*

An historical example of some interest is Fr Jerónimo Gracián, a
Carmelite of the early days of St Teresa's reform of the Order, whom

16. See Jung, *Modern Man in Search of a Soul.*

she praises highly. In Dialogue 15 of his *Peregrinación de Anastasio*
(*Works* in Bib. Mist. Carmelita, Vol. III, p. 238) he enumerated twelve
principal ways of the spirit, which are like "twelve inner windows
letting good desires and light into the will". The tenth of these is:

The dreams which come to a sleeping person. These are of three
kinds: one kind is natural, born of the vapours rising from the
stomach to the brain and arousing or awaking phantasms, or inner
images of the phantasy, and placing them in the imagination; and
because these images are thrown together casually without order or
concert, *it is a sin to believe in dreams.*

Other dreams come from the guardian angel who joins these same
inner figures with order and concert and presents them to the
imagination; they are generally of hidden things, or prophecy, such
as when the angel spoke in dreams to Joseph, spouse of the Virgin
Mary; the dreams of Joseph the Patriarch, son of Jacob; those of
Pharaoh, Nabuchodonosor, etc.

Other dreams are evil, sent by the devil, and often show obscene
images, and some stir up the humours of the body and provoke
sensual movement, against which the Church sings: *Procul recedant
somnia, et noctium phantasmata, hostemque nostrum comprime, ne
polluantur corpora* ("Remove dreams and nocturnal phantasies from
me, and restrain our enemy so that our bodies be not sullied").

What has often happened to me in this respect is that I have not
investigated fully whether my dream was from my good angel, or
from the devil, or natural, but have taken advantage of it on waking
if it was good, and put it out of my memory if it was bad, in accordance with that rule given by St Paul: *Omnia probate, quod bonum
est tenete, ab omni specie mala abstinete vos* ("You must scrutinize all
carefully, retaining only what is good, and rejecting all that has a
look of evil about it") (I Thess. 5. 21-22).

I have often happened to dream that I was arguing in the Schools,
and have remembered the argument, found it excellent, and taken
it to its conclusions. I have also dreamt that I was sinning and con-
fessing my sins, and examining my conscience with regard to hidden
and intricate sins, and remembering my dreams, I have been able to

write a good number of cases of conscience from it. Also I have dreamt that I was awake and that it was not a dream, and this at first made me very unhappy, but afterwards I have remembered the dream on account of the nonsense that was mingled with this thought, and have then realized it was a dream and been relieved of my anxiety. I have also dreamt that I was dying and going to hell for my sins, and this dream has prompted me to repentance and to make a general confession. Not long ago I dreamt that I was in my death agony and trying to perform heroic inner acts and to make the highest and firmest resolutions that I could, and on awaking from that dream I spent a great part of the night continuing to make the same resolution, which gave me very beneficial prayer, and remembering that rule of St Paul which I have quoted, I do not worry about my dreams, nor about those which others tell me they have had. When I was among the Turks, some renegades used to come to me and tell me their dreams, because those who follow the sect of Mahomet attach great importance to their dreams and seek out learned men to interpret them. And if the dream was nonsense, I would interpret it as meaning they should return to the faith of Christ, fleeing from those lands and returning to Catholic lands to save themselves; and by such interpretations I persuaded some to do this, and so succeeded in my aim of saving those souls.

He gave the same opinion to St Teresa concerning her visions: that if they were beneficial, not to worry whether they came from God or the devil. By beneficial he means anything that agrees with the Gospel teaching (*Ibid.*, p. 254).

This is a case of accommodating interpretation which pays more attention to the extreme *ad quem* (something known to be good for the soul) than to the extreme *a quo*, perhaps the real message from the unconscious, but of course respecting the actual content, without which there could be no talk of interpretation. This is the minimum grade of utilizing dreams in spiritual direction. Several of the dreams he relates are obviously good and religious in content: acts of virtue, struggles of conscience, going to hell, etc., and can be spiritually assimilated directly, without any difficulty. But many other dreams

that seventy years ago would have been dismissed as nonsense or
enigmas, can today be turned to spiritual advantage, with adequate
knowledge of the technique of interpretation. And naturally this
improved knowledge will allow greater respect for the term *a quo* as
well as better application of the term *ad quem*.

97. *Everything can be useful*

The task is made easier by the variety of ways in which a dream can
be interpreted. But the educative principle basic to all psychotherapy
holds that this direction of a dream towards a spiritual end will be
more effective if the director tries not to impose his interpretation, but
to make the penitent produce his own. With a little practice, dreams
will always lead to their own interpretation, or at least a possible
interpretation. Like so many other human experiences with an energy
content, dreams are like winds blowing a ship. But the same wind will
blow some ships into harbour and not others; it depends on how the
sails and rudder are set. The sails and the rudder are of course the higher
conscious faculties. Here spiritual direction must help the penitent to
be able to help himself, with God's grace. The psychological principle
of the multivalence of dreams is paralleled, to make the task easier, by the
spiritual principle laid down by St Paul: *Diligentibus Deum omnia
cooperantur in bonum* ("All things do good to those who love God").
If the director never loses sight of the aim of spiritual life—divine
charity—and encourages it in his disciple as much as he can, he will
find a way to make the dreams he has to interpret co-operate for the
good of the soul.

98. *Through creatures to the Creator*

There is another principle more directly concerned with dreams in
relation to spiritual direction: the relation of certain archetypes (one

might almost say all sensory images) to God or something related to God. It is Jung's great achievement to have discovered and studied the divine archetype as a psychic reality. Being an empirical psychologist, he leaves it there, for philosophers and theologians to find out what objective reality corresponds to this archetype, as the eye corresponds to light. When one knows that God created man in his own image and likeness, and that he is man's ultimate destiny, it seems only right that he should be manifested in man's whole being, in his conscious faculties and in the archetypes of his unconscious.

The whole visible creation is sown with analogies and reflections of God, the *logoi spermaticoi* of St Justin, the *rationes seminales* of the Latin Fathers. This is the concept to which St John of the Cross gives poetic expression in his *Spiritual Canticle*:

> Diffusing showers of grace
> In haste among these groves his path he took,
> And only with his face,
> Glancing around the place
> Has clothed them in his beauty with a look.

So the language of the unconscious, and therefore the language of dreams, is essentially analogical, drawing on the infinite variety of figures offered to it by creation, figures which are traces and likenesses of God. Surely it must be possible for the soul to use these figures in its progress towards God, if God put them there for that purpose? God is pure spirit and man is spirit incarnate, bound by the world of sense; to attract man to him, God adapts himself graciously to his nature, in accordance with the theological principle that God *Omnia movet secundum modum eorum*, "moves each thing according to its nature".

St John of the Cross says:

According to these principles, therefore, is it clear that if God is to move and raise the soul from its extreme of lowness to the other extreme of his exaltedness, he will do it in a manner orderly and gentle to the soul. Now since the order by which the soul knows is

made with the forms and images of created things, and since its
way of knowing and understanding is through the senses, it follows
that for God to raise the soul to the supreme knowledge, if he is
to do it gently, he must start from the very lowness of the soul's
senses in order to raise it up in its own manner to the other extreme
of his spiritual wisdom, which the senses cannot grasp. (*Ascent*,
Bk II, Ch. 17, No. 3.)

All spiritual writers say the same, following St Paul himself:
*Invisibilia enim ipsius a creatura mundi per ea quae facta sunt intellecta
conspiciuntur*, "Men have caught sight of his invisible nature as it is
known through his creatures". (Rom. 1. 20.)

Here then, is a first step in spiritual dream-interpretation, with its
theological and psychological bases.

99. *For a more rigorous interpretation*

To decide what a more scientific use of dreams for the same spiritual
purpose should consist of, one might take, for example, Aeppli's book
The Language of Dreams, strip it of all traces of psychologist-vitalist-
naturalist ideology, and reduce it to a purely scientific manual of
oneiromancy. If it were then applied to spiritual direction, it would
give us what we are looking for. It would have to be applied in such a
way as to ensure the maximum adaptation of the two extremes in
question, psychic realities and the aims of spiritual direction. But
evidently one reading, or several, of a book like this would still not
be sufficient to render one fully capable. A deep study of all psychology
would be needed, and then sufficient practice on oneself and others to
obtain a sure feeling for psychic reality. Solid philosophical and theological foundations are even more necessary, to distinguish the numerous
serious religious errors in much modern psychological writing,
particularly in depth psychology, which has paid most attention to
dreams. Knowledge of asceticism and mysticism is also needed; this is
the spiritual director's technical knowledge, and it must be deep both

in theory and practice. Anyone who could satisfy all these requirements would be able to produce the ideal method of using dreams in spiritual direction. Needless to say, neither do I possess such qualities, nor can I list any details of them here: that would need several volumes.

100. *Rules and principles*

To make such a vague conclusion a little more concrete, however, here are some summaries of all that has been said on the subject:

1. The use of dreams in spiritual direction can find good authority in Scripture, theology, philosophy and psychology.

2. The Church has long practised an empirical utilization of dreams for the furtherance of spiritual life.

3. Modern studies and experiments in oneirology and psychotherapeutic dream-interpretation permit a more accurate use of dreams in spiritual direction.

4. In view of the nature of dreams and the conditions imposed by their use, their utilization must nevertheless be regarded as exceptional. Spiritual direction must normally work on the conscious mind by the traditional means, natural and supernatural.

5. There must be grave reasons for having recourse to dreams. Given the competence of the director, this could be advisable or permissible in the following cases:

(a) When a penitent spontaneously relates a dream that has impressed him.

(b) When the penitent has particular psychological knowledge.

(c) When the penitent is desperate, lost in some crisis, finds that

P

ordinary methods no longer have any effect, and wants something more; this provided that there are no counter-indications, such as the penitent's age, mentality, mental illness or danger of it, moral danger for the penitent or the confessor, etc.

6. If dreams are used, the penitent should first be given a religious and psychological introduction to the subject. He should be taught rules to enable him to interpret dream symbolism for himself, under the director's guidance.

7. The best method appears to be to write dreams down, and keep a diary of them. This should be shown frequently to the director— once a week, fortnight, or month.

8. As far as possible, the director should see that the interpretation is not all done by him, but at least shared by the penitent; however, he must never lose sight of the aims of spiritual direction.

9. Generally speaking, the director should follow rules laid down by good authorities on psychotherapy.

10. The use of dreams should not become a normal method either if it leads to an abnormal activation of the penitent's unconscious or if, after a reasonable period of trial, his dreams are still "insignificant".

11. The rules laid down by spiritual writers for discerning spiritual intervention and judging imaginative visions are particularly applicable to spiritual oneiromancy.

12. The director should take care not to be both spiritual director and treating psychotherapist at the same time, even if he is legitimately competent and authorized to do so.

13. Freudian theory—without reference to its truth—should be avoided in interpreting dreams for spiritual purposes, especially when

the complexity of the psyche and the corresponding variety of possible interpretations makes another approach possible.

101. *A biblical text and a theological quotation*

It would be possible to devise many other theoretical and practical rules, but those thirteen will serve as a basis. Finally, I should like to quote two passages in support, one from Scripture and the other from a contemporary theologian.

The scriptural text is from the book of Job; in it Eliu explains the ways in which God speaks to man:

Per somnium in visione nocturna, quando irruit sopor super homines et dormiunt in lectulo, tunc aperit aures virorum, et erudiens eos instruit disciplina, ut avertat hominem ab his quae facit, et liberet eum de superbia, eruens animam eius a corruptione et vitam ipsius ut non transeat in gladium (Job 33. 15-18.)

(*By a dream in a vision by night, when deep sleep falleth upon men and they are sleeping in their beds, then he openeth the ears of men and teaching instructeth them in what they are to learn, that he may withdraw a man from the things he is doing, and may deliver him from pride, rescuing his soul from corruption, and his life from passing to the sword.*)

This magnificent passage appears to refer not only to supernatural dreams, but also to natural good dreams, which can also be a source of divine grace. This is indicated not only by the tone of its expressions, but also by the fact that the sacred author goes on to explain that illnesses are another way in which God can give warnings to men. And obviously he is not referring to supernatural illnesses, which would destroy the whole force of the Book's argument.

It seems to me that this text can, without forcing the interpretation, be shown to enumerate the functions of dreams that concern spiritual direction.

By a dream . . . he openeth the ears of men: God prevents men from continually refusing to listen to the inner voice of God and conscience

—*introversive function*, which interiorizes, makes man examine his inner state.

Teaching instructeth them in what they are to learn: this part is clear in itself; it is the *theoretical-didactic function*.

That he may withdraw a man from the things he is doing: this is the *ethical function*, which reprimands, and encourages man to leave evil ways and follow good.

And . . . deliver him from pride: reductive function, very typical of dreams, as Jung's studies show. I would include it in the ethical function.

Rescuing his soul from corruption, and his life from passing to the sword: here the *prospective function* can be seen, warning against the two sources of future ills—corruption, or mental ills, and "the sword", which symbolizes physical harm.

This text, it should be noted, is spoken by Eliu, the most "orthodox" of Job's interlocutors, so to speak—so much so in fact that when God himself intervenes, he takes over Eliu's line of argument, using what Eliu has just said.

The other text is from *God and the Unconscious*, by Fr Victor White, o.p. "There seems to be no reason why the theologian should deny to dream symbolism the *ex opere operantis* efficacy he must allow to the sacraments of the Old Law, the baptism of John, the sacramentals of the Church or—it may be added—the dream symbols of the Scriptures."[17]

17. *God and the Unconscious*, London, 1952, p. 172.

CONCLUSION

102. *Dreams and "the unknown depths of man"*

Many patient efforts are still needed before "the unknown depths of man" yield up all their secrets. Dreams and the study of dreams have revealed many of them, and will certainly reveal many more. But dreams must not be given greater importance than they deserve. Jung himself, who in his earlier works exalted the unconscious at the expense of the conscious, has recently warned against this very process to unreasonable extremes. Remember the passage I have already quoted, in which he says that experience has taught him that when people have a little knowledge of dream psychology, they tend to overstress the importance of the unconscious, to the detriment of conscious decision. It should not be forgotten that the unconscious only functions satisfactorily when the conscious is fulfilling its role to the limit of its ability.[1]

Delfina Bunge, in her delightful book *La vida en los sueños* (*Life in Dreams*), says the same:

"I certainly believe that some attention should be given to dreams; at least their origins should be sought, even if they cannot be interpreted. Always provided that they are not considered more important than anything in real life, for the unconscious must not be considered more important than the conscious: there is no point in loosing one's prey to clutch at its shadow. Only in the abnormal cases when the prey cannot be caught should the shadow be asked to provide information. Then all dreams can be expected to have meaning and importance, but they must not always be expected to yield some sensational discovery: when this does happen, there will be no mistaking it. . . ."[2]

1. See Section 89.
2. Delfina Bunge de Gálvez, *La vida en los sueños* (Buenos Aires, 1943), p. 95.

INDEX OF PERSONS